Growth Theory

Growth Theory

Solow and His Modern Exponents

Dipankar Dasgupta

OXFORD
UNIVERSITY PRESS

OXFORD
UNIVERSITY PRESS

YMCA Library Building, Jai Singh Road, New Delhi 110001

Oxford University Press is a department of the University of Oxford. It furthers the
University's objective of excellence in research, scholarship, and education by
publishing worldwide in

Oxford New York

Auckland Cape Town Dar es Salaam Hong Kong Karachi
Kuala Lumpur Madrid Melbourne Mexico City Nairobi
New Delhi Shanghai Taipei Toronto

With offices in

Argentina Austria Brazil Chile Czech Republic France Greece
Guatemala Hungary Italy Japan Poland Portugal Singapore
South Korea Switzerland Thailand Turkey Ukraine Vietnam

Published in India
by Oxford University Press, New Delhi

© Oxford University Press 2005

First published 2005

ISBN-13: 978-0-19-567524-5
ISBN-10: 0-19-567524-X

Printed in India at Pauls Press, New Delhi 110 020
Published by Manzar Khan, Oxford University Press
YMCA Library Building, Jai Singh Road, New Delhi 110 001

To

Professor Mihir K. Rakshit
Teacher Par Excellence

Preface

This book constitutes a *modest* attempt at presenting some *recent* advances in Growth Theory. The word "modest" is used in its strict literal sense. The book is modest inasmuch as its coverage is not as exhaustive as one might wish it to be. By deliberate choice, it is concerned with approximately the seven-year period 1986-92 during which a number of classic papers on New Growth Economics appeared in journals. Of course, to present these ideas in their proper perspective, the book travels both backward and forward in time. To the extent that all the authors focussed on used the Solow (1956) scaffolding to build up their ideas, the book starts off with a detailed discussion of the relevant tenets of that seminal work. This constitutes the backward journey. As far as the "forward" trip goes, the book outlines a limited number of attempts to tackle new questions with the methodology of the classic papers it is primarily concerned with.

Regarding the use of the word "recent" in the opening sentence, it is prudent to point out that, given the phenomenal speed of research in the area, articles published even as late as the closing years of the twentieth century should probably be considered dated. Consequently, works included in the book may not qualify as particularly recent. Especially so, since some of them have already made their way into standard textbooks. The decision to set out on a fresh voyage to excavate trodden areas is motivated by two considerations. First, the works addressed by the book do not receive uniform treatment in standard references. In matters of details, the student is often compelled to seek help from other sources, which in turn depend on alternative notational structures as well as conceptual frameworks. These can lead to unforeseen difficulties, especially for the beginner. The book hopefully resolves some of these by presenting a self-contained development of the subject matter, including an exposition of the basic mathematics (viz. Control Theory) needed to study the subject. At the same time, the different authors' contributions are presented with reference to a common platform, consisting of viewing a state of dynamic equilibrium for the economy as a simple supply-demand cross, where the notions of supply and demand apply to the rate of growth itself. Since students of economics are exposed to the tools of supply and demand starting from the most elementary of courses, it is expected that they will readily grasp the messages of Modern Growth Theory when presented in this familiar language.[1] A second consideration that led to the book was the emphasis it accords to the role played by externalities in most of the recent literature. The externality arises from the fact that the subject derives its fundamental motivation from a need to grapple with the force of technical progress in a market environment. By its very nature, knowledge regarding improvements in productive technology often assumes the form of a public good. As in the case of most public goods, technological changes generate non-internalisable externalities, which constitute one of the primary reasons for the failure of the competitive market system. The failure lead to a natural quest for policies to sustain efficient solutions with minimal interventions by the Government. A pervading theme pursued by the book consists of the market failure characteristic. For many of the models presented, the failure is linked to the non-marketability of technical change. However, the book also brings into focus a class of models which bear formal similarity with the models of technical change, though the market failure they suffer from may be traced back to other forms of externalities, in particular the ones associated with public infrastructure, a vital input into the process of economic growth.

Neither this Preface nor the book itself is concerned with history of thought. Hence, only a cursory treatment of the events that led to the evolution of ideas would suffice. Formal growth theory began with Harrod (1939)), who looked into the possibility of economic growth with full employment of resources. His analysis depended on the Keynesian multiplier theory of aggregate demand. At the same time he postulated that the path of capital accumulation was guided by

---

[1]The diagrammatic device that this viewpoint leads to was used, probably for the first time, by Romer (1990), but later on by Barro & Sala-i-Martin (1992) and Rivera-Batiz & Romer (1991) also. However, the identification of the diagram as a supply-demand apparatus is an original contribution of this book.

entrepreneurs' expectations regarding change in demand over time. He found that a dynamic equilibrium path with these features would not be consistent with the requirement of full employment of resources. In fact, he demonstrated that an attempt to follow such a path in a free enterprise society would be self-defeating, leading chronic unemployment or inflation. In other words, Harrod believed that a free enterprise system would more likely than not be characterised by cyclical fluctuations as opposed to steady growth.

Harrod was not so much concerned with capacity improvement over time. It was Domar (1946) who looked into this issue explicitly for the first time. He linked any steadily maintained growth path of investment to a well-defined rate of capacity creation. On the other hand, like Harrod, Domar too visualised a path of output demand by appealing to Keynesian multiplier theory. His major concern was to ensure if the path of demand would match the capacity at each instant of time. Somewhat in Harrod's fashion, he concluded on a negative note that such a path was implausible. In addition, he pointed out that capacity improvement brought about by investment programmes often relates to the advent of new technologies. Such technological change renders existing technologies obsolete. Consequently, the economic costs of unutilised capacity might be aggravated further by capital scrapping in the face of competition, leading to inadequate returns to investment.

A number of authors wrote on the Harrodian instability problem, suggesting the existence of inbuilt mechanisms in the free competitive system that might correct it towards full employment growth. Notable amongst them was Kaldor (1956), who suggested a Keynesian theory of distribution that could affect the savings rate of the economy in a stabilising fashion and keep the economy rolling along an equilibrium growth path with full employment. Nonetheless, the Harrodian scepticism continued to dominate the profession for a long time. It is in this context that Solow (1956) occupies a truly revolutionary position in growth economics. It was Solow's neoclassical model of growth that argued for the first time that the unbridled process of competitive capital accumulation leads to a stable long run path of economic growth. The Solow exercise not only presented an example of a competitive growth model that was free of fluctuations in the long run. In addition, it incorporated the Domarian emphasis on capacity creation by allowing for explicit growth in the productivity of technology over time. (See Chapters 1 and 2 below.)

Of the multifarious directions in which Solow's work provoked new research,[2] there were none so important as the attempts made to capture the nature of technological progress itself. Like Domar, Solow was content to point out the possibility of productivity growth associated with investment. However, the precise link between investment and productivity was left unclear. Future researchers, including Solow (1959) himself, Drandakis & Phelps (1966) and others, devoted considerable energy towards clarifying the role of investment in productivity improvements. However, the credit for first success in this quest goes perhaps to Arrow's model (Arrow (1962)) of Learning by doing. Arrow's explanation of the force of technical change led first of all to a logical determination of the productivity growth rate of an economic system. Secondly, it offered a clear explanation of the reasons underlying technological progress. (See Chapter 3 below.) Uzawa's (Uzawa (1965)) work on the effect of education on growth constituted another instance of a breakthrough, though it received less attention than the Arrow work at the time it initially appeared. (See Chapter 4 below.)

Despite the Arrow and Uzawa successes, however, Growth Theory stood at a standstill for a little over two decades. Indeed, interest in economic growth dwindled considerably (though a parallel literature in economic development flourished) till the mid-eighties when Romer (1986) rekindled interest in economic growth problems by generalising the scope of the Arrow paradigm. Around the same time, Lucas (1988) broadened Uzawa's framework to study the links between human capital formation and economic growth. (See Chapter 3 below for a discussion of Romer (1986) and Chapter 4 for Lucas (1988).) These works were only the beginning of a long line

---

[2]One recalls in particular the Uzawa (1961-a, 1963) exercises aimed at generalising Solow's stability result to multi-sector growth models.

of papers on the subject. In particular, Romer's multi-sector model (Romer (1990)) opened up a new horizon by explaining productivity improvements in terms of specialisation. Further, it broadened the scope of Growth Theory by introducing non-competitive market structures to accommodate the problem of patent protection. The richness of Romer's exercise has lent to it the aura of a classic paper in the area of what is now commonly referred to as *Endogenous* Growth Theory. (See Chapter 5 below for a discussion of Romer's model as well as a similar exercise due to Grossman & Helpman (1991-b)).

An echo of Domar's concern for obsolescence is heard in the work of Aghion & Howitt (1992), though these authors themselves trace their lineage further back to Schumpeter (1934). One comes across forces of uncertainty in this work, connected to the success date for research endeavours. The corresponding equilibrium turns out to be stochastic in nature and captures clearly the losses arising from obsolescence. Once again, Grossman & Helpman (1991-a, 1991-b) carry out a similar investigation and arrive at comparable conclusions. (See Chapter 6 for a discussion of these models.)

While the main line of the literature on Endogenous Growth Theory is concerned with explaining technical progress, Barro (1990) initiated a research programme by attempting to capture the need for infrastructure in economic growth. Barro's work was pursued further by Barro & Sala-i-Martin (1992, 2003), Futagami *et al* (1993), Dasgupta (1999, 2001), Dasgupta & Marjit (2004) and others. (See Chapters 3 and 4 for a report on these exercises.)

A particularly interesting piece of analysis goes back to Rebelo (1991) who succeeded in providing a comprehensive view of the essential components of any exercise in Endogenous Growth Theory. This book owes its overall point of view largely to the Rebelo contribution. (See Chapter 4 below for a discussion of this model.) As already noted, some of the above ideas find place here in a unified framework to help connect common analytical themes running through them. Details are worked out as far as practicable to help the student. These have added to the size of the book, to compensate for which, the book abstracts from the details of certain analytical issues. One such is the problem of stability of dynamic paths. While the issue is not neglected altogether, it is certainly de-emphasised, particularly so in view of the fact that many of the stability results in Modern Growth Theory are highly local in nature.[3]

Certain other omissions in the book deserve special mention. First, the book does not present the *convergence* problem. This literature has both theoretical as well as empirical components, connected to the hypothesis that economies in their initial stages of development grow faster than when they turn mature. The convergence related investigations generated controversies as well as a large volume of empirical literature. Barro & Sala-i-Martin (2003) consider these results in extensive detail.[4] Covering the convergence problem in this book would be space consuming, given the attention the book pays to details. Moreover, convergence analysis does not fit naturally into the flow of ideas pursued by this book. Hence, its exclusion does not constitute a serious shortcoming.

A second major exclusion in the book concerns the area of political economy of growth, which analyses links between income inequality and the rate of growth of the economy. One comes across conflicting strands of thought in this literature, both empirical as well as theoretical. Alesina & Rodrik (1994), Galor & Zeira (1993), Perotti (1993, 1996), Persson & Tabellini (1994) etc. constitute some of the works worth pursuing. It would be interesting to include these in the book, but considerations of space stood in the way. More positively, it might be worth the students' effort to follow up these references with a view to applying the unified framework of this book.

A third important omission concerns the theory of growth in an open economy. Grossman & Helpman (1991-b) did pio-

---

[3]The stability of the growth path in Solow's model is by contrast a global result. The result is presented in detail in Chapter 2. The treatment to be found here has depended heavily on the Barro & Sala-i-Martin (2003) analysis of the problem. Bond *et al* (1996) and Mino (1996) represent nontrivial examples of stability analysis for Endogenous Growth models.

[4]See also, Galor (1996), Quah (1996) and other articles in the symposium issue of Economic Journal, Volume 106.

neering work on the topic. The presentation in this book does cover parts of the Grossman-Helpman contribution on growth in a closed economy. Students who master the relevant chapters (Chapters 5 and 6) of this book, should find it relatively simple to familiarise themselves with the rest of the Grossman-Helpman contribution. The literature on trade and growth, however, is yet to reach a conclusive state. This, along with space considerations, guided the decision to restrict attention to closed economies. Interested readers are referred to contributions by Feenstra (1996), Bond *et al* (2002), Dinopoulos & Segerstrom (2004), Grossman & Helpman (1991-b), Rivera-Batiz & Romer (1991), Stokey (1996) and others.

Finally, the book is devoted entirely to the dynastic household genre of Endogenous growth Theory. While this may be described as the mainstream approach of Growth Economics, there has been a parallel development based on the overlapping generations model. There is an interesting body of results that needs reporting in this context. However, given the limited scope of the present work, this has been avoided. Readers who wish to pursue these models are referred to de la Croix & Michel (2002).

The book has depended almost entirely on the author's experiences in the classroom.[5] Thus, student inputs have been vital to its final emergence. The author has taught regular courses on the subject at the Delhi and Kolkata campuses of the Indian Statistical Institute and at the Jawaharlal Nehru University. He has also had the opportunity of addressing research scholars (as well as the faculty) at the Delhi School of Economics. Consequently, he has benefited significantly from a large collection of students and fellow professionals. Amongst students in particular, he acknowledges fondly the help re-

---

[5]Every teacher has his unique set of experiences to respond to as he strives to communicate and his originality is largely traceable to such fortuitous events. Nonetheless, no teacher can possibly disown the impact of other pedagogic works on his train of thoughts. It is best, therefore, to record here the additional help received by the author from the celebrated books by Grossman & Helpman (1991), Aghion & Howitt (1998) and Barro & Sala-i-Martin (2003). The author's exposition, both in the courses he offered as well as in the present book, has been significantly influenced by these works.

ceived from Ranajoy Basu, Debipriya Chatterjee, Sayan Datta, Kaushik Gangopadhyay, Sambuddha Ghosh, Raman Khaddaria, Shubhashis Modak Chaudhury and Gurbachan Singh. Further, he owes a special note of thanks to Vidya Atal and Arpita Chatterjee for their detailed comments on several versions of the manuscript. As far as professional colleagues go, Professor Kaushik Basu, Professor Amitava Bose, Professor Satya P. Das, Professor Pradip Maiti, Professor Sugata Marjit, Professor Anjan Mukherji, Professor Deepak Nayyar, Professor Prabhat Patnaik and Professor Abhirup Sarkar have contributed directly and indirectly to this project. The final version of the work was completed during the author's visit to the Research Institute for Economics and Business Administration, Kobe University, Japan. The author is particularly indebted to Professor Koji Shimomura for organising a lecture series based on the material for the book. His thought provoking comments as well as the ones received from the participants led to nontrivial revisions before the manuscript was sent to the press.

Last, but not least, a word of thanks to Sankari, without for whose help, generosity and courage, none of this would have taken off in the first place, nor survived the turbulence of the journey.

Kobe
Japan

Contents

Part I: The Solow Model and Optimal Control Theory

Chapter 1

Long Run Growth: Objectives and Received Theory

1.1 Introduction

A rise in the annual growth rate of an economy's real per capita GDP signals, to a large extent, an improvement in the standard of living enjoyed by the inhabitants of the society. Per capita GDP growth, by itself, is of course an imperfect indicator of welfare improvement. Distribution of the GDP across the population matters a great deal also. A large value of per capita GDP, accompanied by severe inequality of distribution, may sometimes signify a deterioration of human well being rather than advancement. Nonetheless, most nations which are reasonably advanced in terms of a wide variety of social indicators do exhibit significantly large values of real per capita GDP also. Consequently, attempts to maintain, and if possible raise, the growth rate of an economy's per capita GDP continue to occupy policy planners, economists and governments in power.[1]

It is helpful in this context to quote some numbers. According to the Human Development Report 2003, the US per capita *GDP* was $ 35,277.00 in 2001. Norway enjoyed a per capita *GDP* of $ 36,815.00. Japan's per capita *GDP* was $ 32,601.00, Switzerland's $ 34,171.00. At the other end of the spectrum, the per capita *GDP* for Ethiopia was a mere $ 95.00. In terms of PPP US $, the Ethiopian GDP translated into the somewhat higher figure of $ 810.00 of course, but this fact should offer us cold comfort, since even graduate students in an average US university receive scholarships in the range of $ 15,000.00 - $ 20,000.00 per academic year. Similarly, Sierra Leone had a per capita *GDP* of $ 146.00, the Democratic Republic of Congo's per capita *GDP* was $ 99.00.

The differences in the numbers at the two extremes are disconcerting to say the least. As one studies these figures, it becomes impossible to resist asking questions like: "Why? What explains the difference?" "How did the US economy manage to reach this level of *GDP*, when Ethiopia lagged so far behind, along with a large number of sub-Saharan African countries." Will it be possible for the per capita *GDP* of Ethiopia to ever reach the US figure? In other words, what makes the real *GDP* of a society rise significantly over time? As the Nobel Laureate Professor Robert E. Lucas observed, "The consequences for human welfare involved in questions like these are simply staggering: Once one starts to think about them, it is hard to think about anything else." (Lucas (1988))

Some would seek answers to these questions in the political histories of the countries, the exploitation that today's poor

---

[1]Lucas (2002) has pointed out that, as opposed to the modern interest in a growing per capita *GDP*, scholars such as Malthus (1798) and Ricardo (1817) were mostly concerned with a stationary per capita *GDP*. A reason underlying this preoccupation, according to Lucas, might have been the historically stable level of per capita world *GDP* spanning the period 1000 AD through as late as 1800 AD. The Malthusian theory of population and Ricardo's use of the iron law of wages were examples of early attempts at explaining the constancy of per capita *GDP*. A theory of growth for Malthus and Ricardo was a theory of population growth. As we shall see, Modern Growth Theory, by contrast, is a theory of per head productivity growth.

societies suffered during the colonial age at the hands of today's rich. To an extent, there would be an element of truth in this perception. However, it would not offer us a clue about what the poor societies ought to do *now*, in this postcolonial age, to cure themselves of the economic illness of acute poverty and the associated human suffering.

The problem is serious enough to exercise the minds of a large number of economists. Growth economics is mostly an outgrowth of these economists' efforts to explain the factors that boost or inhibit growth in particular societies. As with most of economics, the explanations offered by the economists centre around two of the most basic tools of economic analysis, supply and demand. If demand could be stimulated to rise over time, producers will produce more, the supply of goods and services will go up and along with it the GDP. Moreover, if the population does not grow faster than the GDP, then per capita GDP will register an increase also. On the other hand, if demand keeps growing without commensurate increases in supply, then GDP can rise at best in nominal terms without a matching rise in real goods and services. Consequently, to explain the growth or decay of economies over time, economists are led to study the causes underlying the growth of demand and supply over time.

Let us begin with demand. Clearly, a temporary rise in demand cannot be an interesting phenomenon to study when the subject of analysis is its growth over time. Growth over time must refer at the least to a positive growth rate sustained over several years. As already noted, however, growth in demand alone would not suffice unless it is accompanied by a corresponding increase in supply. Further, when demand induced GDP grows steadily over time, it is not adequate to view the corresponding supply responses as movements along a supply curve. Indeed, sooner or later, it would be infeasible for supply to respond to demand rises unless the production capacity is also raised. This means that a study of sustainable growth of per capita real GDP calls for an inquiry into the factors responsible for a growth in the *capacity* to produce, or *shifts* in the supply curve.

The book is devoted to studying alternative theoretical explanations of these factors. Before plunging into these explanations, however, it is of interest to present a few more figures
to convince ourselves that it will be worth our while to spend
the time in pursuing the subject. We do this by looking into
the magnitude of change in per capita GDP brought about by
sustained growth over several years. To begin with, we present
the findings of Barro & Sala-i-Martin (2003) in their discussion
of inter-country growth performance data. The US economy
grew at an approximate trend rate of 1.8 % over the period
1870 through 2000. Measured in 1996 US dollars, it had a
per capita GDP of $ 3340.00 in 1870 and its per capita GDP
in 2000 was 10 times higher at $ 33,330.00. The last figure
demonstrates that the US economy had achieved a very high
standard of living by 2000. Moreover, the fact that this level
of per capita GDP was reached through steady growth over
a long period of time lends to it an element of robustness. It
represents a level of GDP from which the economy cannot be
dislodged (either upwards or downwards) in a significant manner by short run changes. It is impossible that the US GDP
could fall anywhere near the Ethiopian level quoted earlier or
vice versa at short notice. In other words, the level of per
capita GDP achieved on the basis of steady long-term growth
has an element of *firmness* about it. It indicates a standard
of living that has *come to stay*, that the populace has gotten
used to. One cannot make a similar statement about a rise in
per capita GDP that is brought about by an abrupt rise in the
annual rate of growth. Thus, if we have to understand why an
average American is substantially better off than an average
Ethiopian, we must be prepared to undertake a comparative
study of the trend rates of growth of the two societies over a
number of years.

Needless to say, the long-term rate of growth alone cannot explain the entire difference between the wealthiness of
two economies. There are other factors, such as the initial per
capita GDP in the two economies for the period under consideration. Yet other explanations could be based on political
factors, as already noted. Despite these possibilities, however,
the fact remains that the trend rate of growth is one of the

most important explanatory variables of the standard of living that a society has grown accustomed to. It is hard in fact to overestimate its importance, for even small changes in the long run rate of growth lead to substantial changes in the level of living. As Barro & Sala-i-Martin observe, had the US economy, starting from the same level of $ 3340.00 in 1870, grown at the trend rate of 0.8 % (instead of 1.8 %), its per capita *GDP* in 2000 would have been $ 9450.00, which is only 2.8 times higher than where it started. As opposed to this, if it had grown at the rate 2.8 %, it would have reached the level of $ 127,000.00 in 2000, which is 38 times higher than that in 1870. Thus, small changes in the long run growth rate can lead to significant changes in a society's established way of life, whereas even large changes in the short run growth rate may lead to transitory improvements at best.

It is hard to replicate the Barro & Sala-i-Martin exercise for most developing countries. Fortunately, however, the EPW Research Foundation has recently published a data series for the Indian Economy at 1993-94 prices, spanning the 51-year period 1950-51 through 2001-2002. Based on these figures, the trend rate of growth for the entire period of per capita *GDP* at factor cost turns out to be 2.1%, which is higher than the growth rate of the US economy over the 130 year period indicated above, though it falls short of the Japanese long term growth rate of 2.95% calculated over the 100 year period 1890-1990. In 1950-51, India's per capita *GDP* (at factor cost) was Rs. 3912.7 (1993-94 prices). Using the prevailing rupee-US dollar exchange rate of Rs. 31.37 per dollar in 1993-94, the US dollar equivalent of the Indian per capita *GDP* was $ 124.7. As opposed to this, the per capita *GDP* in 2001-2002 was $ 386.7. Thus, over the 51 year period 1950-51 through 2001-2002, the trend growth rate of 2.1% helped to raise India's per capita *GDP* by a factor of 3.1. In absolute terms though, the per capita *GDP* attained over the 51 period compares poorly with some of the fast growing nations of Southeast Asia, such as South Korea, Taiwan, Singapore etc. These economies displayed trend rates of growth lying between 5% and 6.3% during the years 1960-1990. Such sustained levels of high growth had, amongst other factors, caused the per capita *GDP* of Singapore to rise to as high a level as $ 20,733.00 in 2001 and that of South Korea to reach the level of $ 8,917.00 (at current prices).

India lags far behind these figures, its per capita *GDP* at current prices having been only around $ 462.00 in 2001. Where would India be, had its 2.1% trend rate of growth continued, say till 2070, i.e., a period of 120 years beginning 1950-51? Using the EPW data set presented above, the figure turns out to be $ 1547.1 approximately at 1993-94 prices and exchange rates. This figure is nowhere near India's intended goal of catching up with the developed economies. The only way therefore that India can do better is to try and raise its trend rate of growth.

What should be its desired rate of growth? The answer depends on two factors: the per capita *GDP* level it wishes to achieve and the number of years it allows itself to reach the goal. In the year 2001-2002, its per capita *GDP* was Rs. 12133.4, i.e. $ 386.8 at the 1993-94 exchange rate. Suppose India were to decide to reach a per capita *GDP* of $ 3000.00, which is around 7.75 times higher than its per capita *GDP* in 2001-2002. How long should it allow itself to achieve the target? Following the example of the Southeast Asian miracle during the period 1960-1990, suppose the policy makers were to set a 30-year target. It is a simple exercise to calculate that the required growth rate would be 6.8%. On the other hand, if the growth rate were to be 8%, the required number of years to reach the goal would be around 25.

Obviously, even at a growth rate as high as 8%, India's performance would be somewhat unimpressive in terms of the per capita *GDP* achievable over periods as long as 25-30 years. One of the reasons underlying the problem is the size of its population. In the year 2001-2002, the Indian population had already crossed 1 billion, while the population of Singapore was a paltry 4.1 million, with an average growth rate of 2.2% over a 25 year period. Interestingly enough, India's population growth rate during the same period was also around 2%, but whereas the population of Singapore was 2.3 million in 1975, India's population stood at 620 million.

It is no wonder therefore that even with a significantly high growth rate, India cannot reach the standard of living prevailing in Singapore or other developed nations in the foreseeable future. Nonetheless, while controlling the rate of population growth is essential for *GDP* growth enhancement to have a significant impact on the level of living of a nation, it is clear that raising the standard of living calls for other important steps also. This is clearly demonstrated by China, which had a population of 1,285 million in 2001, but a per capita *GDP* that was nearly twice as large as India's. Accordingly, growth theorists look for other important reasons underlying a nation's success or failure in improving its standard of living. The most important of these consists of discovering ways of pushing forward the boundary of an economy's production frontier. Throughout the book we will be concerned with this technological problem alone. To emphasise this fact, we shall often assume a constant labour force over time. This is not to say that the demographic problem is unimportant. It is merely an admission of the fact that finding solutions to the problem of population growth is beyond the scope of this exercise.

1.2   A Suitable Model of Long-term Growth

As with the numbers quoted above, we shall be concerned in our theoretical models mostly with the trend rate of growth of *GDP*. In order to concentrate on factors which explain the long-term trend, it is best to abstract from problems of short run fluctuations, caused, say, by Keynesian effective demand inadequacies. This procedure helps a clear identification of the analytical framework required to study long-term trends.[2] The time worn neoclassical model of economic growth due to Solow (1956) turns out to be a convenient tool for the purpose. [3]

---

[2] The Real Business Cycle theorists do not recognise such a separation of issues. According to this school of thought, the analytical underpinnings of short run fluctuations are indistinguishable from those of long run growth. See Long & Plosser (1983).

[3] Swan (1956) represents an alternative analysis of the neoclassical model with implications similar to the Solow model.

The present section describes the major technological features of the Solow economy.[4]

At each instant of time t, the economy produces a single aggregative commodity Y by means of capital and labour. Denoting the capital stock at t by $K(t)$, the economy faces an instantaneous constraint on aggregate consumption and capital accumulation or investment ($Z(t)$) given by

$$C(t) + Z(t) = Y(t), \tag{1.1}$$

where $Y(t)$ stands for the flow of output at t. No borrowing against future is permitted to enhance current expenditure. It is standard practice to refer to $Z(t)$ as gross investment. A fraction $\delta > 0$ of the capital stock depreciates through use per instant of time. (The depreciation parameter does not play any important role from the analytical point of view and will be dropped from Chapter 3 onwards.) Hence, $Z(t)$ leads to a *net* addition of

$$\dot{K}(t) = Z(t) - \delta K(t) \tag{1.2}$$

to the capital stock at each t. Accordingly, $\dot{K}(t)$ stands for net investment. Equation (1.1) is rewritten as

$$C(t) + \dot{K}(t) = Y(t) - \delta K(t). \tag{1.3}$$

The population at time t, assumed to be identical with the labour force, is denoted $L(t)$. Both K and L are fully employed and the labour force grows at the exogenously given rate n determined by demographic forces. The technology for producing Y is represented by an aggregate production function

$$Y(t) = F(K(t), A(t)L(t)), \tag{1.4}$$

---

[4]The discussion of the Solow model in this chapter and the next expands on Dasgupta (2004).

where $K(t)$ and $L(t)$ are the flows of capital and labour services entering the production process at t. Observe that the use of the same notations for capital stock and services as well as for population size and labour services implies that the stock-flow ratios for both factors are assumed to be constants (normalised to unity). The coefficient $A(t)$ of $L(t)$ represents technological progress and satisfies

Assumption **T** $\dot{A}(t)/A(t) = \mu > 0$.

There are different ways in which the notion of technical progress may be formalised. Equation (1.4) in particular captures it by introducing a distinction between the apparent size of the labour force and its effective size. An improvement in work efficiency is tantamount to a reduction in the time taken to complete a given job. Alternatively, a worker finishes two jobs (say) as opposed to one during any fixed interval of time as her/his efficiency improves. Consequently, from the point of view of work performed, the efficient worker may be treated as two less efficient ones. Viewed this way, technical progress is referred to as labour augmenting. When labour augmentation assumes the form $A(t)L(t)$, technical progress is called Harrod-neutral. Assumption **T** says that the labour force is effectively augmented at the rate μ on account of a rise in work efficiency generated by technological change.[5]

Particular values attained by variables at a time point such as t_0 will be represented by C_{t_0}, K_{t_0} etc. Nonetheless, the time index will often be dropped to achieve notational simplicity, unless essential for the argument. The function $F(.,.)$ satisfies the standard neoclassical properties, viz.

---

[5]Technical progress is neutral when the share of wages and profits in national income are unaffected by improved productivity of factors(s). Under Harrod-neutrality, the shares are unchanging along growth paths which leave the capital-output ratio unaffected. Such paths will be called balanced growth paths in the sequel. Appendix 1.2 provides a brief introduction to the notion of technical progress. For a useful discussion of technical change, see Burmeister & Dobell (1970), Chapter 3. See also Barro & Sala-i-Martin (2003).

Assumption **F1** $F(.,.)$ is continuous and differentiable. $F(0, AL) = F(K, 0) = 0$ and F displays constant returns to scale in K and AL.

Assumption **F2** $F_1 > 0, F_2 > 0, F_{11} < 0, F_{22} < 0.$

Assumptions $F_{11} < 0$ and $F_{22} < 0$ imply the law of diminishing returns.[6]

In a static environment, the assumption predicts diminishing marginal product of a factor as increasing doses of the factor are combined with constant quantities of the other factor. For a growing economy, however, the factor services K and AL would be increasing simultaneously. In this case, what diminishing returns implies is that the marginal product of capital (say) will rise if AL grows faster than K. In particular, a faster growth in A relative to that in K (as of given L) causes the marginal product of K to increase. In other words, it is the direction of change in K/AL that will determine how marginal products of factors respond to improvements in the size of labour augmenting technical change.

We shall denote per capita variables by small case letters. Thus, $y = Y/L$, $c = C/L$, $k = K/L$ and $z = Z/L$. Also, it will be useful to rewrite (1.4) in terms of quantities per unit of *effective labour* (i.e. AL). Thus, denoting Y/AL and K/AL by $\hat{y}$ and $\hat{k}$ respectively and using Assumption **F1**, we obtain

$$\hat{y} = F(\hat{k}, 1) = f(\hat{k}), \ f(0) = 0,$$

---

[6]Assumptions **1** and **2** imply together that the isoquants relating K and AL are strictly convex to the origin. To see this, note that under *CRS*,

$$F_{11}K + F_{12}(AL) = 0$$
$$F_{21}K + F_{22}(AL) = 0.$$

Hence, $F_{12} = F_{21} > 0$. Thus,

$$\frac{d^2(AL)}{dK^2}\big|_{\bar{Y}} = -\frac{1}{F_2^3}\left[F_{11} - F_2^2 - 2F_{12} + F_{22}F_1^2\right] > 0.$$

f is continuous and differentiable . (1.5)

Assumption **F2** implies

Property **f1** f is a strictly concave function with $f'(\hat{k}) > 0$.

In addition to Assumptions **F1** and **F2**, we will impose

Assumption **F2** $f'(\hat{k}) \to \infty$ as $\hat{k} \to 0$ and $f'(\hat{k}) \to 0$ as $\hat{k} \to \infty$.

It is easy to verify (using the assumption of constant returns to scale) that $\partial F/\partial K = f'(\hat{k})$ and $\partial F/\partial(AL) = f(\hat{k}) - \hat{k} f'(\hat{k})$. Thus, Assumption **F2** implies that the marginal product of capital increases without bound as capital becomes indefinitely scarce relative to the factor AL. On the other hand, using Euler's theorem, we see that

$$\frac{\hat{k} f'(\hat{k})}{\hat{y}} + \frac{f(\hat{k}) - \hat{k} f'(\hat{k})}{\hat{y}} = 1.$$

This means that $0 \leq (f(\hat{k}) - \hat{k} f'(\hat{k}))/\hat{y} = 1 - \hat{k} f'(\hat{k})/\hat{y} \leq 1$. Hence, $\partial F/\partial(AL) = f(\hat{k}) - \hat{k} f'(\hat{k}) = f(\hat{k})\{1 - \hat{k} f'(\hat{k})/\hat{y}\} \to 0$ as $\hat{k} \to 0$. In other words, as $\hat{k} \to 0$, the marginal product of effective labour turns indefinitely small. Put differently, the marginal product of capital rises and that of effective labour falls boundlessly as K *relative to AL* becomes indefinitely scarce (irrespective of the *absolute* values of K and AL).

Assumption **F2** is referred to as an Inada condition and constitutes a regularity requirement. It guarantees that the model has mathematically meaningful solutions. Using (1.4), we rewrite (1.1) as

$$C(t) + Z(t) = F(K(t), A_t L_t). \qquad (1.6)$$

At each t, this equation can be viewed as the transformation frontier between $C(t)$ and $Z(t)$ given $K(t)$. Deflating both sides by $A_t L_t$, (1.6) reduces to

$$\frac{c(t)}{A_t} + \hat{z}(t) = f(\hat{k}(t)), \tag{1.7}$$

where $\hat{z}(t) = Z(t)/A_t L_t$. Since

$$
\begin{aligned}
\hat{z} &= \frac{\dot{K} + \delta\, K}{A\, L} \\[2mm]
&= \frac{\dot{K}}{K}\,\frac{K}{A\, L} + \delta\, \hat{k} \\[2mm]
&= \left(\frac{\dot{K}}{K} - (\mu + n)\right)\hat{k} + (\mu + \delta + n)\hat{k} \\[2mm]
&= \frac{\dot{\hat{k}}}{\hat{k}}\, \hat{k} + (\mu + n + \delta)\hat{k} \\[2mm]
&= \dot{\hat{k}} + (\mu + n + \delta)\hat{k}, \tag{1.8}
\end{aligned}
$$

an alternative representation of (1.7) is

$$\frac{c(t)}{A_t} + \dot{\hat{k}}(t) + (\mu + n + \delta)\hat{k}(t) = f(\hat{k}(t)),$$

or,

$$c(t) + A_t\, \dot{\hat{k}}(t) = A_t\{f(\hat{k}(t)) - (\mu + n + \delta)\hat{k}(t)\}, \tag{1.9}$$

where, according to (1.8), $(\mu + n + \delta)\,\hat{k}(t)$ represents the minimum level of gross investment per unit of effective labour, (i.e., $\hat{z}$), that leaves $\hat{k}(t)$ unchanged. It is convenient at this stage to consider two cases depending on whether investment is reversible or irreversible. When investment is irreversible, installed capital cannot be "eaten into" except through depreciation. The maximum fall in capital stock permitted under irreversible investment equals $-\delta K$.[7] In this case, $\dot{K} = -\delta K$ and $Z = \dot{K} + \delta K = 0$. Thus, Z can hit a lower bound and corner solutions can create special problems. Reversible investment, by contrast, permits direct capital consumption. The literature on growth theory with which this book is concerned has developed mostly under the assumption of reversible investment. Accordingly, the book will not present the case of irreversible investment in any depth. However, in the interest

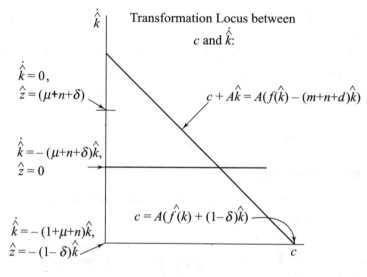

Figure 1.1

---

of students who wish to follow through the technicalities of irreversible investment, the appendices to the present chapter and the next one will prove a few results on optimal growth with irreversible investment.

Under reversible investment, it is possible to have $\dot{K} < -\delta K$, $Z < 0$. Since δK stands for physical depreciation of capital, the maximum amount of the capital stock that can be directly consumed by the household is $(1 - \delta)K$. Hence, the maximum sustainable net disinvestment equals $\dot{K} = -[(1 - \delta)K + \delta K] = -K$. Consequently, $Z = \dot{K} + \delta K = -(1 - \delta)K$. Alternatively, $\hat{z} = -(1 - \delta)\hat{k}$ and $\dot{\hat{k}} = -(1 + \mu + n)\hat{k}$, using (1.8). The corresponding maximum possible level of per capita consumption is $c = A(f(\hat{k}) + (1 - \delta)\hat{k})$. The transformation locus between c and $\dot{\hat{k}}$ is illustrated in Figure 1.1.

A consumption path c must satisfy the condition

$$0 \le c \le A(f(\hat{k}) + (1 - \delta)\hat{k}), \tag{1.10}$$

if investment is reversible.

We end this section by deriving an important restriction on the path of $\hat{k}$.

PROPOSITION **1.1** *Any feasible path* $\hat{k}(t)$ *satisfying 1.9 is bounded above.*

Proof: Referring back to (1.9), the maximum value of $\hat{k}(t)$, hence $\dot{\hat{k}}(t)$, possible at each t is found by equating c/A to zero for all t. This may be called the path of pure capital accumulation. Denote the path by $\hat{k}_p(t)$. It satisfies the equation

$$\dot{\hat{k}}_p(t) = f(\hat{k}_p(t)) - \lambda\hat{k}_p(t).$$

where $\lambda = \mu + n + \delta$. By virtue of Assumption **F2**, $\exists$ a $\bar{\hat{k}}$

such that $\hat{k}_p(t) > \bar{\bar{k}} \Rightarrow \dot{\hat{k}}_p(t) < 0$. Thus, max $\{\hat{k}(0), \bar{\bar{k}}\}$ is the claimed upper bound on $\hat{k}(t)$. ∎

The intuitive argument underlying Proposition 1.1 is as follows. If $\hat{k}(t)$ is not bounded above, then $f'(\hat{k}) \to 0$ according to the Inada conditions. A marginal unit of $\hat{k}$ adds $f'(\hat{k})$, but to maintain that extra unit, the required amount of $\hat{z}$ is λ, a positive constant. Since for $\hat{k}$ large enough, $f'(\hat{k}) < \lambda$, an extra $\hat{k}$ cannot be maintained from some $\hat{k}$ onwards. Consequently, $\hat{k}$ must be bounded above.

1.2.1 Economic Organisation

Command Economy

Throughout the book, we shall be referring to two alternative economic set ups, called the Command economy and the Private economy. The Command economy presumes a single decision-maker, to be called the planner, who allocates all resources at each point of time as well as across time. It does not recognise private claim to economic property. To the extent that the omnipotent planner is in a position to achieve all possible allocation of existing resources, he may attain the best one amongst these according to some criterion or the other (to be specified in Chapter 2). In fact, one may view the Command economy to be a theoretical device for locating the best possible allocation of resources in a growing economy.

Private economy

The alternative to the Command economy is the Private economy where resources are privately owned and allocated by private incentive driven forces. A large part of these forces will assume the shape of competitive markets, though, as we shall see (in Chapter 5), the assumption of perfect competition will not always be tenable. The Private economy will represent the way an economy is actually likely to function. The Private economy evolves over time through the interaction of the agents constituting it, viz., the households and the firms. As

in most macro models, we shall abstract completely from interactions between households alone or those between producers
alone at any point of time. Consequently, we will pretend that
there is a single aggregative or representative household (H)
and a single representative business firm (B) in the economy.
The behaviour of H will be taken up in the next chapter.

The business firm is assumed to choose $L(t)$ and $K(t)$ to
maximise net profit

$$\Pi(t) \;=\; F(K(t), A_t L(t)) - w(t)L(t) - r(t)K(t) - \delta K(t)$$

$$(1.11)$$

at all t. The FOC's for this exercise are

$$
\begin{aligned}
r(t) \;&=\; \frac{\partial F}{\partial K(t)} - \delta \\[1mm]
&=\; f'(\hat{k}(t)) - \delta, \\[2mm]
w(t) \;&=\; \frac{\partial F}{\partial L_t} \\[1mm]
&=\; A_t\{f(\hat{k}) - \hat{k}f'(\hat{k})\}.
\end{aligned}
\qquad (1.12)
$$

Equation (1.12) represent the competitive demands for capital and labour services on the part of B as functions of the
market rate of interest r and the wage rate w. Factor market
equilibrium requires

Demand for factor services   =   supply of factor
                                                services at each t.

$$(1.13)$$

Factor market equilibrium determines, under **F2** and the assumption of perfect wage-price flexibility, the equilibrium values of r and w at each t. The equilibrium time path of market

returns, viz. $\{r_t^*, w_t^*\}$, has associated with it a time path of $\hat{k}_t^*$ and $\hat{y}_t^*$. Since the economy starts with exogenously given values of L_0 and A_0 and AL grows at an exogenously given rate $\mu + n$, the above paths of $\hat{k}_t^*$ and $\hat{y}_t^*$ imply corresponding paths of K_t^* and Y_t^*, where $K_0^* = K_0$, the exogenously given level of $K(0)$. These paths capture the equilibrium behaviour of the economy over time.

To complete the picture, we need to discuss the theoretical underpinnings of the factor supply functions. As far as labour is concerned, we will make the simplest of assumptions, that the household's total endowment of the factor is supplied inelastically to the market at each t. Capital services too will be assumed to be so supplied. However, the household's endowment of capital at each point of time will not be exogenously given as in the case of labour. It will instead be determined by the household's consumption-savings decision over time. The decision requires solving an optimisation exercise involving the choice of a consumption and saving *path* for the household's planning horizon. The next chapter will be concerned with solving this problem. In the process, it will introduce the reader to elements of Control Theory, an important tool for analysing problems involving optimal choice over time.

Appendix 1. 1   Irreversible Investment

Irreversible investment refers to the case where installed capital cannot be "eaten into" except through depreciation. The smallest possible value $\dot{K}$ can assume is $-\delta K$. At this corner value of net investment, gross investment Z equals zero. This means that $z = 0$ and $\dot{\hat{k}} = -(\mu + n + \delta)\hat{k}$. Consequently, from (1.9), the maximum possible per capita consumption is $c = Af(\hat{k})$. In this case, the consumption path will satisfy the condition

$$0 \le c \le Af(\hat{k}). \tag{A1. 1}$$

Figure 1.1 indicates the maximum possible value of c corresponding to $\dot{\hat{k}} = -(\mu + n + \delta)\hat{k}$. The analytical consequences of C hitting its upper bound will be discussed further in Appendix 2.1.

Appendix 1. 2   Technological Progress

This appendix provides a short introduction to the formalities of technological progress. The treatment is not self-complete and the reader is urged to follow up the references cited. The particular form of technical progress assumed in the text is best understood with reference to "stylised facts" from economic history concerning the *long term* behaviour of an economy. Some of these were noted by Kaldor (1957) and may be listed as follows:

(i) The investment-output ratio remains constant.
(ii) The capital-output ratio remains constant.
(iii) The capital-labour and output-labour ratio rise over time.
(iv) The rate of interest is a constant.
(v) The real wage rate is rising.
(vi) The shares of capital and labour in national income are constants.

Growth theorists have been motivated by the above features in modelling technological change. It is easy to check that in the absence of technical progress, i.e., in the absence of the term $A(t)$ in (1.4), the growth model outlined by the chapter will not satisfy (iii) and (iv) simultaneously, a rise in k implies r falls. In the presence of $A(t)$, however, the capital-labour ratio can increase in the face of a constant value of $\hat{k} = K/A\,L$ and hence, as per (1.12), a constant rate of interest. The form of the aggregate production function (1.4) is a special case of the function

$$Y(t) = F(K(t), L(t); t), \ \frac{\partial F}{\partial t} > 0,$$

$$= L(t)f(k(t); t), \tag{A1. 2}$$

assuming constant returns to scale with respect to capital and labour. The explicit appearance of t in F indicates that the function shifts 'upwards" over time. In other words, application of the same flows of capital and labour services yield larger flows of output with the progress of time. This general form of production function too can accommodate a constant k/y and growing k simultaneously, because the fall in f' caused by k can be arrested by a rising t. In particular, $\pi = k\,f'(k;t)/y$ can remain constant, thus satisfying condition (vi). When the latter is guaranteed, technological progress is neutral (as opposed to being "biased"), since the gains in productivity are being shared equally by the two factors of production in the long run. If this happens along a path that leaves k/y unaffected, the associated technical progress is referred to as Harrod-neutral (Harrod (1948)). Figure 1.2 illustrates the notion of Harrod-neutrality.

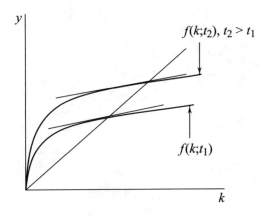

Figure 1.2

It is intuitively obvious that Harrod-neutrality calls for rising labour productivity over time. Consequently, while k increases, the ratio of K to "effective" labour remains unaltered in some sense, thus keeping the rate of interest unaffected. Since factor returns are linked to the slopes of isoquants, the last observation suggests that we try and capture the notion of technical change with reference to the basic isoquant map. Thus, technical change is said to be "factor augmenting" if the isoquants may be drawn with respect to the "effective" factor uses. Given any fixed pair (K, L), let us denote effective capital and labour by $(B(t)K, A(t)L)$, where $B(t)$ and $A(t)$ are increasing functions of time. If output depends on effective factor supplies, as opposed to the "raw" supplies, then the same (K, L) can be associated with physically lower levels of isoquants over time. Alternatively, any given point on the isoquant plane will be associated over time with different

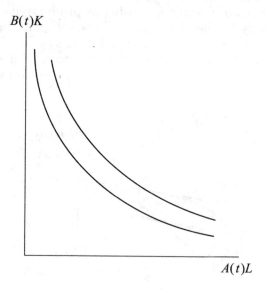

Figure 1.3

quantities of raw factors. See Figure 1.3. In this case, (A1. 2) reduces to[8]

$$
\begin{aligned}
Y(t) &= F(K(t), L(t); t), \\
&= G(B(t)K, A(t)L), \qquad (A1.\ 3)
\end{aligned}
$$

Robinson (1938) conjectured and Uzawa (1961) proved that technical progress is Harrod-neutral *iff* it is labour-augmenting, i.e. it has the form (1.4).[9]

An alternative notion of neutrality has its origin in Hicks (1963). Since π is a constant *iff* $(1-\pi)$ is a constant, it follows that π is a constant *iff* rK/wL is a constant. On the other hand, $rK/wL = k/(w/r)$. The share π will be a constant if the form of technical change is such that for given k, the ratio of factor returns w/r is a constant. When technical change satisfies this property, it is referred to as Hicks-neutral. Going back to (A1. 3), Hicks-neutrality occurs when $B(t) = A(t) \ \forall \ t$.

Let e denote the elasticity of substitution for the two factors. Using the methods of Diamond (1965), it is possible to show that Hicks-neutrality gives rise to

$$
\frac{\dot{\pi}}{\pi} = \frac{\dot{A}}{A}\left(1 - \frac{1}{e}\right), \qquad (A1.\ 4)
$$

if property (ii) above has to hold. When $e < 1$ and $1 - e$ stays bounded away from zero, π reaches zero in finite time. Hence, property (vi) above is violated in finite time. Alternatively, if $e > 1$ and $1 - e$ stays bounded away from zero, π reaches zero asymptotically, so that once again (vi) cannot hold along with (ii). Thus, a Hicks-neutral production function can lead to growth paths consistent with the stylised facts *only if* the

---

[8]A notable feature of (A1. 3) is that technical progress affects the productivity of capital and labour irrespective of their vintages. A new idea improves the efficiency of all pieces of machinery (say), whether they were commissioned recently or in the distant past. The same observation holds true for labour. When technical progress has this characteristic, it is called "disembodied" (as opposed to "embodied").

[9]The reader may refer to Uzawa (1961) for a proof.

elasticity of substitution $e = 1$, i.e., if the production function is Cobb-Douglas. In this case, however, Uzawa (1961) demonstrated that the production function is both Hicks and Harrod-neutral. In fact, Uzawa proved the stronger result that a production function is both Hicks and Harrod-neutral *iff* it is Cobb-Douglas.

In view of these observations, it should be apparent that for the model of this chapter to successfully fit the stylised facts, it should have the form (1.4).[10]

---

[10]See Barro & Sala-i-Martin (2003), Chapter 1, Appendix for an elementary proof of this result.

Chapter 2

Growth in Private and Command Economies

2.1 Equilibrium Growth in a Private Economy

The previous chapter derived the equilibrium path followed by a Private economy under the assumption that there exist well-defined factor supply functions. In the present chapter we will be concerned with deriving the functions. In the process, we shall introduce the reader to elements of Control Theory, an important mathematical tool employed by modern growth theory. In addition, the notion of equilibrium over time will be sharpened further through the introduction of the concept of a balanced growth equilibrium, an idea that will play an all important role in the rest of the book.

Agent H, whose size at t is $L(t)$, is viewed as a dynastic household that expects to live forever and cares (in a limited way) for all subsequent generations. Thus, its welfare function is assumed to be

$$U = \int_o^\infty u(c(t)). \, e^{nt}. \, e^{-\rho t} dt$$

$$= \int_o^\infty u(c(t)) \, e^{-(\rho-n)t} dt, \qquad (2.1)$$

which is a weighted sum of instantaneous (cardinal) utilities derived from $c(t)$. The weights reflect two facts. First, e^{nt} shows that utilities from per capita consumption receive exponentially higher weights with time to take account of the fact that the household size increases at the rate n. Secondly, $\rho > 0$ stands for the rate of time preference arising out of the fact that utilities further down in time are valued less than utilities enjoyed earlier on. As noted above therefore, H is less than altruistic in its attitude towards future generations. This leads to an exponentially decaying weight $e^{-\rho t}$ with the passage of time. The function U is assumed to reflect the intertemporal preferences of H and satisfy the following assumptions:

Assumption u1 $u'(c) > 0$, $u''(c) < 0$,

Assumption u2 $u'(c) \to \infty$ as $c \to 0$ and $u'(c) \to 0$

as $c \to \infty$,

Assumption u3 $\rho > n$.

In other words, utility is a strictly concave function of c, the marginal utility is unboundedly high for small values of c, while it is as close to zero as possible for large c. The first part of **Assumption u2** rules out corner solutions at each point of time. **Assumption u3** ensures that U is well defined.[1] In view of **Assumption T**, the convergence of (2.1) will generally call for a strengthening of **Assumption u3**.[2]

There is only one type of asset in the economy, a share $\mathcal{A}$ issued by B. Each unit of $\mathcal{A}$ represents the ownership right over a unit of K. On the other hand, factor price flexibility and the Inada conditions ensure that all savings are used up in capital formation, i.e. savings = investment.[3] Like B, agent H too treats all prices parametrically. The budget constraint of H at t is parskip.03in

$$\dot{\mathcal{A}}(t) = w(t)L(t) + r(t)\,\mathcal{A}(t) - C(t), \qquad (2.2)$$

---

[1] When $\rho < n$, the function U could be unbounded.

[2] See the discussion in Section 2.3.1.

[3] The latter reflects the non-Keynesian feature of the Solow economy.

where $\dot{\mathcal{A}}(t)$ stands for investment or disinvestment in $\mathcal{A}(t)$, $w(t)\,L(t)$ the income from inelastically supplied labour and $r(t)\,\mathcal{A}(t)$ the income from asset holdings. Denoting per capita asset holding by $a(t)$, equation (2.2) reduces to parskip.03in

$$\dot{a}(t) = w(t) + r(t)\,a(t) - c(t) - n\,a(t), \qquad (2.3)$$

where, following the arguments outlined in footnote 6 of Chapter 1, $n\,a(t)$ is the per capita investment in $\mathcal{A}(t)$ necessary to keep $a(t)$ unchanged. Agent H maximises (2.1) subject to (2.3) (or, (2.2)) being satisfied at each t.

Corresponding to any given K_0 and a path of $r(t)$ and $w(t)$, the solution to the household's problem leads to a choice of $\{C(t), \dot{\mathcal{A}}(t)\}_0^\infty$, hence $\{C(t), \dot{K}(t)\}$ at each t, since all savings are assumed to be invested in this non-Keynesian world. Given the inherited $K(t)$, the chosen $\dot{K}(t)$ and the rate of depreciation δ, the capital stock for the next instant of time is determined. It is assumed to be inelastically supplied and constitutes the supply function in the capital (services) market. Similarly, $L(t)$ is supplied inelastically in the labour market. Accordingly, the notion of an equilibrium of the Private economy which Chapter 1 introduced can be elaborated as follows:

The **equilibrium** of the Private economy consists of

(i) a path of rates of interest and wages $\{r_t^*, w_t^*\}_0^\infty$; (ii) a path of optimal choices by H, viz. $\{c_t^*, \mathcal{A}_t^*\}_0^\infty$, or equivalently, $\{c_t^*, a_t^*\}_0^\infty$, where $\mathcal{A}_t^* = K_t^*$ at each t by definition, or, $\hat{k}_t^* = a_t^*/A_t$ at each t; and
(iii) a path of optimal choices by B, viz. $\{K_t^*, L_t^*\}_0^\infty$, or equivalently, $\{\hat{k}_t^*, L_t^*\}_0^\infty$ satisfying (1.12) and (1.13).

Trivially, the path $\{r_t^*, w_t^*\}_0^\infty$ has the features of a perfect foresight equilibrium. To see this, suppose that H and B forecast the path $\{r_t^*, w_t^*\}_0^\infty$ at $t = 0$. Then, H will choose $\{c_t^*, \mathcal{A}_t^*\}_0^\infty = \{c_t^*, K_t^*\}_0^\infty$ on the basis of its dynamic optimality exercise and B will select $\{\hat{k}_t^*, L_t^*\}_0^\infty$. According to condition (iii) above, factor markets will be in equilibrium. Taking account of the CRS technology, (1.12) and $\mathcal{A}_t^* = K_t^*$, equation

(2.2) reduces to (1.1). The latter implies that the commodity market is in equilibrium. Thus, all markets will be in equilibrium and $\{r_t^*, w_t^*\}_0^\infty$ will be realised if expected.

Before proceeding to solve the household's dynamic problem, viz. maximisation of (2.1) subject to (2.2) or (2.3), it will be convenient to present the corresponding problem for the Planned economy. Once this problem is adequately handled, the solution to the Private economy problem will follow trivially.

2.2   Optimal Growth in a Planned Economy

This section will be concerned with the optimal choice of an accumulation path of $\hat{k}$ and c over time for a Command economy. The exercise goes back to Cass (1965), Koopmans (1965) and Ramsey (1928), who assumed that a consumption (hence, saving) plan is chosen by maximising a welfare integral over a time domain. The economy, being infinitely lived in principle, the planner too will be assumed to have infinite life, as was the case for H. The planner at $t = 0$ is assumed, like H, to plan for the entire future of the economy. In other words, he decides about an optimal consumption path $C(t)$, $t \in [0, \infty)$, where $C(t)$ is the aggregate consumption enjoyed by $L(t)$. Optimality of the path is judged with reference to (2.1), since the planner is supposed to act in the best interest of H.

We saw in Chapter 1 that equation (1.9) can be viewed as the transformation frontier between $c(t)$ and $\dot{\hat{k}}(t)$ given $\hat{k}(t)$. With reversible investment,[4] the optimal value of c must necessarily be an interior point of the transformation frontier. If not, suppose $c = 0$ for some t. Given **Assumption u2**, however, a small decrease in consumption at t accompanied by an increase at a later point of time must be welfare improving. Hence, $c > 0$. Next, let

---

[4]The discussion will be restricted to the case of reversible investment in the main body of the chapter. Problems raised by irreversible investment are covered by the Appendix.

$$c = A(f(\hat{k}) + (1 - \delta)\hat{k}) \qquad (2.4)$$

for some t. This means that all capital gets exhausted at t and the economy cannot produce positive output beyond t. Hence, $c = 0$ subsequent to t, which is suboptimal on account of **Assumption u2**. Consequently, any optimal consumption path c must satisfy the condition

$$0 < c < A(f(\hat{k}) + (1 - \delta)\hat{k}). \qquad (2.5)$$

Thus, the planner's optimisation exercise may be stated as follows:

Optimisation under Reversible Investment:

Find $\{c^*(t)\}_0^\infty$ to maximise (2.1) subject to (1.9) and in $\hat{k}(0) = \hat{k}_0$.

In standard terminology, $c(t)$ is referred to as a control variable and $\hat{k}(t)$ as a state variable.

2.2.1 Necessary Conditions for Optimum: An Intuitive Discussion

This section assumes that the planner has chosen an optimum path $\{c_t^*, \hat{k}_t^*\}_0^\infty$ of per capita consumption and capital per unit of effective labour over time and derives intuitively the properties to be satisfied by that path. Let us fix any time point t. From his own past decisions, the planner has inherited an unalterable level of $\hat{k}(t) = \hat{k}_t^*$. This determines the size of net resources (viz., the RHS of (1.9)) the planner must allocate between $c(t)$ and $\dot{\hat{k}}(t)$. For this purpose, we define a reduced form welfare function governing the planner's behaviour at t. The function, commonly called the Hamiltonian, is written[5]

---

[5]Appendix 2.1 presents a rigorous treatment of this function as well as the following intuitive discussion.

$$\mathcal{H}(c(t), \hat{k}(t), q_t) = u(c(t)) + q_t \dot{\hat{k}}(t), \qquad (2.6)$$

where $\hat{k}$ enters the function $\mathcal{H}$ as an argument, since $\dot{\hat{k}}$ is a function of $\hat{k}$ and c on account of (1.9). The variable q_t is called a co-state variable and represents the shadow price of $\hat{k}$ at t. It is measured in utils and may be calculated as follows. Consider any path $\{c_t, \hat{k}_t\}_0^\infty$. We imagine that the best possible value of aggregate utility across growth paths starting from $\hat{k}_t$ is given by the function $V(\hat{k}_t)$. Then, q_t is the marginal social productivity of $\hat{k}$ at t, i.e., $q_t = d\, V(\hat{k}_t)/d\, \hat{k}_t$. In what follows, we shall loosely refer to $\dot{\hat{k}}$ as investment in $\hat{k}$. Thus, $\mathcal{H}$ stands for the utility derived by the planner from the choice $(c(t), \dot{\hat{k}}(t))$, *under the assumption that the path from t onwards brought about by the investment is optimal.* As defined therefore, $\mathcal{H}$ already incorporates an element of optimality as far as the future is concerned. It says, whatever may be the value of $\dot{\hat{k}}$, the future course of the economy will be optimal.

Different choices of the value of investment, however, will give rise to different optimal values for the future. Which of these should the planner pick up? To answer this question, we have to compare the social productivity of a marginal change in $\dot{\hat{k}}$ with the marginal utility of c at t. This boils down to computing the marginal rate of substitution (MRS) along level curves generated by the Hamiltonian. Differentiate $\mathcal{H}$ totally to get

$$\frac{d\, c(t)}{d\, \dot{\hat{k}}(t)} = -\frac{q_t}{u'(c(t))} < 0$$

and

$$\frac{d^2\, c(t)}{d\, \dot{\hat{k}}(t)^2} = q_t\, \frac{1}{u'(c(t))^2}\, u''(c(t))\, \frac{d\, c(t)}{d\, \dot{\hat{k}}(t)} > 0.$$

Thus, the level curves corresponding to $\mathcal{H}$ are downward falling and strictly convex to the origin. As in any constrained optimisation problem, optimum choice implies equating the MRS with the slope of the constraint. The slope of the linear constraint (1.9) is $(-A_t)$. Hence, a necessary FOC to be satisfied by the optimal path $\{c_t^*, \hat{k}_t^*\}_0^\infty$ is

$$\frac{q_t^*}{u'(c_t^*)} = A_t,$$

$$\text{or,} \quad u'(c_t^*) = \frac{q_t^*}{A_t}, \quad (2.7)$$

where $q_t^* = d\, V(\hat{k}_t^*)/d\, \hat{k}(t)$. Equation (2.7) may also be written as

$$\frac{\partial \mathcal{H}(c_t^*, \hat{k}_t^*, q_t^*)}{\partial c(t)} = 0 \quad \text{at each } t. \quad (2.8)$$

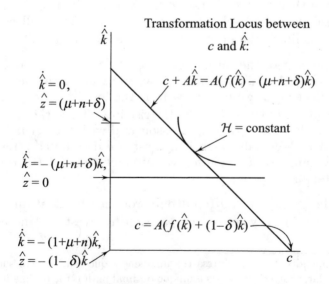

Figure 2.1

In view of the shape of the level curves of $\mathcal{H}$, (2.8) implies that $\mathcal{H}$ is maximised subject to (1.9) at each t. The equilibrium is described in Figure 2.1. For later use we also observe that the maximum in question is unique.[6] Note that the Hamiltonian $\mathcal{H}$ can be interpreted approximately as the value in utils imputed to per capita net national product at t.[7] Thus, an optimal path $\{c_t^*, \hat{k}_t^*\}_0^\infty$ has associated with it a path of $\{q^*(t)\}_0^\infty$ such that the corresponding imputed value of per capita net national product is maximised with respect to $c(t)$ at each point of time. In view of this implication, (2.8) is often referred to as the *Maximal Principle*.

To complete the characterisation of the optimal path, we derive another property that q^* must satisfy. This second property is a necessary condition for the optimality of investment at each t. It says that along the optimal path, the cost of a marginal increase in $\hat{k}$ brought about at any t and maintained ever afterwards must be equal to the discounted present value of the stream of utility returns it brings forth forever. Let us suppose then that $\hat{k}^*$ is raised by Δ at t and that this rise is maintained for all subsequent time points. This will cause a parallel shift in the path of $\hat{k}_s^*$, $s \geq t$ as in Figure 2.2.

The cost of the initial rise is $q_t^* \, \Delta$. Since $q_t^* = A_t \, u'(c_t^*)$, we have $q_t^* \, \Delta = u'(c_t^*) \, A_t \, \Delta$. Now, $A_t \, \Delta$ being the per capita equivalent of Δ, we may view it as the loss in per capita consumption at t necessitated by the rise in $\hat{k}$. Thus, the cost $q_t^* \, \Delta$ is the utility loss $u'(c_t^*) \, A_t \, \Delta$ associated with the net fall $A_t \, \Delta$ in c at t. We shall weigh it against the discounted stream of utility gains to be made forever after netting out the costs of maintenance.

The extra *per capita* output produced by Δ at any $s > t$ is $A_s \, f'(\hat{k}_s^*) \, \Delta$, whereas the *per capita* investment necessary

---

[6] Appendix 2.2 will address the uniqueness question. It will show, in particular, that $\{c_t^*, \hat{k}*t\}_0^\infty$ is a unique optimal path if the optimality conditions derived in this section are satisfied. This would imply from (2.7) that the associated path $\{q_t^*\}$ is also unique.

[7] The qualification "approximate" is needed since $\hat{k}$ is investment per unit of effective labour AL, rather than per capita investment.

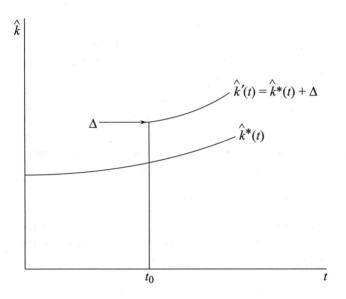

Figure 2.2

to maintain Δ is $A_s \, (\mu + n + \delta) \, \Delta$. Hence, the net *per capita* extra output produced by the additional Δ at each $s > t$ is $A_s \, (f'(\hat{k}_s^*) - (\mu + n + \delta)) \, \Delta$. The extra utility it gives rise to at s is $u'(c_s^*) \, A_s \, (f'(\hat{k}_s^*) - (\mu + n + \delta)) \, \Delta = q_s^* \, \{f'(\hat{k}_s^*) - (\mu + n + \delta)\} \, \Delta$. The discounted present value of the stream of utilities is $\int_t^\infty e^{-(\rho-n)(s-t)} \, q_s^* \, \{f'(\hat{k}_s^*) - (\mu + n + \delta)\} \, \Delta \, ds$. Equating the cost to the discounted returns as explained above, we have

$$q_t^* = \int_t^\infty e^{-(\rho-n)(s-t)} \, q_s^* \, \{f'(\hat{k}_s^*) - (\mu + n + \delta)\} \, ds. \quad (2.9)$$

For q_t^* to be well-defined in (2.9, the integral on the *RHS* must exist for each t. We shall demonstrate in Section 2.3.2

(Proposition 2.4) that the optimality of $\{c_t^*, \hat{k}_t^*\}_0^\infty$ implies that $f'(\hat{k}_s^*) - (\mu + n + \delta)$ is positive and bounded strictly away from zero for s sufficiently large.[8] Anticipating this result, the integral can exist $\forall\, t$ only if

$$e^{-(\rho - n)t} q_t^* \to 0 \text{ as } t \to \infty. \tag{2.10}$$

Equation (2.10) is called the transversality condition and constitutes a restriction on an optimal path. Intuitively, (2.10) implies that efficient paths view capital stocks far out in the future to be increasingly useless relative to present stocks.[9]

The balance between cost and benefits in equation (2.9) implies a restriction on the optimal path. This is seen by differentiating (2.9) with respect to t to get[10]

---

[8]Proposition (J) of Koopmans (1965) proves the result for a model without technical progress. Proposition A2.2.1 of Appendix 2.3 (which looks into the conclusion of Proposition 2.4 more deeply) may be viewed as an extension of Koopmans' result to the case where the production function exhibits technical progress and investment is not necessarily reversible. However, as we shall explain below, our result will hold for a form of the utility function that is less general than the one employed so far in this chapter. Koopmans proved his result for the general utility function. The restriction to be imposed on the utility function subsequently will represent the price to be paid to accommodate technical change.

[9]It is worth noting here that the transversality condition follows from the fact that $f'(\hat{k}_s^*) - (\mu + n + \delta)$ is bounded strictly away from zero, rather than the other way round. Certain sources liken the transversality condition to a no-Ponzi game restriction. The latter is a vacuous restriction for the present model, since it assumes a single macro household or planner which can neither be a net borrower nor a net lender. In any case, as we have demonstrated, optimality implies this condition. It is *not* an exogenous stipulation on the model.

[10]The formula for differentiating a definite integral of the form

$$K(x) = \int_a^{b(x)} F(t, x)\, dt$$

is

$$\frac{dK(x)}{dx} = \int_a^{b(x)} F_x(t, x)\, dt + F(b(x), x) b'(x).$$

See Chiang (1992), (2.11), p.31.

$$\dot{q}_t^* = -q_t^*\{f'(\hat{k}_t^*) - (\mu + n + \delta)\}$$
$$+(\rho - n)\int_t^\infty e^{-(\rho-n)(s-t)}q_s^*\{f'(\hat{k}_s^*)$$
$$-(\mu + n + \delta)\}ds.$$

Substituting from (2.9), the last equation reduces to

$$\dot{q}_t^* = -q_t^*\{f'(\hat{k}_t^*) - (\mu + n + \delta)\} + (\rho - n)q_t^*. \qquad (2.11)$$

In order to interpret (2.11), consider a different scenario where p is the money price of a unit of the commodity that acts both as a consumption and a capital good.[11] For simplicity, the capital good is assumed to be non-depreciating. Suppose further that there exists, alongside the capital good, an alternative monetary asset, a long term bond, yielding a nominal rate of interest $i(t)$ for each t. An infinitely lived agent is engaged in evaluating a chosen path of capital accumulation $\{k(t)\}_0^\infty$. When p units of money are invested in a unit of the capital good at time t, the marginal product is $f'(k(s))$ $\forall$ $s \geq t$, assuming as before that the agent maintains the extra unit of capital for all $s \geq t$ and consumes any residual output brought forth by the extra capital. Then, the agent's return from maintaining an extra unit of k forever from s onwards is $f'(k(s))$ $\forall$ $s \geq t$. In nominal terms, the return equals $p(s)f'(k(s))$ at each s. For the agent to be indifferent between investing in the physical capital and the bond, the two investments must yield the same rate of return per instant of time. The rate of return from the physical capital investment, $r(s)$, is given by

$$p(t) = \int_t^\infty p(s)f'(k(s))e^{-\int_t^s r(x)dx}ds.$$

If the two rates of return are equal, then $r(s) = i(s)$ $\forall$ s. Hence,

$$p(t) = \int_t^\infty p(s)f'(k(s))e^{-\int_t^s i(x)dx}ds. \qquad (2.12)$$

---

[11]This interpretation is based on Solow (1956).

Differentiation of (2.12) with respect to t gives

$$\dot{p}(t) = -p(t)f'(k(t)) + i(t)p(t),$$

or,

$$p(t)f'(k(t)) + \dot{p}(t) = i(t)p(t). \tag{2.13}$$

The first term on the LHS of (2.13) stands for the value of the instantaneous marginal product of investment in k in nominal terms, while the second term represents capital gain (or loss) on account of price change. The LHS then gives the *net* instantaneous nominal return from investing in k. The RHS, on the other hand, is the nominal return at t from holding the bond. The equality implies that the agent is indifferent between the two ways of investing.[12]

The logic underlying (2.13) may be applied to (2.11), which we rewrite as

$$q_t^* \{f'(\hat{k}_t^*) - (\mu + n + \delta)\} + \dot{q}_t^* = (\rho - n)\, q_t^*. \tag{2.14}$$

The LHS now gives the instantaneous *net* return in utils of a unit of investment in $\hat{k}(t)$, where $\dot{q}_t^*$ is the capital gain or loss measured in utils. On the RHS, the term $\rho - n$ is the rate at which utils *ought to grow* in the planner's judgement. It is the counterpart of $i(t)$ in (2.13). This rate applied to the shadow price of capital yields the instantaneous return that the planner finds acceptable, the imputed opportunity cost of investment in physical capital. Hence, (2.14) says that the rate of return from investment along the optimal path equals the household's minimum acceptable return. When (2.11) or (2.14) holds therefore, the planner has no incentive to divert away from the chosen path of asset accumulation.

2.2.2 Necessary Conditions in terms of the Hamiltonian

We present in this section a compact version of the necessary conditions in terms of the Hamiltonian function. Equation

---

[12]A more common way of writing (2.13) is $f'(k(t)) + \dot{p}(t)/p(t) = i(t)$, usually called the Fisher equation, after Irving Fisher.

(2.8) has already used the Hamiltonian to restate (2.7). Going over to (2.9), we note that

$$
\begin{aligned}
\frac{\partial \mathcal{H}(c_s^*, \hat{k}_s^*, q_s^*)}{\partial \hat{k}(s)} &= u'(c_s^*)\, \frac{\partial c_s^*}{\partial \hat{k}(s)} + q_s^* \, \{ f'(\hat{k}_s^*) - (\mu + n + \delta) \\
&\qquad - \frac{1}{A_s} \frac{\partial c_s^*}{\partial \hat{k}(s)} \} \\
&= q_s^* \, \{ f'(\hat{k}_s^*) - (\mu + n + \delta) \},
\end{aligned}
\tag{2.15}
$$

using (1.9) and (2.7).

Consequently, (2.9) reduces to

$$
q_t^* = \int_t^\infty \partial \mathcal{H}(c_s^*, \hat{k}_s^*, q_s^*) / \partial \hat{k}(s) \; e^{-(\rho-n)(s-t)} ds. \tag{2.16}
$$

Similarly, using (2.16) and (2.15) in succession, (2.11) may be expressed as

$$
\begin{aligned}
\dot{q}_t^* &= \frac{d(\int_t^\infty \partial \mathcal{H}(c_s^*, \hat{k}_s^*, q_s^*)/\partial \hat{k}(s) \; e^{-(\rho-n)(s-t)} ds)}{dt} \\
&= -\frac{\partial \mathcal{H}(c_t^*, \hat{k}_t^*, q_t^*)}{\partial \hat{k}(t)} + (\rho - n)\, q_t^* \\
&= -f'(\hat{k}_t^*)\, q_t^* + (\mu + \rho + \delta)\, q_t^*,
\end{aligned}
\tag{2.17}
$$

Finally, since (1.9) implies

$$
\dot{\hat{k}}_t^* = f(\hat{k}_t^*) - \frac{c_t^*}{A_t} - (\mu + n + \delta)\hat{k}_t^*, \tag{2.18}
$$

the equation is reproduced by writing

$$\dot{\hat{k}}_t^* = \frac{\partial \mathcal{H}(c_t^*, \hat{k}_t^*, q_t^*)}{\partial q(t)}. \qquad (2.19)$$

Let us collect the necessary conditions stated in terms of the Hamiltonian function as[13]

PROPOSITION **2.1** *Suppose* $\{c_t^*, \hat{k}_t^*\}_0^\infty$ *solves the problem. Then, there exists a path of co-state variables* q_t^* *such that* (*2.8*), (*2.19*), (*2.17*) *and* (*2.10*) *are satisfied.*

Proposition A.2 proves that a path satisfying the conditions of Proposition 2.1 is the unique solution to the planner's problem. Some authors prefer an alternative version of Proposition 2.1. This is best understood by replacing $\mathcal{H}(c_t^*, \hat{k}_t^*, q_t^*)$, which is the value of welfare from t onwards evaluated *at* t, by its present value at 0, viz.,

$$\begin{aligned}
\mathcal{H}_d(c_t^*, \hat{k}_t^*, q_t^*) &= \mathcal{H}(c_t^*, \hat{k}_t^*, q_t^*) \, e^{-(\rho-n)t} \\
&= u(c^*(t)) \, e^{-(\rho-n)t} + q_t^* \, e^{-(\rho-n)t} \dot{\hat{k}}^*(t).
\end{aligned} \qquad (2.20)$$

In this new formulation, $q_t^* \, e^{-(\rho-n)t}$ stands for the value of the costate variable at t discounted back to 0. It is easy to see that (2.7) follows if (2.8) is substituted by

$$\frac{\partial \mathcal{H}_d(c_t^*, \hat{k}_t^*, q_t^*)}{\partial c(t)} = 0 \quad \text{at each } t. \qquad (2.21)$$

---

[13]The conditions resemble standard representations of the necessary conditions, except for (2.17). Equation (2.17) is borrowed from Cass (1965, 1966). The advantage of choosing the form (2.17) is that it makes direct reference to the economic interpretation of a co-state variable. Moreover, as will be evident from Appendix 2.1, it uses a single differential equation to describe the evolution of the co-state variable for both reversible and irreversible investment. Also, the reader should note once again that this book derives (2.10) of Theorem 2.1 for a special class of utility functions.

Similarly, (1.9) is obtained by substituting

$$\dot{\hat{k}}_t^* = \frac{\partial \mathcal{H}_d(c_t^*, \hat{k}_t^*, q_t^*)}{\partial (q(t) \ e^{-(\rho-n)t})} \tag{2.22}$$

for (2.19). Condition (2.10) is unrelated to the form of the Hamiltonian and remains unchanged. Finally, (2.11) results from

$$\frac{d \ (q_t^* \ e^{-(\rho-n)t})}{d \ t} + \frac{\partial \mathcal{H}_d(c_t^*, \hat{k}_t^*, q_t^*)}{\partial \hat{k}(t)} = 0. \tag{2.23}$$

Thus, an alternative form of Proposition 2.1 is

PROPOSITION **2.2** *Suppose* $\{c_t^*, \hat{k}_t^*\}_0^\infty$ *solves the problem. Then, there exists a path of co-state variables* q_t^* *such that* (2.21), (2.22), (2.23) *and* (2.10) *are satisfied.*

2.3 The Optimal Time Path

The ideas developed till now may be utilised to study the optimal path of capital accumulation for the Command economy. From here onwards, however, the utility function will be restricted till the rest of the book to the form

$$u(c) = \frac{c^{1-\theta} - 1}{1 - \theta}, \tag{2.24}$$

where θ is a positive constant.[14] It is easy to check that θ stands for the elasticity of marginal utility, or, alternatively, $1/\theta$ the elasticity of intertemporal substitution, and that $(c^{1-\theta} - 1)/(1 - \theta) \to \log c$ as $\theta \to 1$. Most of the exercises below will

---

[14]The need to restrict ourselves to the class of such utility functions will be explained below.

be carried out under the assumption that $\theta \neq 1$. The results for the case $\theta = 1$ can usually be derived by substituting $\theta = 1$ in the equations for the general case. Hence, we do not explicitly discuss this special case. However, in parts of Chapters 5 and 6, we will need to part company with the more general formulation and restrict ourselves to the log c case alone.

The analysis will be broken up into two parts to be identified as a balanced growth equilibrium path and an out of balanced growth.

2.3.1   The Optimal Balanced Growth Path

We shall start with a

Definition: An economy is said to display balanced growth if aggregate output, the aggregate capital stock and aggregate consumption grow at constant rates over time.

Notice that the definition implies that the rates of growth of the per capita variables y, k and c as well as the variables $\hat{y}$, $\hat{k}$ and $\hat{c}$ must also be constants under balanced growth.

In what follows, we shall try to find out if the optimally chosen paths of the Command economy variables can be consistent with balanced growth. To appreciate the point, differentiate (2.7) subject to (2.24) to obtain

$$-\theta \, \frac{\dot{c}}{c} = \frac{\dot{q}}{q} - \mu, \qquad (2.25)$$

dropping the superscript "*" for simplicity. Similarly, (2.17) gives

$$\frac{\dot{q}}{q} - \mu \; = \; -\{f'(\hat{k}) - (\mu + \rho + \delta)\} - \mu$$

$$= \; -\{f'(\hat{k}) - (\rho + \delta)\}. \qquad (2.26)$$

Combining (2.25) and (2.26),[15]

$$\frac{\dot{c}}{c} = \frac{1}{\theta}\ \{f'(\hat{k}) - (\rho + \delta)\}. \qquad (2.27)$$

Equation (2.27) describes the behaviour of $\dot{c}/c$ along an optimal path. It says that the economy's desire to grow is positively linked to the difference between the net marginal productivity of capital and the rate of discounting. A rise in the former raises the desired rate of growth. On the other hand, a rise in the discount rate implies a shift of preference towards current

---

[15]The economic intuition underlying (2.27) may also be understood as follows. Assume the following perturbation in the optimal growth path $\{c^*, \hat{k}^*\}$. There is a marginal increase in $\hat{k}$ at t_0, thus causing a reduction of A_{t_0} in $c^*_{t_0}$. The loss in utility is $A_{t_0}\ u'(c^*_{t_0})$. The extra $\hat{k}$ yields a marginal net return of $f'(\hat{k}^*) - (\mu + n + \delta)$ along the optimal balanced growth path. As opposed to the procedure followed in deriving (2.9), i.e., consuming the extra yield, the latter is assumed to be reinvested now, producing (approximately) the same net return per unit as above, viz. $f'(\hat{k}^*) - (\mu + n + \delta)$, if the invested amount is arbitrarily small. This procedure is followed till $t_1 > t_0$, so that an extra amount of per capita output equal to $A_{t_1}\ e^{(f'(\hat{k}^*)-(\mu+n+\delta))(t_1-t_0)} = A_{t_0}\ e^{\mu(t_1-t_0)}\ e^{(f'(\hat{k}^*)-(\mu+n+\delta))(t_1-t_0)}$ is available at t_1 over and above what the original optimal path produced. The extra utility this yields is $A_{t_0}\ e^{\mu(t_1-t_0)}\ e^{(f'(\hat{k}^*)-(\mu+n+\delta))(t_1-t_0)}\ u'(c^*_{t_1})$. Discounted back to t_0, this gives $e^{-(\rho-n)(t_1-t_0)}\ A_{t_0}\ e^{\mu(t_1-t_0)}\ e^{(f'(\hat{k}^*)-(\mu+n+\delta))(t_1-t_0)}\ u'(c^*_{t_1})$. Suppose now that the consumption path is growing at a balanced rate g. For optimality, the perturbation, being small, leaves the planner indifferent. Thus, using (2.24),

$$
\begin{aligned}
A_{t_0}\ c^*(t_0)^{-\theta} &=\ e^{-(\rho-n)(t_1-t_0)}\ A_{t_0}\ e^{\mu(t_1-t_0)} \\
&\quad \times\ e^{(f'(\hat{k}^*)-(\mu+n+\delta))(t_1-t_0)}\ c^*(t_1)^{-\theta} \\
&=\ e^{-(\rho-n)(t_1-t_0)}\ A_{t_0}\ e^{\mu(t_1-t_0)} \\
&\quad \times\ e^{(f'(\hat{k}^*)-(\mu+n+\delta))(t_1-t_0)} \\
&\quad \times c^*(t_0)^{-\theta}\ e^{-\theta\ g(t_1-t_0)}.
\end{aligned}
$$

Cancelling out terms and solving, (2.27) follows. The argument goes back to Ramsey (1928), who in turn quoted Keynes as its inventor.

consumption. This causes the desired rate of growth to fall. Let us consider a special case of an optimal path by restricting attention to balanced growth paths only. Then, $\dot{c}/c$ and hence $\hat{k}$ are constants, thus implying that the set of feasible paths is restricted to those for which k displays balanced growth at the rate μ. We may appeal to (1.9) to conclude that $\dot{c}/c = \mu$ also. Hence, (2.27) may be rewritten

$$f'(\hat{k}) = \rho + \delta + \mu\theta, \qquad (2.28)$$

which solves for the value of $\hat{k} = \hat{k}^*$ associated with the optimal balanced growth path for a Command economy. We may denote the solution to (2.28) by $\hat{k}^*$. Thus, $\hat{k}^*$ stands for the value of $\hat{k}$ the planner would wish to be endowed with at $t = 0$ if he is to restrict himself to an optimal balanced growth path.[16] The accompanying value of $\hat{c}$ will be denoted by $\hat{c}^*$. We have accordingly[17]

PROPOSITION **2.3** *When restricted to balanced growth paths, the Command economy chooses to grow at the rate* $G_c^* = \mu$. *Along the optimal balanced growth path* $\hat{k}$ *satisfies* (2.28).

According to Proposition 2.3, the planner, when restricted to the set of balanced growth paths in his search for an optimal

---

[16]A solution must exist according to **Property f1** and **Assumption F2**.

[17]The need to restrict the analysis to a special class of utility functions for balanced growth equilibrium to be possible is ultimately related to the presence of technical progress in the model. To appreciate this fact, assume that $\mu = 0$. As Cass (1965) shows, balanced growth for this case would imply constant values of k and c. Consequently, (2.27) may be replaced by the more general condition

$$\frac{cu''(c)}{u'(c)} \frac{\dot{c}}{c} = -\{f'(\hat{k}) - (\rho + \delta)\}.$$

A constant c reduces the LHS of the above equation to zero quite independent of the form of the utility function. In this case, the value of $\hat{k} = k$ under optimal balanced growth is found by solving the equation $f'(k) = \rho + \delta$. See Cass (1965).

path, will choose to start at $\hat{k}^*$ and stay there forever, provided of course that initial values of K and L allow the planner the choice of $\hat{k}^*$. To appreciate the nature of the choice, note that the requirement of optimal balanced growth reduces equation (1.9) to

$$\hat{c} = f(\hat{k}) - (\mu + n + \delta)\,\hat{k}. \qquad (2.29)$$

With reference to Figure 2.3, we see that the maximum value of $\hat{c}$ occurs when[18]

$$f'(\hat{k}) = \mu + n + \delta. \qquad (2.30)$$

The solution $\hat{k}^{**}$ to (2.30) is referred to as the Golden rule(GR) value of the effective capital-labour ratio.[19] The corresponding solution $\hat{k}^*$ to (2.28) is called the Modified Golden Rule. (Cass (1965), Koopmans (1965).) The value of $\hat{c}$ associated with $\hat{k}^{**}$ is denoted $\hat{c}^{**}$. The reader will wonder how $\hat{c}^*$ compares with $\hat{c}^{**}$. Indeed, if $\hat{c}^* < \hat{c}^{**}$, then $\hat{k}^{**}$ might appear to be a better choice over $\hat{k}^*$, since it would lead to a larger value of c for all time.

We show first that $\hat{k}^* < \hat{k}^{**}$, so that $\hat{c}^* < \hat{c}^{**}$ is indeed the case. The chosen form (2.24) of the utility function imposes a restriction on the exogenously specified rate of technical progress μ. To see this, observe that aggregate utility along the balanced growth equilibrium path is given by

$$U = \int_0^\infty \frac{c_t^{*1-\theta} - 1}{1 - \theta}\, e^{-(\rho - n)t}\, dt.$$

Using the fact that $c_t^* = c_0^* e^{\mu t}$, the above integral reduces to

---

[18]The reader should be able to verify quite easily that the strict concavity of f along with the Inada conditions guarantees that a maximum exists.

[19]The nomenclature goes back to Phelps (1961, 1965).

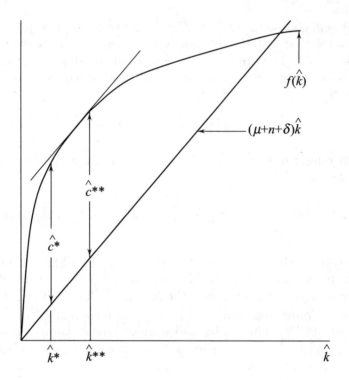

Figure 2.3

$$U = -\frac{1}{1-\theta} \int_0^\infty e^{-(\rho-n)t}dt + \frac{(c_0^*)^{1-\theta}}{1-\theta} \int_0^\infty e^{(1-\theta)\mu t} e^{-(\rho-n)t}dt. \tag{2.31}$$

Clearly, for the integral to be well-defined, it is necessary and sufficient that

$$\rho - n > (1-\theta)\,\mu. \tag{2.32}$$

Since $\rho - n > 0$, inequality (2.32) imposes no restriction on μ when $\theta \geq 1$. However, if $\theta < 1$, (2.32) leads to a nontrivial bound on the allowable rate of technical change.[20] Armed with this inequality, we see that $\mu + n + \delta < \rho + \mu\,\theta + \delta$. Hence, comparing (2.28) with (2.30) and using the concavity of $f(\hat{k})$, it follows that $\hat{k}^* < \hat{k}^{**}$. Since the solution to (2.30) is unique, we conclude that $\hat{c}^{**} > \hat{c}^*$. Thus, along the balanced growth equilibrium path, society enjoys less than the maximum possible per capita consumption.

Why then does the planner prefer $\hat{c}^*$? To answer this question, note that $\{\hat{c}^*, \hat{k}^*\}$ was a *unique* pair that satisfied simultaneously the condition of optimality (i.e., (2.27)) *and* balanced growth. In fact, the optimal rate of growth of c implied by (2.27) at $\hat{k}^{**}$ must be less than μ, since $\hat{k}^{**} > \hat{k}^*$. This means that the planner considers it suboptimal to stay put at $\hat{c}^{**}$. The explanation lies in the form of the planner's objective function, which is a *discounted* sum of utilities. Intuitively speaking, the planner can construct an alternative and better path by (a) consuming a part of the capital stock associated with $\hat{c}^{**}$, thus bringing the capital stock down to a level consistent with $\hat{c}^*$ and (b) maintaining the lower value of $\hat{k}^*$ thereafter forever. There would be an initial gain in consumption in the process (the capital consumed) and subsequent loss (lower consumption corresponding to $\hat{k}^*$). However, the discounted sum of future losses will be more than compensated by the initial gain. Appendix 2.3 will prove this result rigorously. Indeed, as we shall see there, the conclusions remain true whether investment is reversible or not.

In this connection, it should be obvious that, in the absence of discounting, the planner would in fact choose $\{\hat{c}^{**}, \hat{k}^{**}\}$ as the best balanced growth path. The only problem in that case would however be that the associated welfare function would not be a simple generalisation of (2.1), because the infinite integral would be unbounded for any balanced growth path. It is worth noting here that Ramsey considered an undiscounted version of the planner's aggregate welfare function, since he viewed discounting of future utilities to be unethical. Consequently, he had to address the question of the existence of

---

[20]This is the additional restriction that Section 2.2 hinted at while discussing **Assumption u3**.

the infinite integral. He had an ingenious idea to circum-
vent the non-existence problem, for which interested students
are referred to his paper. Much later, undiscounted future
utilities were once again the centre of attraction in connection with an alternative version of the planner's utility function, the so-called *overtaking criterion*, introduced by Atsumi
(1965) and von Weizäcker (1965). In the undiscounted case,
the transversality condition is not expected to hold. The best
way to appreciate this is to note that the value of the co-
state variable corresponding to the optimal GR solution c^{**}
equals $q^{**} = u'(c^{**}) > 0$, which stays bounded away from
zero. Appendix 2.4 discusses another infinite horizon, undiscounted problem (constructed by Halkin (1974)), for which the
transversality condition fails. Contrary to the problem we have
discussed so far, Halkin's objective function assigned a dispro-
portionately high weight on capital in the distant future.

2.3.2   Out of Balanced Growth Equilibrium Path

Pinning down a variable like $\hat{k}$ brings up another problem.
Since, K_0 and $(A_0 \ L_0)$ are exogenously given, $\hat{k}_0$ is fixed at
the outset. Except by accident, $\hat{k}_0$ will not be identical with
the optimal choice of $\hat{k}$. Consequently, the economy will not
move along the balanced growth equilibrium path all the time.
This being the case, we must discover what constitutes out of
balanced growth behaviour and how it relates to the balanced
growth path. The objective of this section is to demonstrate
that optimal behaviour leads the planner to guide the economy
over time towards the MGR pair $(\hat{k}^*, \hat{c}^*)$.

To establish this result, let us subtract μ from both sides
of (2.27) to write

$$\frac{\dot{\hat{c}}}{\hat{c}} = \frac{1}{\theta} \left\{ f'(\hat{k}) - (\rho + \delta + \mu\theta) \right\}, \qquad (2.33)$$

where the superscript "*" has been dropped for all the variables
for simplicity (as in Section 2.3.1). Using (2.25), we see that

$$\frac{\dot{\hat{c}}}{\hat{c}} = -\frac{1}{\theta}\left(\frac{\dot{q}}{q} - (1-\theta)\mu\right) = -\frac{1}{\theta}\frac{\dot{\hat{q}}}{\hat{q}}, \qquad (2.34)$$

where $\hat{q} = q/A^{1-\theta}$. The new variable $\hat{q}$, which is a monotone transformation of q will play a role in our study of the optimal out of balanced growth behaviour of the economy. Given the definition of $\hat{q}$ and (2.34), equation (2.33) reduces to

$$\frac{\dot{\hat{q}}}{\hat{q}} = -\{f'(\hat{k}) - (\rho + \delta + \mu\theta)\}. \qquad (2.35)$$

Next, use (2.7), (2.24) and (1.9) to write

$$\hat{q}(t) = \frac{1}{(f(\hat{k}(t)) - \lambda(\hat{k}(t) - \dot{\hat{k}}(t))^\theta}, \qquad (2.36)$$

recalling $\lambda = \mu + n + \delta$. The study of optimal path reduces now to a study of the pair of differential equations (2.35) and (2.36). The method of analysis to follow will identify the qualitative properties of this path, especially its behaviour in the long run. This is best done with the help of what is known as a phase diagram in the $(\hat{k}, \hat{q})$ plane. See Figure 2.4. The phase diagram displays two curves. One of these, the U-shaped curve, plots the equation (2.36) by putting $\dot{\hat{k}} = 0$. The second is a vertical line through $\hat{k}^*$ obtained by equating the *LHS* of (2.35) to zero. Thus, the first curve represents combinations of $\hat{q}$ and $\hat{k}$ which leave $\hat{k}$ unchanged over time. Similarly, along the second curve, $\hat{q}$ is a constant. The intersection of the two curves represents the balanced growth equilibrium point $(\hat{k}^*, \hat{q}^*)$. If the economy starts out with $\hat{k}^*$, then it continues forever with the combination $(\hat{k}^*, \hat{q}^*)$, or, alternatively, $(\hat{k}^*, \hat{c}^*)$.

The curves divide up the plane into four non-overlapping zones $\mathcal{P}$, $\mathcal{P}'$, $\mathcal{Q}$ and $\mathcal{Q}'$. We want to find out how the economy will behave if it starts with $\hat{k}_0 \neq \hat{k}^*$ and chooses a $\hat{q}_0$ so that the pair $(\hat{k}_0, \hat{q}_0)$ falls in any one of these regions. We shall

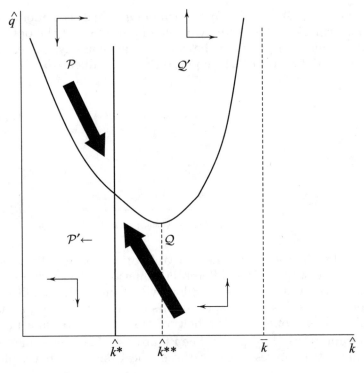

Figure 2.4

present the arguments for $\mathcal{P}$ and leave it to the reader to carry out the arguments for the other cases. In the region $\mathcal{P}$, we have $f'(\hat{k}) > \rho + \delta + \theta\mu$. Hence, (2.35) implies $\dot{\hat{q}} < 0$, which is indicated by an downward pointing arrow. In the same region, (2.36) implies that $\dot{\hat{k}} > 0$. This is indicated by a rightward pointing arrow. The directions of movements in the other three regions are indicated in Figure 2.4.

A path that starts in region $\mathcal{P}$ can either move towards the balanced growth equilibrium point (see thick arrow), or move into either of the two regions $\mathcal{P}'$ or $\mathcal{Q}'$. Once inside the last two regions, the path stays trapped there as the little arrows indicate. Similarly, a path starting in $\mathcal{Q}$ may converge to the balanced growth equilibrium or get trapped in regions $\mathcal{P}'$ or $\mathcal{Q}'$. We will argue that it is either suboptimal or infeasible for a path to enter the regions $\mathcal{P}'$ or $\mathcal{Q}'$.

Suppose to the contrary that an optimal path ends up being trapped in $\mathcal{Q}'$. This means either that $\hat{q} \uparrow \infty$. Hence, (2.36) implies that $\hat{c}$ is arbitrarily small for t large enough. This amounts to suboptimal behaviour, since it is possible to hold $\hat{c}$ at a higher level and maintaining the corresponding $\hat{k}$ ever onwards. Thus, an optimal path cannot move into the zone $\mathcal{Q}'$.

Next suppose that $\{\hat{k}_t^*, \hat{c}_t^*\}$ moves into $\mathcal{P}'$. In this zone, $\hat{q}^* \downarrow 0$, Hence, (2.36) implies that $\hat{c}^* \uparrow \infty$. On the other hand, $\hat{k}^* \downarrow 0$ in the region $\mathcal{P}'$ also. Since the maximum possible value of $\hat{c}$ is $f(\hat{k}) + (1 - \delta)\hat{k}$, the path in question is infeasible.

Thus, the only possibility that remains is that the optimal path converges to $(\hat{k}^*, \hat{q}^*)$. The result arrived at may be stated as

PROPOSITION **2.4** *Starting from any arbitrary initial values of the capital stock and labour force, the optimal path for the Solow economy converges to the Modified Golden rule configuration.*

We have thus proved that the optimal path cannot converge to $\hat{k}^{**}$. Further, for t large enough, $f(\hat{k}_t^*) - (\mu + n + \delta)$ is strictly positive and stays bounded away from zero. This takes us back to the transversality condition discussed in Section 2.2.1 and ensures that (2.10) holds.[21]

---

[21] As already noted, the result is proved more generally in Appendix 2.3 to incorporate irreversible investment.

2.4 Growth in a Private Economy

The present section and the following one will derive the complete set of necessary conditions for the optimality of the dynamic path chosen by the household. The exercise is a relatively simple one, given our derivation of the conditions for the Command economy. Let us replace (1.9) by (2.3) and treat a rather than $\hat{k}$ as the state variable. The control variable for both problems is c. However, to distinguish between the Command and the Private economies, we shall denote the Private economy choice by $\bar{c}$. The necessary condition for a static optimum turns out to be

$$u'(\bar{c}) - \bar{q} = 0, \qquad (2.37)$$

where $\bar{q}(t)$ is the co-state variable for the problem, i.e., the shadow price of a unit of $a(t)$ at t.

The derivation of the dynamic optimisation condition too mimics the corresponding derivation for the Command Economy. For H to be willing to hold $\bar{a}$ at each t, the optimal price of a unit of a at each t should equal the discounted present value of the stream of returns from the investment, after correction for depreciation on account of population growth. In other words,

$$\bar{q}_t = \int_t^\infty e^{-(\rho-n)(s-t)} (r_s - n)\, \bar{q}_s ds. \qquad (2.38)$$

Differentiating this equation, we get

$$\dot{\bar{q}}_t = -\bar{q}_t\, r_t + \bar{q}_t\, \rho. \qquad (2.39)$$

Equations (2.37), (2.38) and (2.39) correspond to (2.7), (2.9) and (2.11) respectively. We shall show in Section 2.5 that these conditions, along with an appropriate transversality condition constitute the necessary conditions for the optimality of the household's chosen path.

Conditions (2.37) and (2.39) can be written with reference to the relevant Hamiltonian for the market economy:

$$\mathcal{H}_m(c(t), a(t), \bar{q}(t)) = u(c(t)) + \bar{q}(t)[w(t)$$
$$+(r(t) - n)a(t) - c(t)]. \quad (2.40)$$

Condition (2.37) turns out to be

$$\frac{\partial \mathcal{H}_m(\bar{c}_t^*, \bar{a}_t^*, \bar{q}_t^*)}{\partial c} = 0. \quad (2.41)$$

Similarly, (2.39) follows from

$$\dot{\bar{q}}_t^* = \frac{d \int_t^\infty \partial \mathcal{H}_m(\bar{c}_s^*, \bar{a}_s^*, \bar{q}_s^*)/\partial a(s)\ e^{-(\rho-n)(s-t)} ds}{dt}. \quad (2.42)$$

Finally,

$$\dot{\bar{a}}_t^* = \frac{\partial \mathcal{H}_m(\bar{c}_t^*, \bar{a}_t^*, \bar{q}_t^*)}{\partial \bar{q}(t)} \quad (2.43)$$

yields (2.3).

We end up this section with a discussion of the optimal balanced growth path for the Private economy. Given (2.24), equations (2.37) and (2.39) may be manipulated to yield

$$\frac{\dot{c}}{c} = \frac{r - \rho}{\theta}. \quad (2.44)$$

The above equation expresses the rate at which the household wishes to grow given the market rate of interest r. Consequently, we shall denote it by $g_c^d(r)$ and call it the demand rate of growth for the Private economy.

Somewhat in the spirit of the Command economy exercise, we may ask if a balanced growth path could constitute the equilibrium growth path for the Private economy. Suppose then that the Private economy equilibrium path displays balanced growth. As (2.44) shows, such a path will be associated with a constant r. Though each value of r gives rise to a corresponding demand rate of growth, not all of them will constitute an equilibrium. Equilibrium will only correspond to values of r for which the supply of consumption goods by B increases at the same rate as the rise in their demand. Using the equilibrium condition (1.12), a constant r will imply a constant $\hat{k}$ for profit maximisation. Consequently, k will grow at the rate μ. The latter implies from (1.9), however, that c must grow at the rate μ too. Hence, from supply side considerations, c grows at the constant rate μ for any arbitrary constant value of r. We may refer to this perfectly inelastic relationship as the supply rate of balanced growth $g_c^s(r)$.

As argued, for a balanced growth path to be the equilibrium path for a Private economy, $g_c^d(r) = g_c^s(r)$. Figure 2.5 captures the equilibrium. The right hand panel of Figure 2.5 represents the determination of r^*, the equilibrium rate of

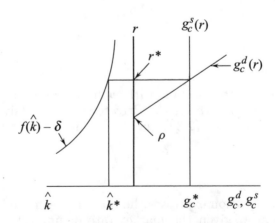

Figure 2.5

interest. Even though the equilibrium rate of growth is viewed as an intersection of a demand and a supply curve, it should be obvious that it is the supply side which dominates. The equilibrium growth rate of c is $g_c^* = \mu$. Thus, a change in the parameters of demand, i.e., shifts or changes in the slope of the demand curve, will leave the equilibrium rate of growth unaffected. An increase in thriftiness, caused, say, by a tax on consumption, will fail to affect the equilibrium rate of growth of the system. In other words, the equilibrium rate of growth is uncontrollable. This diagrammatic device will find extensive use in the subsequent chapters.

The left hand panel captures the determination of $\hat{k}^*$ associated with a balanced growth equilibrium. The value of $\hat{k}^*$ follows from the equilibrium value of r^*, since (1.12) requires that the net marginal product of capital be equated to the market rate of interest.[22]

2.5 Comparison of Growth Paths: Command Economy vs. Private Economy

The purpose of this section is to derive the complete set of optimality conditions for the household's dynamic optimisation exercise in a Private economy and establish that the equilibrium growth path of the Private economy is unique and identically the same as the optimal growth path for the Command economy. The latter result is the dynamic counterpart of the First Fundamental Theorem of Welfare Economics, which states that a competitive equilibrium is Pareto Optimal.

We shall restrict attention to the function (2.24). Define a new variable p^* such that $p_t^*/A_t = \bar{q}_t^*$ at each t. Then, (2.38) reduces to

$$\frac{p_t^*}{A_t} = \int_t^\infty e^{-(\rho-n)(s-t)}(r_s^* - n)\,\frac{p_s^*}{A_s}\,ds. \qquad (2.45)$$

---

[22]To the extent that a balanced growth path is an equilibrium path for a Private economy, it satisfies the property of a perfect foresight equilibrium.

Differentiating with respect to t and taking account of (1.12), we obtain

$$\dot{p}_t^* = -f'(\bar{\bar{k}}_t^*)\, p_t^* + (\mu + \rho + \delta)\, p_t^*. \tag{2.46}$$

Equation (2.37) reduces to

$$u'(\bar{c}_t^*) = \frac{p_t^*}{A_t}. \tag{2.47}$$

Also, as already noted, (2.3) implies (1.1) and the latter boils down (as with (1.9)) to

$$\bar{c}_t^* + A_t\, \dot{\bar{k}}_t^* = A_t\{f(\bar{\bar{k}}_t^*) - (\mu + n + \delta)\bar{\bar{k}}_t^*\}. \tag{2.48}$$

Equations (2.46), (2.47), (2.48) may now be used to show (following Section 2.3.2) that the relevant variables for the Private economy converge to the MGR configuration. In particular, this means that $f'(\bar{\bar{k}}_t^*) - (\mu + \delta + n)$ stays bounded away from 0 as $t \to \infty$. Let us now solve the differential equation (2.46) to obtain[23]

$$p_t^* = p_0^*\, e^{-\int_0^t\, (f'(\bar{\bar{k}}_s^*) - (\mu + \rho + \delta))\, ds}.$$

Multiplying both sides by $e^{-(\rho - n)\, t}$ and simplifying, we get

$$p_t^*\, e^{-(\rho - n)\, t} = p_0^*\, e^{-\int_0^t\, (f'(\bar{\bar{k}}_s^*) - (\mu + \delta + n))\, ds}. \tag{2.49}$$

Since, $f'(\bar{\bar{k}}_t^*) - (\mu + \delta + n)$ is strictly positive from some t onwards and stays bounded away from 0 as $t \to \infty$, it follows

---

[23]See Appendix 1.1.2 of Barro & Sala-i-Martin (2003) for a clear exposition on the method of solution of this differential equation.

that the RHS of the last equation converges to 0 as $t \to \infty$. Hence, p_t^* satisfies (2.10). We now appeal to Appendix 2.2 to claim that (2.46), (2.47), (2.48) and (2.49) imply that the path $\{\bar{c}_t^*, \bar{\bar{k}}_t^*\}_0^\infty$ is unique and solves the Command Economy's problem. Hence, the Private economy path is identically the same as the one followed by the Command economy. Also, the path of $\{r_t^*, w_t^*\}_0^\infty$ determined by (1.12) is unique.

We may further note that (2.38) is rewritten as

$$\bar{q}_t^* = \int_t^\infty e^{-(\rho-n)(s-t)} (f'(\bar{\bar{k}}_t^*) - \delta - n)\, \bar{q}_s^* ds. \qquad (2.50)$$

Moreover, given (2.32), $f'(\bar{\bar{k}}_t^*) \to (\rho + \delta + \mu\ \theta)$ implies that $f'(\bar{\bar{k}}_t^*) - (\delta + n)$ is strictly positive from some t onwards and stays bounded away from 0 as $t \to \infty$. Hence, the variable $\bar{q}_t^*$ must satisfy the transversality condition for (2.50) to hold at each t. Our results for the Private economy may now be collected with reference to the Hamiltonian function $\mathcal{H}_m$:

PROPOSITION **2.5** *Suppose* $\{\bar{c}_t^*, \bar{a}_t^*\}_0^\infty$ *and* $\{r_t^*, w_t^*\}_0^\infty$ *is an equilibrium path for the Private economy. Then, there exists a path of co-state variables* $\bar{q}_t^*$ *such that* (2.41), (2.42), (2.43) *and the transversality condition*

$$e^{-(\rho-n)t} \bar{q}_t^* \to 0 \ as \ t \to \infty \qquad (2.51)$$

are satisfied. The equilibrium paths of the variables chosen by the Private economy are unique. Moreover, the paths of per capita consumption and capital chosen by the Private economy are identically the same as the ones chosen by the Planned Economy.

Thus, the decentralised decisions of a Private economy produce a social optimum, though, as we shall see, many of the growth models to follow violate this property. Moreover, as far as the

Solow model goes, the path followed by the Private economy, being identically the same as the one chosen by the Command economy, will by dynamically stable in the sense of Section 2.3.2.

2.6   The Ways Ahead

Let us first take stock of where we have arrived. We may refer to the growth rate of labour as the exogenous rate and the model determined rate of growth of capital as the endogenous rate. In the absence of technical change, the Solow model predicts the impossibility of the endogenous rate to stay indefinitely higher than the exogenous rate. Under the law of diminishing returns, the latter drives the former down to a level commensurate with itself. Consequently, the Solow exercise leads to the depressing conclusion that the long run growth rate of per capita magnitudes will be exactly zero, a conclusion that would appear to run counter to the very purpose of economic growth.   Fortunately, technical progress helps to get rid of this disturbing conclusion by introducing a "wedge" between the exogenous and the endogenous rates. The force of diminishing returns still prevails, but technical progress distinguishes between the actual labour force and the effective labour force. Capital can now grow permanently faster than the *actual* labour force (the head count if one likes) in apparent violation of the law of diminishing returns! This suggests that any meaningful growth exercise must consist of finding ways of easing the economic system out of the shackles of diminishing returns.

Solow, as we have seen, succeeds in leading us to this vitally important conclusion. Unfortunately, however, he found a way out of the zero growth trap in an ad hoc manner, by supplementing the growth rate of labour by yet another exogenous growth rate, that of technical progress. Both the Private and the Command Economies for the Solow world give rise to economic variables, such as c, k, y etc., that grow ultimately at the rate of growth of A. The latter though is a nebulous entity, consisting of an *exogenously* specified rate of labour augmentation arising from *unexplained* causes. The model fails to shed any light on the nature of economic forces that may affect technological progress. An implication of this observation is that the long run growth rate of the Solow economy cannot be affected by economic policy.[24] This is not a trivial issue, especially so for economies driven by private enterprise, because casual observation suggests that firms do employ resources in the shape of R & D to improve the technology. Thus, one would expect the rate of technological progress to respond to economic incentives, much as the supply of output by a firm does. But, from what we have presented so far, the different supply rates of growth, which depend on the Solow rate of technical progress, behave completely inelastically vis-à-vis changes in known economic variables.

It is this last observation that constitutes the point of departure for Modern Growth theory. It investigates different ways of filling up this missing link in the Solow model and adding refinements to it so as to remove the triviality associated with the rate of technological progress. Let us note the nature of difficulties that could arise in a private economy when we move in the intended direction. First, if we consider A to be the output of a conscious process of production, such as R & D, then it must be paid for. Paying for A in addition to K and L brings up questions of returns to scale with respect to the three factors. The Solow model assumes F to display constant returns to scale with respect to K and AL. But this means that it will give rise to increasing returns if K, A and L are considered separately. Consequently, the assumption of competitive factor markets needs to be given up when we deal with a Private economy. That is, explaining A might require admitting non-competitive market structures. An alternative avenue could be to view A as an unconscious by-product of the process of capital accumulation. Investment undertaken by a firm may attract high quality labour into a given area from which other existing firms benefit. Such investments lead

---

[24]However, a policy that affects, say, saving behaviour, will have an impact on the out of steady state path to the equilibrium. To see this, note that the variable $\dot{k}$ in equation will change in response to changes in the instantaneous savings rate.

to social improvements in productivity, which are external to
the investing firm. In these situations, competitive markets
can function, but the market-generated equilibria will not be
socially optimal, for reasons similar to the failure of the first
fundamental theorem of welfare economics in the presence of
externalities.

In what follows, we shall attempt to introduce the reader to
the different ways in which economic theorists have attempted
to address the basic question raised by the Solow model. In-
variably, however, the answers received fit into one or the other
of the two approaches suggested in the preceding paragraph.
As we shall see in the rest of this book, the *modus operandi*
boils down to investigating if the *scarcity of natural resource*-
imposed law of diminishing returns can be postponed by means
of *human creativity*. Putting it somewhat philosophically,
natural resources, even if growing according to some law, are
ultimately scarce. On the other hand, human wants are boundlessly large. Tapping yet another potentially endless resource,
viz. the unlimited variety of human ingenuity, bridges the gap
between the scarce and the infinite. If human understanding of
the ostensible boundaries imposed by natural phenomena can
keep growing over time through a growth of wilfully acquired
knowledge, then the conflict between the finite and the infinite
could well be resolved. As growth economists would wish us
to believe, knowledge, the most abstract of resources created
by economic agents, serves as the ultimate vehicle for breaking
through the barriers of diminishing returns. It constitutes, in
other words, the crowning refinement in the concept of capital, the only form of capital that is not subject to the laws of
natural scarcity.

The remaining four chapters of the book will present a selected set of attempts by economic theorists to carry forward
the above ideas. In particular, Chapter 4 will collect, except for
the model proposed by Romer (1986), some of the attempts to
view technical progress as an unconscious by product of capital
accumulation. This will lead us to consider the famous Arrow
(1962) exercise on Learning by doing and its extensions. The
chapter will also present models of growth which are formally
similar to the Arrow type models, though motivated by differ-

ent factors. One of these is the exercise due to Dasgupta and Marjit (2004) on the link between quality of life and labour productivity. A famous model it will be concerned with is due to Barro (1990) and Barro and Sala-i-Martin (2004) on the role of infrastructure in capital accumulation. Chapters 4, 5 and 6 will then be concerned with models of consciously produced technical progress. The latter will sometimes assume the form of human capital accumulation (Lucas (1998), Rebelo (1991) in Chapter 4), accumulation of infrastructure (Dasgupta (1999, 2001) in Chapter 4). Other famous exercises they will be concerned with are due to Romer (1990) (in Chapter 5), Grossman and Helpman (1991) (Chapters 5 and 6) and Aghion and Howitt (1992) (Chapter 6). These works will be seen to link growth with profit driven R & D. The models, as we shall see, will call for non-competitive market structures to allow for payment to factors responsible for technical progress. They will also open up the possibility of obsolescence of research ideas in the face of cutthroat competition.

Appendix 2.1　Optimality Conditions: General Treatment

This section has two objectives. First, it provides some of the mathematical details avoided by the intuitive discussion of the necessary first order conditions in Section 2.2.1. Secondly, it gives an integrated analysis that applies to the cases of reversible as well as irreversible investment. Note that for irreversible investment, it is not possible to rule out c hitting the upper bound. At the maximum possible value of c, all output is consumed away, but this does not exhaust the capital stock. The economy bequeaths $(1 - \delta)K$ to posterity. Hence, positive production as well as consumption is feasible at subsequent points of time. However, **Assumption u2** still rules out $c = 0$ at any t. Hence, for irreversible investment, (A1. 1) reduces to

$$0 < c \leq Af(\hat{k}). \tag{A2.1.1}$$

Equation (A2.1.1) shows that the optimum for the irreversible investment case could occur at a point where $\hat{k}$ can no longer be sacrificed to yield extra c. Consequently, the marginal rate of substitution between c and $\hat{k}$ (as measured by the slope of the level curves of the Hamiltonian) may no longer equal the rate of technical substitution between them. At points such as these, the marginal rate of substitution will be treated as the correct price ratio. The implication of this observation will be clearer below. The planner's optimisation exercise for this case is:

Optimisation under Irreversible Investment:

Find $\{c^*(t)\}_0^\infty$ to maximise (2.1)

subject to (1.9), (A2.1.1) and $\hat{k}(0) = \hat{k}_0$.

In what follows, we shall refer to the reversible and the irreversible investment versions of our problem as Version 1 and Version 2 respectively.

Necessary Conditions for Optimum

We begin our discussion with a

Definition: The function $c : R_+ \to R$ is piecewise continuous if
(a) $c(\cdot)$ is continuous except over a finite set of points $\{a_1, \cdots, a_n\}$ and
(b) at each a_i, $\lim c(t)$ exists for $t \uparrow a_i$ as well as for $t \downarrow a_i$, but the two limits are unequal.

In what follows, the control variable $c(t)$ will be restricted to piecewise continuous functions satisfying (1.9). Any such $c(t)$ will be referred to as a *feasible path*.

At $t = 0$, the entire path $\{c(t)\}_0^\infty$ (leading to the associated path $\{\hat{k}(t)\}_{t>0}^\infty$) is the choice variable for the agent. To this extent, the agent is engaged in a dynamic exercise. However, we shall break up the analysis into two parts. The first part will be concerned with *static* optimality conditions, properties that must hold true for a given volume of output at t to be allocated optimally between consumption and investment. The second part will be concerned with *dynamic* conditions of optimal resource allocation across time, i.e., the way in which the optimal choice at a given point of time is linked to choices in the future.

Static Optimisation, the Principle of Optimality and the Functional Equation

Strictly speaking of course, these exercises are not independent. The overall problem being dynamic in nature, even the static optimality conditions need to be derived with reference to a minimal set of dynamic considerations. In this context, we shall begin by developing Bellman's *Principle of Optimality* (Bellman (1957)), a famous mathematical principle underlying multi-stage decision problems. Starting from any time point t_0, the best achievable value of welfare depends on $\hat{k}_{t_0}$. Notice that this is a deeper statement than might appear at first sight. If the planning horizon were finite, say T, then the best value of welfare would depend on $\hat{k}_{t_0}$ *as well as* t_0, since the residual time horizon shrinks with the passage of time (i.e., $T - t_0$ falls as t_0 rises). The infinite horizon problem does not involve this complication. At any value of t, the residual horizon continues to be infinitely long.

Let $V(\hat{k}_{t_0})$ stand for the optimum welfare starting from $\hat{k}_{t_0}$, as in Section 2.2.1. The function is normally referred to as the *value function*. Consider the truncated problem

$$\text{Maximise} \quad \int_{t_o}^{\infty} u(c(t)) \; e^{-(\rho-n)(t-t_0)} \; dt$$

$$\text{subject to} \quad (1.9), \; (2.5)$$

$$\text{(alternatively, } (1.9), \; (A2.1.1))$$

$$\text{and} \quad \hat{k}(t_0) = \hat{k}_{t_0}. \tag{A2.1.2}$$

If $\{\tilde{c}_t\}_{t_0}^{\infty}$ solves this problem, then

$$V(\hat{k}_{t_0}) = \int_{t_o}^{\infty} u(\tilde{c}_t) \; e^{-(\rho-n)(t-t_0)} dt.$$

Bellman's Principle of Optimality says:

An optimal path has the property that whatever be
the initial conditions and control variables over some
initial period, the control variables over the remain-
ing period must be optimal for the remaining problem,
with the state resulting from the early decisions con-
sidered as the initial condition.

Let $\{c_t^*\}_0^{\infty}$ solve either Version 1 or Version 2 of our problem. Suppose, moreover, that it gives rise to the path $\hat{k}_t^*$.
Then, according to the Principle of Optimality,

$$V(\hat{k}_{t_0}^*) = \int_{t_o}^{\infty} u(c_t^*) \; e^{-(\rho-n)(t-t_0)} dt.$$

Proof of the Principle of Optimality: Consider a small
interval $0 \leq t \leq h$, $h > 0$. Denoting the truncated path
$\{c(t)\}_0^h$ by $c_{0,h}$, it is clear that $\hat{k}_h$ is a function of $c_{0,h}$, given
$\hat{k}_0$. Let $\hat{k}(h) = \phi(c_{0,h})$. Then, $V(\hat{k}(h)) = V(\phi(c_{0,h}))$. Suppose
then that the agent chooses $c_{0,h}^*$ over the interval $[0, h]$, but that
contrary to the Principle of Optimality, the aggregate utility
from $\{c_t^*\}_h^{\infty}$ falls short of $V(\phi(c_{0,h}^*))$. If possible, let

$$V(\phi(c_{0,h}^*)) = \int_h^{\infty} u(\bar{c}_t)e^{-(\rho-n)\,(t-h)} \; dt$$

$$> \int_h^{\infty} u(c_t^*)e^{-(\rho-n)\,(t-h)} \; dt,$$

where $\bar{c}_t$ is feasible from $\phi(c_{0,h}^*)$ and $\bar{c}_t \neq c_t^*$ except possibly
over a set of time points which is so small that it may be
ignored. Define

$$c^{**}(t) = \begin{cases} c_t^*, & t \in [0, h] \\ \bar{c}_t & t \in (h, \infty). \end{cases}$$

Clearly, $c^{**}(t)$ is feasible, since $c^{**}(t)$ involves possibly a single point of discontinuity at (at $t = h$) in addition to the finite number of discontinuities c_t^* or $\bar{c}_t$ might admit. Further,

$$\int_0^\infty u(c^{**}(t)) \, e^{-(\rho-n)t} \, dt > \int_0^\infty u(c_t^*) \, e^{-(\rho-n)t} \, dt$$

by construction, which contradicts the presumed optimality of $\{c_t^*\}_0^\infty$. ∎

According to the Principle of Optimality then,

$$\begin{aligned} V(\hat{k}_0) &= \int_o^h u(c_t^*) \, e^{-(\rho-n)t} dt + V(\phi(c_{0,h}^*)) \\ &\geq \int_o^h u(c_t) \, e^{-(\rho-n)t} dt + V(\phi(c_{0,h})), \end{aligned}$$
$$(A2.1.3)$$

given any feasible path $\{c(t)\}_0^\infty$. Alternatively,

$$V(\hat{k}_0) = max_{c_{0,h}} \left\{ \int_o^h u(c(t)) \, e^{-(\rho-n)t} dt + V(\phi(c_{0,h})) \right\},$$
$$(A2.1.4)$$

or, more generally,

$$\begin{aligned} V(\hat{k}_{t_0}) &= max_{c_{t_0,t_0+h}} \left\{ \int_{t_0}^{t_0+h} u(c(t)) \, e^{-(\rho-n)(t-t_0)} dt \right. \\ &\left. + V(\phi(c_{t_0,t_0+h})) \right\}, \end{aligned}$$
$$(A2.1.5)$$

where $max_{c_{a,b}}$ denotes maximisation with respect to $c(t)$, $a \leq t \leq b$. Equation (A2.1.4) (alternatively (A2.1.5)) is referred to as a *functional equation*. This completes our discussion of Bellman's Principle of Optimality.

Necessary Conditions for Static Optimality

In what follows, we shall proceed under

Assumption V $V(\hat{k})$ is continuously differentiable.

Assumption V allows us to make some approximations concerning the *RHS* of (A2.1.5). First, for h small,

$$u(c(t)) \cong u(c(t_0)), \quad t_0 \leq t \leq t_0 + h.$$

If t_0 is a point of discontinuity, we choose c_{t_0} as the right hand limit of $c(t)$ at t_0.[25]

Therefore,

$$\int_{t_o}^{t_0+h} u(c(t)) \, e^{-(\rho-n)(t-t_0)} dt \cong u(c(t_0)) \int_{t_o}^{t_0+h} e^{-(\rho-n)(t-t_0)} dt$$

$$= u(c(t_0))[-\frac{e^{-(\rho-n)(t-t_0)}}{\rho - n}]_{t_0}^{t_0+h}$$

$$= u(c(t_0))[-\frac{e^{-(\rho-n)h}}{\rho - n} + \frac{1}{\rho - n}]$$

$$= u(c(t_0))[\frac{1}{\rho - n}\{1 - e^{-(\rho-n)h}\}]$$

$$\cong u(c(t_0))$$

$$\times [\frac{1}{\rho - n}\{1 - (1 - (\rho - n)h)\}]$$

by Taylor's approximation,

$$= u(c(t_0))h.$$

[25]Note that replacing the optimal value of $c(t_0)$ by the right hand limit does not affect the value of the utility integral.

Thus, (A2.1.5) can be written as

$$V(\hat{k}_{t_0}) \cong max_{c(t_0)} \{h\ u(c(t_0)) + V(\hat{k}(t_0 + h))\}, \quad (A2.1.6)$$

where $\hat{k}(t_0 + h)$ results from the choice of $c_{t_0, t_0+h} = c(t_0)$, $t_0 \leq t \leq t_0 + h$. A necessary condition for this optimum is

$$\frac{h\ \partial u(c(t_0))}{\partial c(t_0)} + \frac{\partial V(\hat{k}(t_0 + h))}{\partial c(t_0)} \geq 0. \quad (A2.1.7)$$

The *inequality* is explained by the fact that under irreversible investment, the optimum value of $c(t_0)$ might hit its upper bound given by (A2.1.1). This being a corner solution, the partial derivative may turn out to be strictly positive.

Next, note that

$$\frac{\partial V(\hat{k}(t_0 + h))}{\partial c(t_0)} = \frac{\partial V(\hat{k}(t_0 + h))}{\partial \hat{k}(t_0 + h)} \cdot \frac{\partial \hat{k}(t_0 + h)}{\partial c(t_0)}.$$

Linearizing again

$$\hat{k}(t_0 + h) \cong \hat{k}(t_0) + h\ \dot{\hat{k}}(t_0),$$

where, according to (1.9),

$$\dot{\hat{k}}(t_0) = f(\hat{k}(t_0)) - (\mu + n + \delta)\hat{k}(t_0) - \frac{c(t_0)}{A_{t_0}}.$$

Thus,

$$\frac{\partial \hat{k}(t_0 + h)}{\partial c(t_0)} \cong -\frac{h}{A_{t_0}}.$$

Denote $\partial V(\hat{k}_t^*)/\partial \hat{k}(t)$ by q_t^*. The variable $q(t)$ stands for the maximum possible change in the social welfare from t onwards on account of a marginal change in $\hat{k}(t)$. In other words, it is the marginal value or shadow price of $\hat{k}$ at t along the optimal path. The assumption that V is differentiable implies that at any given value of $\hat{k}(t)$, the value of $q(t)$ is uniquely defined. Using these facts, the optimality of $\{c_t^*\}_{t_0}^{\infty}$ and the definition of q_t^*, (A2.1.7) reduces to

$$\frac{h\, \partial u(c_{t_0}^*)}{\partial c(t_0)} - q_{t_0+h}^* \frac{h}{A_{t_0}} = \frac{h\, \partial u(c_{t_0}^*)}{\partial c(t_0)} - \frac{h\, q_{t_0}^*}{A_{t_0}} - \frac{h\, (q_{t_0+h}^* - q_{t_0}^*)}{A_{t_0}}$$

$$\geq\ 0,$$

or,

$$\frac{\partial u(c_{t_0}^*)}{\partial c(t_0)} - \frac{q_{t_0}^*}{A_{t_0}} - \frac{(q_{t_0+h}^* - q_{t_0}^*)}{A_{t_0}} \geq 0.$$

Allowing $h \to 0$, replacing t_0 by t and using **Assumption V**, we see that for $\{c_t^*\}_0^{\infty}$ to be optimal,

$$\frac{\partial u(c_t^*)}{\partial c(t)} - \frac{q_t^*}{A_t}\ \geq\ 0, \text{ with equality}$$

$$\text{if } c_t^* \text{ is interior} ,\quad \text{(A2.1.8)}$$

$$\text{and }\ \left(\frac{\partial u(c_t^*)}{\partial c(t)} - \frac{q_t^*}{A_t}\right) z^*(t)\ =\ 0 \qquad \text{(A2.1.9)}$$

must hold for all t.

The Maximal Principle

Section 2.2.1 introduced the reader to the terminology *Maximal Principle* and the connection between the static optimisation exercise and the auxiliary Hamiltonian function. We fill in some of the mathematical details of that discussion here and, in the process, generalise it to apply the case of irreversible investment also.

Consider first the reversible investment case. We shall argue that in this case, c_t^* maximises $\mathcal{H}$ subject to (1.9), $\hat{k}(t) = \hat{k}_t^*$ and $q(t) = q_t^*$ for each t. Moreover, the *FOC* characterising such a solution is identically the same as the equality version of (A2.1.8). To see this, use (1.9) to get

$$\dot{\hat{k}}(t) = \{f(\hat{k}^*(t)) - (\mu + n + \delta)\hat{k}^*(t)\} - \frac{c(t)}{A_t}.$$

Substituting in (2.6), $\mathcal{H}$ reduces to

$$\mathcal{H}(c(t), \hat{k}^*(t), q^*(t)) = u(c(t)) + q^*(t)[\{f(\hat{k}^*(t)) - (\mu + n + \delta)\hat{k}^*(t)\} - \frac{c(t)}{A_t}],$$

which is a function of $c(t)$ alone. Differentiating $\mathcal{H}$ with respect to $c(t)$, we obtain $\partial u(c(t))/\partial c(t) - q^*(t)/A_t$. By assumption, $\exists$ a value of c_t^* satisfying (1.9) and $\hat{k}(t) = \hat{k}_t^*$ such that

$$\frac{\partial u(c_t^*)}{\partial c(t)} - \frac{q_t^*}{A_t} = 0.$$

The shape of the level curves of $\mathcal{H}$ tell us further that c_t^* is a unique solution to the problem

$$\text{Maximise } \mathcal{H}(c(t), \hat{k}_t^*, q_t^*) \text{ subject to (1.9).} \qquad \text{(A2.1.10)}$$

Next, consider a corner solution corresponding to irreversible investment. To relate it to the Hamiltonian, let us reformulate the relevant constraints in the Kuhn-Tucker form. Rewrite (1.9) as the inequality constraint

$$A_t\{f(\hat{k}(t)) - (\mu + n + \delta)\hat{k}(t)\} - c(t) - A_t\,\dot{\hat{k}}(t) \geq 0 \quad \text{(A2.1.11)}$$

Similarly, note that

$$(\mu + n + \delta)\hat{k}(t) + \dot{\hat{k}}(t) \geq 0 \qquad \text{(A2.1.12)}$$

must hold. The inequality (A2.1.8) may now be viewed as the *FOC* satisfying a corner solution to the problem

$$\text{Maximise} \quad \mathcal{H}(c(t), \hat{k}^*(t), q_t^*)$$

$$\text{subject to} \quad (A2.1.11) \text{ and} \quad (A2.1.12).$$

$$\text{(A2.1.13)}$$

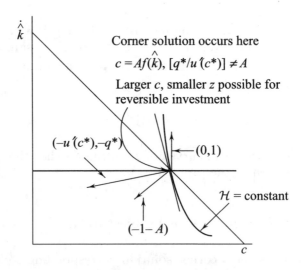

Figure 2.6

Figure 2.6 shows that at the corner solution, both constraints are binding. The gradients to these constraints at the optimum point are $(-1, -A_t)$ and $(0, 1)$ respectively and the gradient to the objective function is $(u'(c_t^*), q_t^*)$. As per the Kuhn-Tucker conditions then, $\exists$ nonnegative Lagrange multipliers λ_1 and λ_2 such that

$$(-u'(c_t^*), -q_t^*) = \lambda_1 (-1, -A_t) + \lambda_2 (0, 1).$$

Moreover, it is easy to read from Figure 2.6 that (A2.1.8) must hold as a strict inequality.

Dynamic Optimality

We shall consider the following perturbation in the optimal path (See Figure 2.2):

(a) at t_0, consumption is lowered and investment increased marginally so as to raise $\hat{k}_{t_0}^*$ to $\hat{k}_{t_0}'$, where $\hat{k}_{t_0}' - \hat{k}_{t_0}^* = \Delta$;

(b) $\hat{k}_s' = \hat{k}_s^* + \Delta \ \forall \ s > t_0$, or, as shown in Figure 2.2, $\hat{k}_s'$ is merely a parallel upward shift in $\hat{k}^*(s)$ for $s > t_0$;

(c) $\forall \ s > t_0$, the extra *per capita* output realised by the higher $\hat{k}_s'$ *after maintaining the additional* Δ *for all time* is consumed away.[26]

The definition of $q(\cdot)$ implies that the price of a unit of $\hat{k}(t_0)$ in units of $c(t_0)$ is $q_{t_0}^*/u'(c_{t_0}^*)$ along the optimal path. Thus, the sacrifice of $c(t_0)$ required to raise $\hat{k}_{t_0}^*$ by Δ equals $(q_{t_0}^*/u'(c_{t_0}^*)) \Delta$. This entails a loss of *utility* equal to $u'(c^*(t_0)) \times \Delta (q_{t_0}^*/u'(c_{t_0}^*)) = \Delta q_{t_0}^*$.

Let us now compute the extra utility provided by the new path $\forall \ s > t_0$. The extra per capita output brought forth by Δ at s equals $A_s f'(\hat{k}_s^*) \Delta$. This extra output is partly invested to maintain $\hat{k}(s)$ at the higher level. In units of z, the required

---

[26]The construction of the perturbed path follows Solow (2000).

investment is $(\mu + n + \delta)$ Δ, which equals $(q_s^*/u'(c_s^*))$ $(\mu + n + \delta)$ Δ in units of c. The extra per capita consumption permitted by the extra output after subtracting the investment is $A_s f'(\hat{k}_s^*)$ $\Delta - (q_s^*/u'(c_s^*))$ $(\mu + n + \delta)$ Δ. Multiplying out by $u'(c_s^*)$, the extra utility from the extra consumption at each s is given by $[A_s\, u'(c_s^*)\, f'(\hat{k}(s)) - q_s^*\, (\mu + n + \delta)]$ Δ. Thus, the total discounted gain in utility at t_0 from the perturbation equals $\Delta \int_{t_0}^{\infty} e^{-(\rho-n)(s-t_0)}\{A_s u'(c_s^*) f'(\hat{k}_s^*) - q_s^* (\mu + n + \delta)\} ds$.

Optimality, as noted, requires that the gain and the loss be equal. Hence,

$$\Delta\, q_{t_0}^* = \Delta \int_{t_0}^{\infty} e^{-(\rho-n)(s-t_0)}\{A_s u'(c_s^*)\, f'(\hat{k}_s^*) - q_s^* (\mu + n + \delta)\} ds,$$

or,

$$q_{t_0}^* = \int_{t_0}^{\infty} e^{-(\rho-n)(s-t_0)}\{A_s u'(c_s^*)\, f'(\hat{k}_s^*) - q_s^* (\mu + n + \delta)\} ds.$$

$$(A2.1.14)$$

Replacing t_0 by t for notational ease, consistency between (A2.1.8) and (A2.1.14) implies

$$q_t^* \geq \int_{t}^{\infty} e^{-(\rho-n)(s-t)} q_s^* \{f'(\hat{k}_s^*) - (\mu + n + \delta)\} ds. \quad (A2.1.15)$$

For q_t^* to be well-defined, the integral on the *RHS* must exist for each t. We shall demonstrate in Appendix 2.2 (Proposition A2.2.1) that the optimality of $\{c_t^*, \hat{k}_t^*\}_0^{\infty}$ implies $f'(\hat{k}_s^*) - (\mu + n + \delta)$ is bounded strictly away from zero for s sufficiently large. Anticipating this result, the integral can exist $\forall$ t only if the transversality condition (2.10) is satisfied. Differentiating (A2.1.14) with respect to t to get

$$\dot{q}_t^* = -\{A_t u'(c_t^*) f'(\hat{k}_t^*) - q_t^*(\mu + n + \delta)\}$$

$$+(\rho - n) \int_t^\infty e^{-(\rho-n)(s-t)} \{A_s u'(c_s^*) f'(\hat{k}_s^*)$$
$$-q_s^*(\mu + n + \delta)\} ds.$$

Using (A2.1.14), the last equation reduces to

$$\dot{q}_t^* = -\{A_t u'(c_t^*) f'(\hat{k}_t^*) - q_t^*(\mu+n+\delta)\} + (\rho-n)q_t^*. \quad \text{(A2.1.16)}$$

The necessary conditions for static and dynamic optimality are renumbered and stated below for easy reference as

PROPOSITION **A2.1.1** *If* $\{c_t^*, \hat{k}_t^*\}_0^\infty$ *is optimal, then there exists a path of co-state variables* $\{q_t^*\}_0^\infty$ *such that*

$$u'(c_t^*) \geq \frac{q_t^*}{A_t}, \text{ with equality for an interior } c_t^*; \quad \text{(A2.1.17)}$$

$$\dot{\hat{k}}_t^* = f(\hat{k}_t^*) - \frac{c_t^*}{A_t} - (\mu + n + \delta)\hat{k}_t^*; \quad \text{(A2.1.18)}$$

$$\dot{q}_t^* = -\{A_t u'(c_t^*) f'(\hat{k}_t^*) - q_t^*(\mu + n + \delta)\}$$
$$+ (\rho - n)q_t^*$$

$$= -A_t u'(c_t^*) f'(\hat{k}_t^*) + (\mu + \rho + \delta)q_t^*; \quad \text{(A2.1.19)}$$

and $\quad e^{-(\rho-n)t} q_t^* \to 0 \text{ as } t \to \infty.$ (A2.1.20)

The Hamiltonian Function Again

The link between (A2.1.17) of Proposition A2.1.1 and the Hamiltonian was already indicated by (A2.1.10) and (A2.1.13). The remaining parts of this proposition can also be stated in terms of the same Hamiltonian function. Equation (A2.1.18) follows from (2.19).

Equation (2.17) established the link between (A2.1.19) and the Hamiltonian for the reversible investment case. For irreversible investment, use (1.9) and (A2.1.1) to get

$$\mathcal{H} = u(Af(\hat{k})) - q(\mu + n + \delta)\hat{k}, \text{ when } c \text{ has a corner solution.}$$

Differentiating $\mathcal{H}$ with respect to $\hat{k}$, we see that

$$\frac{\partial \mathcal{H}(c_s^*, \hat{k}_s^*, q_s^*)}{\partial \hat{k}(s)} = u'(c_s^*)\, A_s\, f'(\hat{k}_s^*) - q_s^*(\mu + n + \delta).$$

Using (A2.1.14) now, $q_t^* = \int_t^\infty (\partial \mathcal{H}/\partial \hat{k}(s))\, e^{-(\rho-n)(s-t)}ds$. Thus,

$$
\begin{aligned}
\dot{q}_t^* &= \frac{d(\int_t^\infty (\partial \mathcal{H}(c_s^*, \hat{k}_s^*, q_s^*)/\partial \hat{k}(s))\, e^{-(\rho-n)(s-t)}ds)}{dt} \\[2mm]
&= -\frac{\partial \mathcal{H}(c_t^*, \hat{k}_t^*, q_t^*)}{\partial \hat{k}(t)} + (\rho - n)\, q_t^* \\[2mm]
&= -A_t u'(c_t^*) f'(\hat{k}_t^*) + (\mu + \rho + \delta) q_t^*, \qquad \text{(A2.1.21)}
\end{aligned}
$$

which is none other than equation (A2.1.19). Let us collect the necessary conditions stated in terms of the Hamiltonian function as[27]

PROPOSITION **A2.1.2** *Suppose* $\{c_t^*, \hat{k}_t^*\}_0^\infty$ *solves Version 1 or Version 2 of the problem. Then, there exists a path of co-state variables* q_t^* *such that (A2.1.10) (alternatively (A2.1.13)), (2.19), (A2.1.21) and (A2.1.20) are satisfied.*

---

[27]The conditions resemble standard representations of the first three necessary conditions, except for (A2.1.21). Equation (A2.1.21) is borrowed from Cass (1965, 1966). The advantage of choosing the form (A2.1.21) is that it makes direct reference to the economic interpretation of a co-state variable. Moreover, it uses a single differential equation to describe the evolution of the co-state variable for both reversible and irreversible investment.

Appendix 2.2 Sufficient Conditions for an Optimum

We proceed now to prove that under **Assumptions u1** and **F1**, any path $\{c_t^*, \hat{k}_t^*, q_t^*\}_0^\infty$ satisfying (2.8), (2.19), (2.17) and (2.10) constitutes a unique solution to the problems stated as Version 1 and Version 2 above. Assume then that $\{c(t), \hat{k}(t)\}_0^\infty$ is any feasible path. Then, equation (1.7) gives

$$A(f(\hat{k}) - \hat{z}) - c = 0, \tag{A2.2.1}$$

where the time index t has been dropped for convenience. In what follows, we shall also use the fact that **u1** and **F1** imply

$$u(c^*) - u(c) - u'(c^*)(c^* - c) \;>\; 0$$

$$f(\hat{k}^*) - f(\hat{k}) - f'(\hat{k}^*)(\hat{k}^* - \hat{k}) \;>\; 0. \tag{A2.2.2}$$

Our claim is established if we can show that

$$D \;=\; \int_0^\infty \{u(c^*) - u(c)\}\, e^{-(\rho-n)t} dt$$

$$>\; 0.$$

By adding and subtracting terms, we may use (A2.2.1) and the identity $\hat{z} = \dot{\hat{k}} + (\mu + n + \delta)\hat{k}$ to write

$$D \;=\; \int_0^\infty [\{u(c^*) - u(c)\} + u'(c^*)\{(A(f(\hat{k}^*) - \hat{z}^*) - c^*)$$

$$-(A(f(\hat{k}) - \hat{z}) - c)\} + q^*\{(\hat{z}^* - \lambda\,\hat{k}^* - \dot{\hat{k}}^*)$$

$$-(\hat{z} - \lambda\,\hat{k} - \dot{\hat{k}})\}]\, e^{-(\rho-n)t}\, dt,$$

where $\lambda = \mu + n + \delta$. Collecting terms,

$$
\begin{aligned}
D = \int_0^\infty & [\{u(c^*) - u(c) - u'(c^*)(c^* - c)\} + \{q^*(\hat{z}^* - \hat{z}) \\
& - Au'(c^*)(\hat{z}^* - \hat{z})\} - q^*\{\lambda(\hat{k}^* - \hat{k}) + (\dot{\hat{k}}^* - \dot{\hat{k}})\} \\
& + Au'(c^*)\{f(\hat{k}^*) - f(\hat{k})\}]\, e^{-(\rho-n)t}dt, \qquad \text{(A2.2.3)}
\end{aligned}
$$

Equation (A2.2.3) may be reduced further by integrating $\int_0^\infty q^*(\dot{\hat{k}}^* - \dot{\hat{k}})e^{-(\rho-n)t}dt$ by parts. Thus,

$$
\begin{aligned}
\int_0^\infty q^*(\dot{\hat{k}}^* - \dot{\hat{k}})e^{-(\rho-n)t}dt = \; & e^{-(\rho-n)t}q^*(\hat{k}^* - \hat{k})\,|_0^\infty \\
& - \int_0^\infty (\hat{k}^* - \hat{k})\{\dot{q}^* e^{-(\rho-n)t} \\
& - (\rho - n)q^* e^{-(\rho-n)t}\}dt.
\end{aligned}
$$

Proposition 1 has demonstrated that any feasible path $\{\hat{k}\}$ is bounded above. Using (2.10), the last equation reduces to

$$
\begin{aligned}
\int_0^\infty q^*(\dot{\hat{k}}^* - \dot{\hat{k}})e^{-(\rho-n)t}dt = \; & - \int_0^\infty (\hat{k}^* - \hat{k})\{\dot{q}^* e^{-(\rho-n)t} \\
& - (\rho - n)q^* e^{-(\rho-n)t}\}dt.
\end{aligned}
$$

$$\text{(A2.2.4)}$$

Plugging (A2.2.4) into (A2.2.3), we get

$$
\begin{aligned}
D &= \int_0^\infty [\{u(c^*) - u(c) - u'(c^*)(c^* - c)\} + \{q^* - Au'(c^*)\} \\
&\quad \times (\hat{z}^* - \hat{z}) - q^*\lambda(\hat{k}^* - \hat{k}) + (\dot{\hat{q}}^* - (\rho - n)q^*)(\hat{k}^* - \hat{k}) \\
&\quad + Au'(c^*)\{f(\hat{k}^*) - f(\hat{k})\}] \, e^{-(\rho-n)t} dt \\
&= \int_0^\infty [\{u(c^*) - u(c) - u'(c^*)(c^* - c)\} + \{q^* - Au'(c^*)\} \\
&\quad (\hat{z}^* - \hat{z}) + (\hat{k}^* - \hat{k})\{\dot{\hat{q}}^* - (\rho + \lambda - n)q^* + Au'(c^*)f'(\hat{k}^*)\} \\
&\quad + Au'(c^*)\{f(\hat{k}^*) - f(\hat{k}) - f'(\hat{k}^*)(\hat{k}^* - \hat{k})\}] \, e^{-(\rho-n)t} \, dt,
\end{aligned}
$$

$$ (A2.2.5) $$

adding and subtracting $Au'(c^*)f'(\hat{k}^*)(\hat{k}^* - \hat{k})$. Note that $(q^* - Au'(c^*))\hat{z}^* = 0$ according to (A2.1.9). Further, $(q^* - Au'(c^*))\hat{z} = 0$ for reversible investment. In case of irreversible investment, $q^* - Au'(c^*) \leq 0$ and $\hat{z} \geq 0$. Hence, $(q^* - Au'(c^*))(\hat{z}^* - \hat{z}) \geq 0$ in all cases. Appealing to this fact along with (A2.2.2), the definition of λ and (A2.1.19), equation (A2.2.5) implies

$$
\begin{aligned}
D &> \int_0^\infty [(\hat{k}^* - \hat{k})\{\dot{\hat{q}}^* - (\rho + \lambda - n)q^* \\
&\quad + Au'(c^*)f'(\hat{k}^*)\}] \, e^{-(\rho-n)t} \, dt \\
&= \int_0^\infty [(\hat{k}^* - \hat{k})\{\dot{\hat{q}}^* - (\rho + \delta + \mu)q^* \\
&\quad + Au'(c^*)f'(\hat{k}^*)\}] \, e^{-(\rho-n)t} \, dt \\
&= \int_0^\infty (\hat{k}^* - \hat{k})\{\dot{\hat{q}}^* - \dot{\hat{q}}^*\} \, dt \\
&= 0.
\end{aligned}
$$

This establishes that $\{c_t^*, \hat{k}_t^*\}_0^\infty$ is a unique optimum path. We may note in passing that the last inequality will be weak if both u and f are weakly concave. Thus, we have proved the following result[28]:

PROPOSITION **A2.2** *The conditions enumerated in Proposition 2.1, along with the strict concavity of u and f, are sufficient for the existence of a unique solution to the planner's problem.*

Appendix 2.3   Suboptimality of Golden Rule

We are now ready to prove the following

PROPOSITION **A2.3** *For any optimal path $\{c_t^*, \hat{k}_t^*\}_0^\infty$, $\exists$ a t_0 such that $f'(\hat{k}_t^*) - (\mu + n + \delta)$ is bounded strictly away from zero $\forall\, t > t_0$. In other words, the optimal path of capital accumulation stays away from the GR in the long run.*

Proof: Although the arguments will be posed in terms of a Command economy, they will hold *mutatis mutandis* for a Private economy also. The proof holds for both reversible and irreversible investment. The result will be derived in two steps. The first will demonstrate that the GR per capita consumption path $\{A_t \hat{c}^{**}\}$ associated with indefinite maintenance of $\hat{k}^{**}$ is a suboptimal policy. The second step will then show that a path for which $f'(\hat{k}_t^*) \to (\mu + n + \delta)$ is suboptimal.

Step 1.

In what follows, we shall abbreviate by writing $\lambda = \mu + n + \delta$. Equation (2.29) implies that along the GR path

$$\hat{c}^{**} + \lambda \hat{k}^{**} = f(\hat{k}^{**}), \qquad (\text{A2.3.1})$$

---

[28]Mangasarian (1966) proved the corresponding result for the finite horizon problem.

As an alternative to the path $\{A_t\hat{c}^{**}, \hat{k}^{**}\}$, consider a path which raises per capita consumption at $t = 0$ above $A_0\,\hat{c}^{**}$ by reducing $\hat{k}^{**}$ to $\hat{k}' = \hat{k}^{**} - \Delta$. It is possible to achieve this by reducing $\hat{z}$ below $\lambda\,\hat{k}^{**}$.[29] Thus, we have

$$
\begin{aligned}
f(\hat{k}^{**}) &= \hat{c}^{**} + \lambda\hat{k}' + \lambda(\hat{k}^{**} - \hat{k}') \\
&= \hat{c}^{**} + \lambda\Delta + \lambda\hat{k}'.
\end{aligned}
$$

Thus, the change in $\hat{c}^{**}$ is $\lambda\Delta$ and the rise in per capita consumption at $t = 0$ is $A_0\,\lambda\,\Delta$.

The alternative path is constructed to maintain $\hat{k}$ at this constant value $\hat{k}'\ \forall\,t > 0$. Per capita consumption for all $t > 0$ is $A_t\hat{c}'$ along the alternative path, where $(\hat{c}', \hat{k}')$ solves (A2.3.1). Linearizing around $A_0\hat{c}^{**}$, the gain in utility at $t = 0$ from the change is

$$
\begin{aligned}
\mathcal{G}(0) &= u(A_0\hat{c}^{**} + A_0\,\lambda\,\Delta) - u(A_0\hat{c}^{**}) \\
&\cong u(A_0\hat{c}^{**}) + A_0\,\lambda\,\Delta\,u'(A_0\hat{c}^{**}) - u(A_0\hat{c}^{**}) \\
&= A_0\,\lambda\,\Delta\,u'(A_0\hat{c}^{**}). \tag{A2.3.2}
\end{aligned}
$$

Denote $u'(A_0\hat{c}^{**})$ by u'^{**}.

We proceed now to compare the initial gain $A_0\,\lambda\,\Delta\,u'^{**}$ with subsequent losses. The loss in utility from the change at each $t > 0$ is

$$
\begin{aligned}
\mathcal{L}(t) &= u(A_t\hat{c}^{**}) - u(A_t\hat{c}') \\
&= u(A_t\hat{c}^{**}) - u(A_t(f(\hat{k}') - \lambda\hat{k}')).
\end{aligned}
$$

---

[29]One may consume part of the capital also in the reversible case, but we do not follow up this possibility. The proof we construct instead works for both reversible as well as irreversible investment.

Linearizing around $\hat{k}^{**}$,

$$\mathcal{L}(t) \;\cong\; u(A_t \hat{c}^{**}) - u[A_t(f(\hat{k}^{**}) - \Delta f'(\hat{k}^{**}) + \frac{\Delta^2}{2} f''(\hat{k}^{**})$$

$$-\lambda \hat{k}^{**} + \lambda \Delta)]$$

$$=\; u(A_t \hat{c}^{**}) - u[A_t((f(\hat{k}^{**}) - \lambda \hat{k}^{**}) - \Delta(f'(\hat{k}^{**})$$

$$-\lambda) + \frac{\Delta^2}{2} f''(\hat{k}^{**}))]$$

$$=\; u(A_t \hat{c}^{**}) - u(A_t(\hat{c}^{**} + \frac{\Delta^2}{2} f''(\hat{k}^{**}))), \;\; \text{using (2.30),}$$

$$\cong\; u(A_t \hat{c}^{**}) - (u(A_t \hat{c}^{**}) + \frac{\Delta^2}{2} A_t \; f''(\hat{k}^{**}) u'(A_t \hat{c}^{**})),$$

(linearizing around $A_t \hat{c}^{**}$),

$$=\; -\frac{\Delta^2}{2} A_t f''^{**} u'(A_t \hat{c}^{**}), \qquad\qquad\qquad \text{(A2.3.3)}$$

where $f''^{**} = f''(\hat{k}^{**})$. The discounted stream of losses incurred during $(0, \infty)$ is

$$\int_0^\infty \mathcal{L}(t) \; e^{-(\rho-n)t} dt \;=\; \frac{\Delta^2}{2} \int_0^\infty (-f''^{**} A_t \; u'(A_t \; \hat{c}^{**}) \; e^{-(\rho-n)t} dt$$

$$>\; 0, \qquad\qquad\qquad\qquad\qquad \text{(A2.3.4)}$$

since $f'' < 0$ by **Assumption F1**. The net change in welfare to the household from the perturbation is

$$\omega \;=\; \mathcal{G}(0) - \int_0^\infty \mathcal{L}(t) \; e^{-(\rho-n)t} dt$$

$$= A_0 \lambda \Delta u'^{**} - (\Delta^2/2) \int_0^\infty (-f''^{**} A_t\, u'(A_t\, \hat{c}^{**}) e^{-(\rho-n)t} dt.$$

Let

$$\xi^* = \int_0^\infty (-f''^{**} A_t u'(A_t\, \hat{c}^{**}) e^{-(\rho-n)t} dt,$$

so that

$$\omega = A_0 \lambda \Delta u'^{**} - (\Delta^2/2)\, \xi^*$$

$$= \Delta\, \xi^* (A_0 \lambda\, u'^{**}/\xi^* - \Delta/2).$$

Since A_0, λ, u'^{**} and ξ^* are fixed, $\exists$ an ϵ such that $\Delta < \epsilon$ $\Rightarrow \omega > 0$. So long as the reduction in $\hat{k}$ falls short of ϵ, the perturbation from the path $\{A_t\, \hat{c}^{**}, \hat{k}^{**}\}$ constructed above is welfare improving.

Step 2.

Suppose now that the proposition is false. Then, $\exists$ an optimal path $\{\hat{c}_t^*, \hat{k}_t^*\}$ such that $|\hat{c}_t^* - \hat{c}^{**}|$ and $|\hat{k}_t^* - \hat{k}^{**}|$ are arbitrarily small for t large enough. Consider the following perturbation. At a large enough t_0, disinvest down to $\hat{k}'$ (defined in Step 1) and maintain $\{\hat{c}', \hat{k}'\}$ then onwards. The extra consumption generated is Δ_{t_0}, where $|\Delta_{t_0} - A_{t_0}\, \lambda\, \Delta|$ is arbitrarily small for t_0 large enough (given the definition of Δ in Step 1).

The per capita consumption at t_0 changes to $A_{t_0}\hat{c}_{t_0}^* + \Delta_{t_0}$ and the gain in utility from the increased consumption is $u(A_{t_0}\hat{c}_{t_0}^* + \Delta_{t_0}) - u(A_{t_0}\hat{c}_{t_0}^*) = \nu$ (say). For large enough t_0, the value of $\nu \cong (u(A_{t_0}\hat{c}^{**} + A_{t_0}\,\lambda\,\Delta) - u(A_{t_0}\hat{c}^{**})$. Thus, using Step 1 again, we may assume $\nu \cong A_{t_0}\lambda\, \Delta u'(A_{t_0}\, \hat{c}^{**})$.

Since $\hat{k}_t^* \to \hat{k}^{**}$, it is possible to assume *wlog* that $u(c_t^*) - u(A_t\hat{c}') > 0\ \forall\ t > t_0$. Thus, utility falls by $u(c_t^*) - u(A_t\hat{c}')$

at each $t > t_0$. The discounted present value of the stream of losses is $\int_{t_0}^{\infty}(u(c_t^*) - u(A_t\hat{c}'))e^{-(\rho-n)(t-t_0)}dt$. We have, by definition GR,

$$\int_{t_0}^{\infty}(u(A_t\hat{c}^{**}) - u(A_t\hat{c}'))\ e^{-(\rho-n)(t-t_0)}dt$$
$$> \int_{t_0}^{\infty}(u(c_t^*) - u(A_t\hat{c}'))e^{-(\rho-n)(t-t_0)}dt,$$

or,

$$-\int_{t_0}^{\infty}(u(A_t\hat{c}^{**}) - u(A_t\hat{c}'))\ e^{-(\rho-n)(t-t_0)}dt$$
$$< -\int_{t_0}^{\infty}(u(c_t^*) - u(A_t\hat{c}'))e^{-(\rho-n)(t-t_0)}dt,$$

or,

$$-(\Delta^2/2)\,\xi_{t_0}^* < -\int_{t_0}^{\infty}(u(c_t^*) - u(A_t\hat{c}'))\ e^{-(\rho-n)(t-t_0)}dt,$$

where $\xi_{t_0}^*$ corresponds to ξ^* of Step 1 with due alteration of details. Thus, the net gain is approximately equal to

$$A_{t_0}\,\lambda\,\Delta\,u'(A_{t_0}\hat{c}^{**}) - \int_{t_0}^{\infty}(u(c_t^*) - u(A_t\hat{c}'))\ e^{-(\rho-n)(t-t_0)}dt$$
$$> A_{t_0}\,\lambda\,\Delta\,u'(A_{t_0}\hat{c}^{**}) - (\Delta^2/2)\,\xi_{t_0}^* > 0$$

for an appropriately small value of Δ.

This completes the proof. ∎

Appendix 2.4   Halkin's Counter-example

Section 2.3.1 ended with an example of an optimum path that does not satisfy the transversality condition. This section discusses one more case, a famous example due to Halkin (1974), for which the transversality condition is not a necessary characterisation of optimality.

Before stating the details of the example, let us go back to (A2.1.15) and analyse the reason why it leads to (2.10). The inequality (A2.1.15) is a relationship between the shadow price of investment q_t^* and all subsequent shadow prices over infinite time. Note that, given the objective function and the technology, (2.10) holds because optimality imposes nontrivial restrictions on the behaviour of the capital accumulation path for all $t > t_0$. (See Proposition A2.3 above.) Halkin, on the other hand, constructs an objective function that leaves the path of accumulation unrestricted.

To get a feel for Halkin's example, consider an agent engaged in wealth accumulation. Her lifetime utility depends on the difference between the terminal (i.e. limiting) value of her wealth and the initial wealth she owns. Suppose that the maximum possible value of the terminal wealth is $\bar{K}$ and that her initial wealth is K_0. Then, the optimum value of her welfare is $\bar{K} - K_0$. The important characteristic of this objective function is that the agent's welfare is independent of the path followed for approaching $\bar{K}$. The marginal social product of a rise in K_0 is thus $q(0) = \partial(\bar{K} - K_0)/\partial K_0 = -1$, which is independent of the marginal social productivities of K along the way to the optimum $\bar{K}$. Consequently, the value of the shadow price at $t = 0$ does not put any restriction on future values of the shadow price. The same argument holds for the shadow price at any later point in time. In other words, $q(t) = \partial(\bar{K} - K(s))/\partial K(s) = -1 \; \forall s > t$. Hence, for this problem, the co-state variable does not converge to zero.

Let us now state and work out the example algebraically. The problem is stated as follows:

$$\text{Maximise } \int_0^\infty (1 - y) \, u \, dt$$

subject to

$$\dot{y} = (1 - y) \, u, \; y(0) = 0, \; u \in [0, 1].$$

Obviously, u and y are respectively the control and state variables for this problem.

Solution:

Substituting the state equation in the objective function,

$$\int_0^\infty \dot{y} \, dt \; = \; y|_0^\infty$$

$$= \; \lim{}_{t\to\infty} \, y(t).$$

The problem thus reduces to maximising $\lim{}_{t\to\infty} \, y(t)$. To find the upper bound of y, we solve the equation

$$\dot{y} + (y - 1) \, u = 0.$$

Substituting $z = y - 1$, the equation reduces to

$$\dot{z} + zu = 0.$$

The solution to this equation is

$$z(t) = be^{-\int_0^t u(\nu)d\nu}, \; b = \text{constant},$$

or,

$$y(t) = 1 + b \, e^{-\int_0^t u(\nu) \, d\nu}.$$

At $t = 0$, $y(0) = 0 = 1 + b$, or, $b = -1$. Hence, the general solution is $y(t) = 1 - e^{-\int_0^t u(\nu)d\nu}$. Writing $\int_0^t u(\nu)d\nu = h(t) \geq 0$, the solution is $y(t) = 1 - e^{-h(t)}$, whence $y(t) \in [0, 1)$. Thus, the upper bound of $y(t)$ is unity and any path leading to it is a solution to the problem. There is no unique optimum path. Indeed, any constant $u \in (0, 1)$ is a solution to the problem. Suppose such a constant u^* is selected.

The Hamiltonian for the problem is

$$\mathcal{H} = (1-y)\,u + \lambda\,(1-y)\,u$$
$$= ((1-y)(1+\lambda))\,u.$$

The *FOC*'s are:

$$\dot{y} = u\,(1-y),$$
$$\dot{\lambda} = (1+\lambda)\,u,$$
$$(1-y)(1+\lambda) = 0.$$

Choose $\lambda^* = -1\ \forall\ t$. Then $(u, \lambda) = (u^*, -1)$ satisfies all the optimality conditions, but $\lim_{t\to\infty} \lambda(t) \neq 0$. Note that the value of the co-state variable tallies with the one we obtained above from purely economic arguments. This completes the counter-example.

Part II: Selected Models of New Growth Theory

Chapter 3

Technical Progress as a Spillover

3.1 Introduction

Chapter 2 concluded with the suggestion that there are two possible avenues for modelling technical progress. First, one might view it as the conscious result of R & D, attempts to acquire knowledge based skill and so on, requiring expenditure on factors responsible for the activities in question. We noted that the latter might in turn call for the introduction of market structures that are radically different from the Solow type conventional perfectly competitive markets. The second approach suggested was to view technical progress as an unplanned by-product of the process of privately conducted economic activities, a possible example of which was suggested in Section 2.6. Typically, when technical progress is brought forth unconsciously by the private actions of one economic agent or the other, it assumes the form of a non-internalisable externality generated by the relevant agent. In that event, the Private Economy can continue to be supported by standard competitive markets. Consequently, one can breathe life into the notion of technical progress with minimal changes in the one sector competitive Solow model. We shall accordingly present a series of models in this chapter which avoid the complexities of alternative market structures and view technological progress as a spillover or externality. The models will try to capture two types of externalities. The first of them (Sections 3.2 and 3.3) will be induced by the process of private investment activities, a class of models initiated by Arrow (1962) and Frankel (1962) and carried forward by Romer (1986), d'Autume & Michel (1993) and others. The nature of technical progress introduced by these models is referred to as Learning by doing, a terminology that goes back to Arrow's seminal paper. Under the Learning by doing hypothesis, technical progress is viewed as an improvement in workers' skills caused by exposure to new generations of machines brought into existence by continuing investment activity. A second type of externality (Section 3.4) adds to this notion the possibility that work incentive could respond to the quality of life enjoyed by a society. A society, where workers are accustomed to underprivileged living conditions, is likely to be characterised by work attitudes that are, *on the average*, somewhat indifferent compared to the work culture prevailing in societies where the quality of life is superior. The type of externality in question will attempt to identify simultaneity between the growth rate of an economy and the living standard enjoyed by it. While it is straightforward that the latter is positively related to the former, we will argue that a reverse causation is also not ruled out. The idea of such externalities is discussed by Dasgupta & Marjit (2004).

Some of the above models will often share a common feature that the literature characterises as the AK structure. We shall clarify below the essential components of such models and show how they can be utilised to study other models of economic growth, where the growth rate is solved for by the model, though not necessarily linked to technical progress. The well-known exercise by Barro (1990) relating growth to infrastructure falls in this category and will be the subject studied in Section 3.5.1. This will be followed by a discussion in Section 3.5.2 of a different class of AK-models based on (the so called Leontief) technologies characterised by fixed coefficients of production. Finally, the Appendix will prove results not proved in the main body of the chapter, which continues to stress on basic economic intuition.

3.2   Learning by Doing

In Section 1.2 and Appendix 1.2, we discussed the nature of Harrod-neutral technical change and identified it as a factor of labour augmentation. However, we noted later that the parameter A reflecting technological growth is itself an unexplained phenomenon. While the original exercise did not search deeper into the nature of A, in a subsequent paper Solow did try to repair the shortcoming of the earlier paper by linking technical progress to the process of capital accumulation itself (Solow (1960)). Higher productivity was *embodied* only in new equipment. The rate of increase in productivity, however, was assumed to be exogenous to the system. In the face of diminishing returns, the equilibrium growth rate remained tied up with such exogenous factors alone, while the mechanical association of new investment to technical progress failed to identify the factors responsible for a rise in productivity. Thus, from the point of view of a theory of technical progress, the approach of Solow did not qualify as an improvement over Solow (1956).[1]

Arrow (1962) took a significant step towards offering a theory of labour augmentation, thereby endogenising the equilibrium rate of technical progress for the economy. He attributed productivity increases over time to learning, i.e., the accumulation of experience, on the part of the labour force. Experience is gathered in workshops while producing output with the help of machinery and equipment. Hence, technical progress amounts to "Learning by doing". Every new piece of equipment has to be "broken in" so to speak, thus creating room for learning.[2] Since it is in the course of machinery handling that learning takes place, Arrow considers the value of cumulative gross investment (CGI) at any point of time to be the index of

---

[1]Other similar attempts at explaining technical progress may be found in Phelps (1962) and Drandakis & Phelps (1966).

[2]In Arrow's words: "Each new machine put to use changes the production environment, thereby inducing the workers to learn."

experience.[3] As he viewed it, an increase in investment today raises the size of CGI from tomorrow onwards above what it would be had the investment not taken place. More specifically, suppose the economy's capital stock is growing along the path $K(t)$. Imagine now that at $t = t_0$, an entrepreneur changes his investment decision and raises it by Δ, but that the investment decisions of all future entrepreneurs remain unchanged. Then, the path of capital stock t_0 onwards gets altered to $K(t) + \Delta$. The CGI for the economy is thus increased by Δ units for all $t > t_0$. Consequently, the labour force at all time points subsequent to t_0 will have the opportunity of being exposed to a larger CGI than what would have been the case had the extra investment not occurred at t_0. In this sense, the altered investment plan by the entrepreneur at t_0 has the effect of bequeathing a more experienced and productive labour force to the future, compared to the experience they would otherwise possess. The extra investor will of course gain from the act of his investment, but he would be causing gains in future also. The latter though would be accruing to the future entrepreneurs only. They cannot be internalised by the investor at t_0. This form of technical change generates an *intertemporal externality*, causing later machines to be more productive than earlier ones.

3.2.1   Description of the Economy

In what follows, however, a *disembodied* version of the Arrow exercise (suggested by Sheshinski (1967)) will be considered. Technical change is still an externality, but it is atemporal. An investment activity, irrespective of the firm in which it is located, adds to the CGI for the entire economy, and the benefit of increased labour productivity in the initiating firm *spills over* to *all* coexisting firms, increasing the effective size of the labour force in each firm. It is this last fact that makes technical change disembodied; it raises the output generated by

---

[3]Thus, in the presence of physical depreciation of capital, experience is measured by the aggregate capital stock that *would be* in existence in its absence. Arrow also offers reasons as to why cumulative gross output is not a satisfactory index of learning.

all machines in existence, *irrespective* of their vintages, even if the firms in which they are located have not raised their investments. The exact manner in which this happens may be understood by visualising workers from different organisations interacting beyond office hours and learning from one another as an outcome of the social intercourse.[4]

Formally speaking, the only change this introduces in the Solow (1956) model is in the specification of $A(t)$, which is now a function of CGI at t. In the absence of physical depreciation, the latter is equal to the aggregate capital stock $K(t)$. The exact functional form assumed by Arrow and Sheshinski is

$$A(t) = K(t)^\alpha, \quad \alpha > 0. \tag{3.1}$$

Capital accumulation has diminishing, constant or increasing productivity in the *learning activity* depending on whether $\alpha < 1, = 1,$ or, > 1.

The technology is given by

$$Y = F(K, K^\alpha L), \tag{3.2}$$

where (3.2) satisfies Assumptions **F1** and **F2** of Chapter 1. The function $F(.,.)$ can be expressed as in (1.5), with no change in the definitions of $\hat{y}$ and $\hat{k}$. The properties of $f(\hat{k})$ remain unaltered too vis-à-vis the variable $\hat{k} = K/K^\alpha L$. As with the case of intertemporal externality discussed above, equation (3.2) introduces a distinction between the private and the social marginal productivity of capital. A private producer, in computing the profitability of an additional dose of capital, will be ignoring the gain it generates for other producers. Intuitively speaking, the productive sector may be imagined to be made up of M identical firms, each producing according to $F(K/M, K^\alpha(L/M))$. Given constant returns in K and $K^\alpha L$, this means that aggregate production is still represented by (3.2). An increase in $\frac{K}{M}$ in all firms brings about a corresponding rise in K, but each firm, being negligibly small, is

---

[4]In concrete terms, it might help to think of labourers from different organisations converging to the local pub as it were, where they get a chance to exchange information.

aware only of the change in its own capital stock. Hence, it does not take into account the effect of the social marginal productivity of the change in the private capital stock. As a result, $\partial F/\partial K|_{K^\alpha=constant} = F_1$ measures the private marginal product of capital.

As opposed to the private return, however, the *social* marginal productivity of capital is $\partial F/\partial K = \alpha f(\hat{k})/\hat{k} + (1 - \alpha)f'(\hat{k})$. It is strictly greater than the *private* marginal product $F_1 = f'(\hat{k})$, since f is strictly concave. This happens because the very process of capital accumulation has a spillover effect on the level attained by AL. Such spillovers may or may not give rise to nondecreasing *social* returns to capital. But the returns are external to individual firms. Consequently, the equilibrium for the system is sustainable by a perfectly competitive Private Economy. In other words, the private marginal productivity of capital $(F_1(.,.) = f'(k))$ will still be equated to the market rate of interest by private producers. To appreciate the nature of social returns to capital on the other hand, consider the expression

$$\frac{Y}{K} = F(1, K^{\alpha-1}L), \qquad (3.3)$$

which decreases, remains constant or increases with K according as α falls short of, equals or exceeds unity.

The learning by doing hypothesis is expected to change the Solow conclusion on the equilibrium rate of balanced growth. The crucial factor underlying Solow's result was that under the law of diminishing returns, sustained growth would require K to grow at the exogenously specified combined rate of growth of A and L. In the Learning by doing scenario, the law of diminishing returns continues to hold. What changes, however, is the status accorded to the rate of growth of A. It is no longer an exogenous parameter for the model and depends instead on the rate of growth of K itself. Consequently, while diminishing returns still predicts a constant value of K/AL, the rate of growth of K has a feedback effect on the rate of growth of A, instead of the causality being unidirectional as in the Solow case.

We will divide up the discussion into three parts depending on the value of α.

3.2.2 Case 1– $\alpha < 1$: The Private Economy

This was the case considered by Arrow as well as Sheshinski. As already indicated, the rate of growth of efficient labour is a blend as it were of an endogenous factor, viz., the rate of growth of learning, which is a function of the rate of capital accumulation, and the exogenous population growth rate. Thus, while the supply rate of capital growth is determined by the rate of growth of efficient labour, the latter is itself influenced by the former. As a result, the rates of growth of capital and efficient labour are solutions to a pair of simultaneous equations and hence, endogenously determined. In other words and as distinct from Solow, the rate of technical progress is *solved for* by the model. As such, Arrow's view of technical change is less arbitrary than Solow's. Nevertheless, as will be seen, the growth rates of the relevant variables continue to be impervious to policy changes.

Thus, similar to Solow's Private Economy, the position of the supply rate of balanced growth curve is determined by a constant value of μ in Arrow's work also. But the progress achieved by Arrow is that the value of μ is determined internally and specified in terms of other parameters of the model. This is the content of the next result.

PROPOSITION **3.1** *The supply rate of balanced growth in a Command Economy with learning is given by*

$$\mu = \frac{n\alpha}{1-\alpha}.$$

Proof: Profit maximisation at constant r implies $K/AL =$ *constant*, i.e.,

$$\frac{\dot{K}}{K} = \mu + n.$$

On the other hand, (3.1) yields

$$\mu = \alpha \frac{\dot{K}}{K}.$$

Solving these simultaneous equations in $\dot{K}/K$ and μ,

$$\frac{\dot{K}}{K} = \frac{n}{1-\alpha} \tag{3.4}$$

$$\text{and} \qquad \mu = \frac{n\alpha}{1-\alpha}, \tag{3.5}$$

as was to be proved.

Since μ is completely determined by demographic and technological factors, Arrow's conclusions were somewhat disappointing insofar as they failed to suggest how policy prescriptions (say the response of the demand rate of growth to a tax on interest income) might influence the *equilibrium* balanced growth rate. However, there are other interesting features of the Arrow model that we now proceed to highlight.

Consider first the balanced growth equilibrium in the Private Economy. As in Solow's case, the demand rate of growth is given by $g_c^d = (r - \rho)/\theta$. When equated with the supply rate of growth established by Proposition 3.1, we see after taking account of the entrepreneurs' condition for profit maximisation $r = f'(\hat{k})$, that the equilibrium balanced growth rate of c is $g_c^* = n\alpha/1 - \alpha$. The associated value of k is the solution $\hat{k}^*$ of the equation

$$f'(\hat{k}) = \rho + \frac{n\alpha\theta}{1-\alpha}. \tag{3.6}$$

Thus, although demand has no implication for the rate of growth, it interacts with supply to determine the optimal balanced growth level of $\hat{k} = \hat{k}^*$ as in Solow. See Figure 3.1.

3.2.3   Case 1− $\alpha < 1$: The Command Economy

We have already noted that the social marginal productivity of capital is higher in Arrow's economy than its private marginal

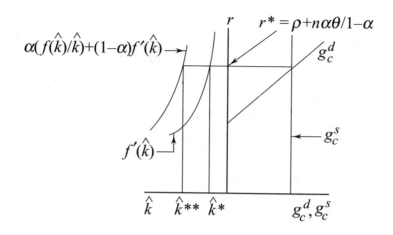

Figure 3.1

productivity. There is no way the private sector can internalise this externality. However, an all perceiving social planner, were she/he to exist, would be in a position to do so. Keeping this in mind, we may write the planner's optimisation exercise as:

Maximise (2.1) subject to (1.9), (2.24) and (3.2).

In the planner's problem, there is no free market equating the marginal product of capital to the rate of interest. Secondly, the planner internalises all externalities and replaces the private marginal product of capital by its social marginal product.

To appreciate the manner in which the planner internalises the externality, let us go back to equation (1.9). While μ is an exogenous parameter as far as the Command Economy is concerned, the planner is aware of the exact manner in which μ is affected by the process of capital accumulation. In particular, he is aware that $A = K^\alpha = (\hat{k}L)^{\alpha/1-\alpha}$, so that

$$\mu = \dot{A}/A$$

$$= \frac{\alpha}{1-\alpha}\left(\frac{\dot{\hat{k}}}{\hat{k}} + n\right). \tag{3.7}$$

Substituting for this in (1.9) and solving for $\dot{\hat{k}}$, we get

$$\dot{\hat{k}} = (1-\alpha)\,f(\hat{k}) - n\,\hat{k} - (1-\alpha)\,\frac{c}{(\hat{k}L)^{\alpha/1-\alpha}}. \tag{3.8}$$

The Hamiltonian for the planner's problem is accordingly

$$\mathcal{H} = \frac{c^{1-\theta} - 1}{1-\theta}$$

$$+ q\left((1-\alpha)f(\hat{k}) - n\,\hat{k} - (1-\alpha)\,\frac{c}{(\hat{k}L)^{\alpha/1-\alpha}}\right). \tag{3.9}$$

The static condition for optimality, i.e.,

$$\frac{\partial \mathcal{H}}{\partial c} = 0$$

yields

$$c^{-\theta} = (1-\alpha)\,\frac{q}{(\hat{k}L)^{\alpha/1-\alpha}}$$

$$= (1-\alpha)\,\frac{q}{A}. \tag{3.10}$$

The condition for dynamic optimality implies

$$
\dot{q} = -\frac{\partial \mathcal{H}}{\partial \hat{k}} + (\rho - n)\, q
$$

$$
= -\left((1 - \alpha)\, f'(\hat{k}) - n + \alpha\, \frac{c}{A\, \hat{k}} \right) q + (\rho - n)\, q.
$$

$$(3.11)$$

Denote the Command Economy's optimal balanced growth rate of c by G^*. Differentiating (3.10) with respect to t and substituting from (3.11) we obtain

$$
G^* = \frac{\alpha\, f(\hat{k}^{**})/\hat{k}^{**} + (1 - \alpha) f'(\hat{k}^{**}) - \rho}{\theta}, \qquad (3.12)
$$

where $\hat{k}^{**}$ stands for the optimal level of $\hat{k}$ corresponding to G^*. Following the arguments of Section 2.3.1, we conclude that $G^* = \mu = n\alpha/1 - \alpha$. Thus, the balanced growth rate for the Command Economy is identical with the rate achieved by the Command Economy in equilibrium. There will nonetheless be a difference between the solutions achieved by the two systems. To see this, substitute $G^* = \mu = n\alpha/1 - \alpha$ in (3.12) to get

$$
\left(\alpha\frac{f(\hat{k}^{**})}{\hat{k}^{**}} + (1 - \alpha) f'(\hat{k}^{**}) \right) = \rho + \frac{n\alpha\theta}{1 - \alpha} \qquad (3.13)
$$

Equations (3.6) and (3.13) demonstrate that the balanced growth equilibrium value of $\hat{k}$ for the Command Economy is larger than that for the Command Economy.

3.2.4 Comparison of Command and Private Economies

The planner's balanced growth equilibrium is the best possible balanced growth path for the economy since it corresponds to the internalisation of all externalities. The social marginal product of capital being larger than the private marginal product, it follows that in balanced growth equilibrium, $\hat{k}^{**} > \hat{k}^{*}$. In other words, the Private Economy is unable to achieve the socially optimal value of $\hat{k}$. The result amounts to a failure of the first fundamental theorem of welfare economics. The market failure creates room for policy intervention in Arrow's model. The rise in social marginal productivity brought about by labour augmentation is not recognised by the market. Hence, the market pays capital less than its true marginal product, while it awards to labour the marginal product of efficient labour, which in turn is created by the investment generated learning process. The market solution can be improved by a tax-subsidy scheme. The private producers will raise their investments to increase $\hat{k}^{*}$ to the level $\hat{k}^{**}$, if the private return at $\hat{k}^{**}$, viz. $f'(\hat{k}^{**})$, were to be supplemented by a subsidy to raise the effective return to $\alpha(f(\hat{k}^{**})/\hat{k}^{**}) + (1 - \alpha)f'(\hat{k}^{**})$. The subsidy can be provided by taxing labour income appropriately.

PROPOSITION **3.2** *The market equilibrium balanced growth path is not socially optimal in the Arrow model. A market equilibrium supported by wage taxation and capital subsidisation can restore the social optimum.*

Apart from the equilibrium rate of growth turning out to be inert to policy manipulations,[5] a second major shortcoming of the Arrow theory is that technical progress, though endogenously generated, is viewed as an inevitable (or, unavoidable) *byproduct* of the process of capital accumulation. It is not linked to the *rational* actions of economic agents who are known in real life to innovate in search of higher profits from production.

As indicated in Chapter 2, a part of the difficulty lies in the structure of markets. We may end this section by drawing the readers' attention to a difficulty that will arise in the context of appropriate designing of markets. Arrow's technical change is

---

[5] As with the Solow model, policy has a role to play in out of steady state dynamics in Arrow's model.

a non-marketable commodity in that it is both nonrival as well as nonexcludable, i.e., it is a pure public good. It is non-rival since all firms enjoy it simultaneously; and it is non-excludable, since it has the form of an external effect. Thus, the classic public good problem will need to be handled appropriately if a Command Economy has to accommodate the technical progress issue. This important question is addressed by Romer (1986, 1990). We shall review these contributions in Section 3.2.8 and Chapter 5.

3.2.5   Case 2– $\alpha = 1$: The Private Economy

Romer (1986) raised an important criticism against the Arrow exercise. Since, except for the determination of the equilibrium value of μ, Arrow's model shares all the features of the Solow world, it is possible to carry out an out of balanced growth analysis and prove that both the Private and the Command Economies eventually grow at the rate $\mu = n\,\alpha/(1-\alpha)$. Arrow therefore predicts that, given α, the per capita consumption c in economies characterised by a low value of n will grow at negligible rates in the long run. The prediction is clearly not borne out by facts, because the richest economies in the world have a low population growth rate, though they are known to experience significant growth rates of c.

The problem arises on account of the restriction $\alpha < 1$ imposed by Arrow, for as we shall see now, the above criticism does not apply when $\alpha \geq 1$. In this connection, we begin with the work of d'Autume and Michel (1993), who assume $\alpha = 1$. For this specification of the value of the parameter α, the Arrow production function exhibits a strong spillover effect. In the interest of continuity, the neoclassical framework will be maintained, although the original results were presented in Arrow's embodied form.

By definition, $\mu = \dot{K}/K = constant$ along a balanced growth path. However, with $\alpha = 1$, the assumption of balanced growth does not yield the value of the supply rate of growth as in the earlier models. Of course, the supply rate of growth continues to be equal to μ, but the value of μ re-

mains unknown until $\dot{K}/K$ is determined. More precisely, the
requirement that $\dot{K}/K = \dot{A}/A + \dot{L}/L$ leads to

$$\frac{\dot{K}}{K} = \mu + n$$

$$= \frac{\dot{K}}{K} + n, \text{ since } \alpha = 1 \qquad (3.14)$$

and this can happen with $\dot{K}/K > 0$ only if $n = 0$. On the
other hand, (3.14) cannot solve for $\dot{K}/K$ with $n = 0$.

A necessary condition for balanced growth being a *stationary* level of population, $L = \bar{L} = constant$. As a result, and
as opposed to the case $\alpha < 1$, $\hat{k}^* = K/(K\bar{L}) = 1/\bar{L}$. This
represents, once again, a departure from the models studied
so far, where the equilibrium value of $\hat{k}$ depended on demand
as well as supply parameters. Further, (1.12) admits a unique
profit maximising value of r, viz., $r^* = f'(1/\bar{L})$, quite independently of the value assumed by μ. (Compare with Figure 2.5.)
Alternatively, r^* can sustain *any* rate of balanced growth of k.
Note, moreover, that with $n = \delta = 0$, (1.9) implies

$$\frac{\hat{c}}{\hat{k}} = \frac{f(\hat{k})}{\hat{k}} - \mu, \qquad (3.15)$$

where $\mu = dotK/K = constant$, along a balanced growth
path. The above equation fixes the value of $\hat{c}/\hat{k}$ (since $\hat{k} = \hat{k}^* = 1/\bar{L}$). A fixed value of $\hat{c}/\hat{k}$, while assuring us that c and k
grow at an equal rate in balanced growth equilibrium does not
throw any light on the exact magnitude of that growth rate
(i.e., μ). This implies that g_c^s is a perfectly elastic function at
r^*. Hence, g_c^s is a horizontal curve passing through r^*.

The g_c^d curve is identically the same as in the earlier models. Consequently, the equilibrium rate of balanced growth,
$g_c^* = (r^* - \rho)/\theta$, is determined once again by the intersection of
demand and supply. However, as opposed to the earlier cases,
and this is the second crucial departure from earlier models, it
is demand now that has the driver's seat in the determination

of the equilibrium growth rate.[6] Indeed, a change in ρ and θ would now have an effect on the growth rate. So would policy,

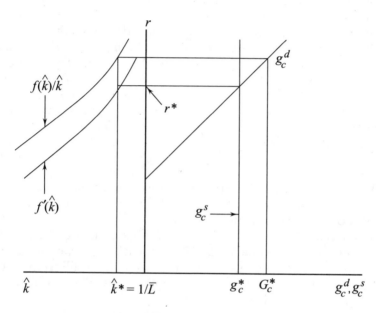

Figure 3.2

[6]The reader cannot fail to note the diametrically opposite roles played by g_c^d and g_c^s for the two cases $\alpha < 1$ and $\alpha = 1$. In the former, they interact to fix the equilibrium value of $\hat{k}$, leaving the rate of growth of the economy to be determined by exogenous supply side parameters. In the latter, the opposite is the case.

such as a proportional tax on interest income.[7] As opposed to Arrow's case, the growth rate is *controllable*. The equilibrium is depicted in Figure 3.2.

It follows now that, despite the fact that the rate of population growth is zero, the equilibrium rate of growth is non-zero. Hence, the criticism raised by Romer (1986) against Arrow's exercise (with which this section started) does not apply to the d'Autume & Michel model.[8] Note, however, that while the equilibrium solution is no longer tied to the *rate* of population growth, it does still depend on the *size* of the labour force, since the latter determines the equilibrium rate of interest and hence the equilibrium growth rate. In this connection, recall the restriction (2.32) discussed in Chapter 2, which reduces now to

$$g_c^* \, (1 - \theta) < \rho. \tag{3.16}$$

The rate g_c^* being endogenously determined, there is no guarantee that the above restriction will be satisfied. Of course, a low enough value of r^* will ensure that the restriction will not be violated. A low r^* follows from a high value of $1/\bar{L}$, which amounts to a low value of $\bar{L}$. Consequently, one way of ensuring that the model gives rise to a meaningful equilibrium is to impose an upper bound on $\bar{L}$.[9] Another possibility to explore is to impose bounds on ρ and θ.

The link between g_c^* and $\bar{L}$ imply a comparative static result. A higher $\bar{L}$ leads, *ceteris paribus*, to a higher value of g_c^* via a larger value of r^*. One may interpret this to mean that the effect of Learning by doing is higher when the labour force is larger, i.e., the aggregate of skills acquired is higher. This phenomenon will show up in a major way again when we discuss Romer (1990) in Chapter 5. As Romer argues, a rise in the stock of *human capital* or skilled work force has a growth

---

[7]The impact of a proportional tax of the expression for the demand rate of growth is discussed in some of the remaining models to be discussed in this chapter.

[8]Moreover, as will be evident from Section 3.2.7, the model does not permit out of balanced growth dynamics in any case.

[9]The reader will doubtlessly ask whether parameter restrictions need to be imposed in the Arrow model of the previous section. The answer to this question is left as an exercise.

rate enhancing effect.

The conclusions are summarised below.

PROPOSITION **3.3** *When* $\alpha = 1$, *balanced growth equilibrium implies zero growth of population. Further, the rate of equilibrium growth of c, k and y is determined by demand as well as technological parameters. A change in preference parameters affects the growth rate, while a change in the size of the labour force affects both the growth rate as well as the equilibrium value of the effective capital-labour ratio.*

3.2.6 Command Economy and Private Economy

Once again, the Command Economy takes into account the externality factor in its optimality calculation and this shows up in the form of a higher value accorded to the social marginal product of capital as compared to the market economy. Since the production function can be rewritten as $Y = K\bar{L}f(1/\bar{L})$, the social marginal product is a constant $\bar{L}f(1/\bar{L})$ and equals the social average productivity $f(\hat{k})/\hat{k}$. As a result, the optimal balanced growth rate for the Command Economy is

$$G_c^* = \frac{\bar{L}f(1/\bar{L}) - \rho}{\theta}.$$

Since the average product is larger than the marginal product, the following proposition emerges:

PROPOSITION **3.4** *The equilibrium rate of growth in a Private Economy is strictly less than the equilibrium growth rate in a Command Economy.*

As opposed to the case $\alpha < 1$, it is now the *rate of growth* that is higher in the Command Economy rather than the equilibrium value of $\hat{k}$. The Command Economy and Command Economy equilibria are compared in Figure 3.2. Figure 3.3 is an alternative depiction of the model. This diagram shows that the ratio $K/K\bar{L} = 1/\bar{L}$ is a ray through the origin along which the economy moves. The wage-rental ratio is tangential to the isoquants at their points of intersection with the ray $1/\bar{L}$. There is full employment of both factors along the balanced growth path. The rate at which the economy moves along the ray is determined by the rate of interest corresponding to the wage-rental ratio quoted above. The Command Economy too moves along the same ray, but the rate of change is determined by the social marginal productivity of capital $\bar{L}f(1/\bar{L})$ which is larger than the rate of interest in the Private Economy.

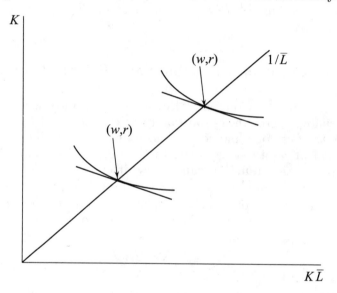

Figure 3.3

3.2.7   Lessons from Case 2

An important feature of the model is that it adjusts to the equilibrium rate of growth $g_c^* = (f'(\hat{k}^*) - \rho)/\theta$ instantaneously at time point $t = 0$. This follows because $\hat{k} = 1/\bar{L}$. Given g_c^*,

(3.15) yields $c_0 = k_0 \, (f(\hat{k})/\hat{k} - \mu)$.[10] The entire paths of k_t^* and c_t^* are solved for then onwards. The Command Economy jumps on to the balanced growth path independent of the value of K_0 and continues on that path forever. There is no scope for out of balanced growth behaviour.

Exactly the same observation holds, *mutatis mutandis*, for the Command solution. The only difference lies in the values chosen of the variable G^* and the paths of $K(t)$ and $C(t)$, beginning from a given K_0.

Two features of the model stand out vis-à-vis the Solow and the Arrow models. First, demand parameters now affect the growth of technology in a straightforward manner and this in turn influences the growth rate of important macro variables like the GDP, capital stock, consumption etc. In this sense, this is the first example of an endogenous growth model that we have come across in this book. Secondly, and as already noted, the model links up the endogenously determined growth rate to the exogenously given *level* of the work force. In particular, the higher the latter, the higher is the growth rate that the economy enjoys (subject to (3.16) being satisfied). This second feature has the important implication that scarce resources (labour in this case) impose an upper bound on the achievable growth rate of technology, GDP and so on. The bound can be relaxed therefore through an expansion of the resource base.[11] Apart from this, there is no technological constraint on an economy's rate of growth. In subsequent chapters, we shall have occasions to refer back to these two basic characteristics of the model. As we shall observe in connection with our discussion of more sophisticated models, not all of them are capable of incorporating the two features equally well. It should be obvious that even if a model succeeds in determining the growth rate endogenously, its predictions would be somewhat pessimistic if it ends up by imposing a *technological* bound on the rate of growth of *technology* itself.[12]

---

[10]Writing $\Lambda = f(\hat{k})/\hat{k} - \mu$, $\hat{c} = \Lambda \, \hat{k}$ may be looked upon as the consumption function for the economy under balanced growth.

[11]See, however, footnote 9 in Chapter 5 for criticisms of the second feature of the model.

[12]A model that may be considered to be a close parallel of the d'Autume

3.2.8   Case 3– $\alpha > 1$: Private and Command Economies

This case takes us back to Romer (1986) and constitutes the most technically demanding of the three alternatives under consideration. Since the mathematical derivations involved are nontrivial, we shall present the bare essence of the model only. The externality is the strongest in the present case. Using (3.2),[13]

$$\frac{\dot{\hat{k}}}{\hat{k}} = \frac{\dot{K}}{K} - \alpha\frac{\dot{K}}{K} - n < 0, \qquad (3.17)$$

whenever $\dot{K}/K > 0$. Thus, $\hat{k}$ must continuously fall over time thereby making it necessary for the demand rate of growth to change over time.[14] Thus, this system can never hope to be

---

& Michel model is one due to Frankel (1962). The only difference between the two lies in the value of the coefficient of labour augmentation. Frankel takes it to be per capita capital K/L, rather than K. As a result, the Frankel production function reduces to

$$Y \;=\; F(K, (K/L)L)$$

$$\;=\; F(K, K).$$

The equilibrium market rate of interest reduces now to $f'(1)$, the average product of capital to $f(1)$ and the planner's production to $Y = Kf(1)$. Apart from these specific details, the model shares all the properties of the d'Autume-Michel exercise.

[13]Romer (1986) specifies a production function that is more general than (3.2) in two respects. First, the function is posed at the micro firm level. Secondly, in his most general treatment, Romer does not assume any specific form for the learning by doing effect. In our presentation, we stick to the Arrow form of the function for simplicity as well as for comparability with Cases 1 and 2.

[14]To the extent that $f'(\hat{k})$ rises as $\hat{k}$ falls, one expects the growth rate of the economy to rise over time. By the very choice of the value of α, the effective labour force keeps rising at a rate higher than the rate of growth of capital. Thus, the marginal productivity of capital increases forever. For models represented so far, this could make the marginal product of K rise unboundedly (via Inada conditions), causing the demand rate of growth to explode also. The utility integral will correspondingly diverge and no optimal path would exist. Romer avoids this problem, as we shall see below in equation (3.20), by doing away with the one to one transformation of saving into new capital.

in balanced growth equilibrium. However, paths of c, k and y satisfying the definition of a perfect foresight equilibrium will exist and we characterise these below.

A notable feature of Romer's model is the replacement of physical by knowledge capital.[15] Unlike Arrow, where technical progress is an unplanned by-product of physical capital accumulation, it is the accumulation of *knowledge* through an explicit R & D activity that contributes to an increase in labour productivity in Romer's economy.[16] In the changed scenario, I still stands for investment in the sense of foregone consumption. However, unlike the previous models, Romer abstracts from physical capital accumulation. Instead, I is used up completely in the accumulation of more knowledge, represented by K.[17] Thus, savings (S) translates one-to-one into investment (I) as in Solow, but I is not identically the same as $\dot{K}$.

To keep matters as simple as possible, let us assume that $n = 0$, though it is not logically necessary to do so as in d'Autume & Michel, since, in any case, the Romer model rules out balanced growth. In particular, normalise $\bar{L} = 1$. Thus, (3.2) reduces to

$$Y = F(K, K^\alpha), \ \alpha > 1, \tag{3.18}$$

where Y is viewed as being produced by means of knowledge capital and efficient labour. Savings being equal to investment,

$$\begin{aligned} I &= F(K, K^\alpha) - C \\ &= F(K, K^\alpha) - c. \end{aligned} \tag{3.19}$$

New knowledge capital (i.e., $\dot{K}$) is developed through research. Explicitly, it is assumed to be a linear homogeneous function of I and the *entire* stock of knowledge capital (i.e., K) and

---

[15]The models of Chapters 5 and 6 will have more to report on the subject.

[16]In view of this feature, the Romer (1986) model belongs more naturally to Chapter 5.

[17]At this stage of Romer's work, the precise nature of knowledge capital is left somewhat vague.

concave in each argument. The R & D production function is written $G(I, K)$. In other words,

$$\dot{K} = G(I, K) = K g \left(\frac{I}{K} \right), \qquad (3.20)$$

where $g(I/K) = G(I/K, 1)$ is assumed to be bounded above to ensure that the utility integral is well-defined.

The fact that the whole of K is present simultaneously in both F and G indicates that it is being viewed as a nonrival good. The household sells the services of K and $\bar{L}$ to firms producing Y. The income so derived is spent wholly on C and I. The latter is used in producing $\dot{K}$, with the help of the nonrival K, which implies that K is a free input as far as the production of $\dot{K}$ is concerned. Since K has to be paid for in producing Y but not $\dot{K}$, knowledge capital is a *partially excludable* commodity in the model.[18] Following Arrow's basic idea, however, the labour augmenting effect of capital accumulation (viz. K^α) is external to the firm. Consequently, the market structure may still be assumed to be perfectly competitive as in Solow (1956).

As indicated above, the algebra of the Romer model is complicated. We work out below some of its salient features, though these had best be treated as initial steps designed to help students interested in details. Concretely speaking, the problem of the Command Economy will be solved in the same way as the planner would solve the Command Economy exercise, subject to the restriction that producers are unable to internalise the external effect of learning. This amounts to doing away with the household-firm separation and solving a grand optimisation exercise similar to the one studied in Section 2.2.[19] Let

$$\mathcal{H} = \frac{c^{1-\theta} - 1}{1 - \theta} + \bar{q} \, K \, g \left(\frac{I}{K} \right)$$

---

[18]The conceptual implication of a nonrival and partially excludable K is brought out in great detail in Romer (1990). See Chapter 5.

[19]The procedure will be repeated later on in the book also. See Chapter 4, Section 4.2.

$$= \frac{c^{1-\theta} - 1}{1 - \theta} + \bar{q} \, K \, g \left(\frac{F(K, K^\alpha) - c}{K} \right). \quad (3.21)$$

The condition of static optimality yields

$$\frac{\partial \mathcal{H}}{\partial c} = 0,$$

which reduces to

$$c^{-\theta} = \bar{q} \, g' \left(\frac{I}{K} \right). \quad (3.22)$$

The condition for dynamic optimality leads to

$$\dot{\bar{q}} = -\frac{\partial \mathcal{H}}{\partial K} + \rho \, \bar{q},$$

or, using (3.21),

$$\frac{\dot{\bar{q}}}{\bar{q}} = -g \left(\frac{I}{K} \right) - g' \left(\frac{I}{K} \right) \{ F_1(K, K^\alpha) - \frac{I}{K} \} + \rho. \quad (3.23)$$

Differentiating (3.22), we have

$$-\theta \, \frac{\dot{c}}{c} = \frac{\dot{\bar{q}}}{\bar{q}} + \frac{(I/K) \, g''(I/K)}{g'(I/K)} \, \frac{(\dot{I}/K)}{I/K}$$

$$= \frac{\dot{\bar{q}}}{\bar{q}} + \frac{(I/K) \, g''(I/K)}{g'(I/K)} \left(\frac{\dot{I}}{I} - \frac{\dot{K}}{K} \right)$$

$$= \frac{\dot{\bar{q}}}{\bar{q}} + \frac{(I/K) \, g''(I/K)}{g'(I/K)} \left(F_1(K, K^\alpha) \frac{\dot{K}}{I} - \frac{\dot{c}}{c} \frac{c}{I} - \frac{\dot{K}}{K} \right),$$

using (3.19). (3.24)

Substituting for $\dot{\bar{q}}/\bar{q}$, I and $\dot{K}/K$ from (3.23), (3.19) and (3.20) respectively, we may express $\dot{c}/c$ as a function of K and c:

$$\frac{\dot{c}}{c} = \Phi(K, c). \quad (3.25)$$

On the other hand, (3.20) is similarly rewritten

$$\frac{\dot{K}}{K} = g(\frac{I}{K}),$$

$$= \Psi(K, c). \tag{3.26}$$

The two equations (3.25) and (3.26) represent the fundamental equations of motion for the system. These are difficult to solve analytically. Hence, Romer illustrates their behaviour through a series of examples using specific functional forms for F and g and values of θ. The resulting paths, as already noted, do not display balanced growth equilibrium. To the extent that they are solved for by the model, the rates of growth of c and K at each t are endogenously determined.[20] Moreover, unlike Arrow's case, despite the absence of population growth, the economy does not converge to a zero-growth equilibrium in the long run.[21]

The Command Economy solves exactly the same problem as above, but for the internalisation of the externality. As a result, Romer is able to argue that the rate of research will be higher for the Command Economy and the level of consumption lower. Summarising, we have

PROPOSITION **3.5** *When $\alpha > 1$, the economy is not in balanced growth equilibrium at any finite t. The out of balanced growth equilibrium paths of both the Private and Command Economies are endogenously determined and are different from one another. The economy does not converge to zero growth equilibrium even though the population growth rate is zero.*

As far as balanced growth is concerned, there was a *logical* need in d'Autume & Michel for assuming the rate of population growth to be zero. Although there is no such necessity in

---

[20]In particular, the rate of technological progress is determined endogenously at each instant of time. Note that the out of steady state path in Case 1 had the same characteristic.

[21]In general, K and c are seen to diverge for all of Romer's examples. The examples differ, however, in terms of whether they impose asymptotic bounds on the rates of growth, though the possibility of increasing growth rates is not ruled out.

the remaining models, it is convenient to make the assumption in any case. Apart from simplifying the algebra, it helps to establish the fact that an exogenous specification of the population growth rate has no role to play in determining the growth rate of an economy. Also, it isolates clearly the role of technology in generating economic growth. Accordingly, we shall henceforth restrict our discussions to the case where $n = 0$.

3.3　Quality of Life: A Generalisation

Development economists (Banerjee and Gupta (1997), Dasgupta and Ray (1986), Ray (1998) and others) have adequately analysed the implication of improved consumption on work effort under the assumption that higher wages permit higher nutritional standards and labour supply, while the supply drops dramatically at low wages. Under neoclassical assumptions on technology, an augmented labour supply is likely to raise the marginal productivity of capital by lowering the capital-labour ratio. This in turn, following principles laid down so far, is expected to have a beneficial effect on the rate of growth of an economy, provided a majority of production organisations resort to payment of efficiency wages.

In this section, however, we move one step further by conjecturing the possibility of *social effects* of a higher quality of life on labour supply. This accords additional emphasis to the development economists' proposition that a consumption wise better provided *individual* works more efficiently on account of improved nutrition than one who is not. The extra dimension added now is that higher wages normally generate surplus incomes as well, available for spending on amenities of life other than basic consumption. This observation attains particular significance in a macro context, where the surpluses earned by *a large number of* individuals add up to a significant size. The latter creates room for extensive social intercourse *outside* the office amongst well provided individuals, through entertainment and cultural activities, thus extending the boundaries of basic necessities to include a variety of *superior* items of consumption. We conjecture that the consequent opportunities of social intercourse amongst well provided individuals achieves additional effects by elevating the average person culturally, intellectually and attitudinally, both outside as well as inside the workplace. Specifically, the quality and quantity of work effort is expected to be upgraded beyond levels that the pure nutrition theory suggests. To the extent that this effect is present, a *society* of individuals that grows accustomed to higher standards of living is likely to create a positive externality flow from the Household sector to the Business sector. Unlike the efficiency wage proposed by development economics, though, the externality will be non-internalisable.

Developing societies are more likely to experience the effect described as compared to developed ones. The latter too profits from improvements in the range of consumption, but the gains might work predominantly through the single channel of utility functions, without carrying any other social implication. The mindset and in particular work attitudes of people already accustomed to high standards may not undergo a large scale metamorphosis due to improvements in consumption standards. However, a society of individuals accustomed to indifferent living standards may well experience the phenomenon in question.[22]

To clarify the viewpoint further, compare a worker who uses an overcrowded public transport system in a tropical country to commute to work with another who uses an air-conditioned private car. The second worker will be less tired at the workplace and hence perform better; in addition, the quality of his leisure hours will improve. He might be able to give more time to his family and hence raise the overall lifestyle his family maintains. As a result, he will be better rested than the first worker when he arrives for work on the subsequent day. For all these reasons, an hour of labour supply by the second worker effectively exceeds an hour's labour supply by

---

[22]As we shall see in the following chapter, Lucas (1988) allowed for a comparable external effect caused by the aggregate quantum of human capital in the society. As a society grows richer in human capital, the overall environment in which people live and work has a beneficial effect on the productivity of each individual firm, even though the firm employs only a negligible fraction of the total work force.

the first. The marginal productivity of capital will increase if a firm substitutes the first type of worker by the second. Moreover, to the extent that the increase in marginal productivity of capital is caused by this substitution, it might make sense to award that increase to the worker as an incentive wage.

Imagine now that there are N identical firms. Also, assume that each firm substitutes the first type of worker by the second. There will then be a general improvement in the quality (i.e., effective quantity) of labour supply. As before, the marginal productivity of capital will rise in each firm. However, the rise in this second case will be substantially higher than in the first case. The reason for this is to be found in the fact that in addition to each worker being able to improve the quality of leisure enjoyed, there will be extensive scope for social interaction. Families can meet and plan for cooperative avenues of enjoyment. Such increased social interactions will improve the quality of workers, not only through the Arrow-Sheshinski route, but also because society as a whole attains a higher standard of life. Generally speaking, the manner in which workers spend their time away from work will affect their performance while at work.

The consumption externality is modelled like the Arrow-d'Autume & Michel-Romer-Sheshinski approach above by generalising the learning by doing *coefficient* of labour augmenting technical progress to a function of both the cumulative gross investment (i.e., aggregate capital) *and* aggregate consumption, the latter acting as an index of the general standard of living. Of course, the consumption effect is characterised by diminishing marginal productivity, the higher the attained level of consumption, the smaller the marginal impact of additional consumption on work attitudes.

Certain interesting results emerge from the approach developed. Noteworthy amongst these are the following: (i) a low level growth trap can be corrected by diverting resources from investment to consumption, (ii) the growth rate rises in response to a rise in the discount parameter in the welfare function and (iii) the Command Economy growth rate may dominate the Command Economy rate.[23] Also, one may offer a decentralisation scheme for sustaining the social optimum as a market equilibrium. The scheme advocates either labour taxation and capital subsidisation (as in the learning by doing models) or capital taxation and household subsidisation, depending on the relative strengths of the learning by doing and consumption effects.

3.3.1   The Private Economy

The household sector operates exactly the same way as the one for the d'Autume-Michel model, where, for simplicity, we assume that $L_t = \bar{L}$ $\forall$ t. Moreover, for most of the results, except for the ones involving the comparative statics of changes in $\bar{L}$, we shall normalise $\bar{L} = 1$. The aggregate production function for the model is

$$Y = F(K, K^\alpha C^{1-\alpha}\bar{L}), \ \ 0 \le \alpha < 1,$$

$$= F(K, K^\alpha C^{1-\alpha}), \text{ when } \bar{L} = 1. \qquad (3.27)$$

The function F satisfies the standard properties listed earlier. Note as before that the rates of growth of C and c are identical as of given $\bar{L}$.

The function reduces to the d'Autume-Michel case of learning by doing when $\alpha = 1$. Under the usual neoclassical assump-

---

[23]Chapter 6 below discusses the work of Aghion & Howitt (1992) who show that the Command Economy can grow faster than the Market Economy. The result is similar to the one proved by Aghion & Howitt in the context of Schumpeterian growth. Two additional features of our model in this context are that, unlike Aghion & Howitt, the rate of interest is determined endogenously by our model. Moreover, and once again contrary to Aghion & Howitt, the solution to the Command Economy problem is independent of the rate of interest for the Market Economy. Needless to say, however, the problem addressed by this paper being different from the one studied by Aghion & Howitt, the models are not strictly comparable.

tions on F as spelt out in Chapter 1, equation (3.27) reduces to[24]

$$Y = KF(1, (C/K)^{1-\alpha}),$$
$$= Kf(\hat{c}), \qquad (3.29)$$

where $\hat{c}$ stands for $(C/K)^{1-\alpha}$. The function f is assumed to satisfy the Inada conditions, i.e.,

$$f'(\hat{c}) \to \infty \text{ as } \hat{c} \to 0$$
$$f'(\hat{c}) \to 0 \text{ as } \hat{c} \to \infty.$$

Product and factor markets are perfectly competitive, which is a permissible assumption since externalities in the model are not internal to the firm.[25] Given that $\bar{L}$ is a constant, we have *wlog* that $c(t) = C(t) \ \forall \ t$. The solution to the Household's problem results in the choice of the steady rate of per capita consumption growth:

$$g_c^d(r) = \frac{r - \rho}{\theta}. \qquad (3.30)$$

A profit maximising competitive entrepreneur equates the

---

[24]In the Cobb-Douglas case, the assumed production function boils down to

$$Y = A K^{\beta}(K^{\alpha}C^{1-\alpha})^{1-\beta}, \ 0 < \beta < 1, A > 0$$
$$= A K \hat{c}^{(1-\beta)(1-\alpha)}$$
$$= AK\hat{c}^{\gamma}, \ 0 < \gamma = (1-\beta)(1-\alpha) < 1. \qquad (3.28)$$

[25]Note that w stands for the marginal product of the resource $K^{\alpha}C^{1-\alpha} \ \bar{L} = K^{\alpha}C^{1-\alpha}$. In other words, labour's compensation exceeds the marginal product of L, either due to the Learning by doing effect or the Social Consumption effect. In any case, the RHS of (1.3) exhausts the total output by virtue of the product exhaustion theorem.

private marginal product of capital to the market rate of interest. Thus,

$$r = \left(\frac{\partial Y}{\partial K}\right)_{K^\alpha \ C^{1-\alpha}=constant}$$

$$= f(\hat{c}) - \hat{c}f'(\hat{c}),$$

$$= f(\hat{c})\left(1 - \frac{\hat{c}f'(\hat{c})}{f(\hat{c})}\right). \tag{3.31}$$

where $(\hat{c}f'(\hat{c}))/f(\hat{c}) \in [0,1]$, being a factor share. Further,

$$\frac{\partial r}{\partial \hat{c}} = -\hat{c}f''(\hat{c}) > 0. \tag{3.32}$$

Hence, using (3.31), r is a monotone increasing function of $\hat{c}$, with $r \to 0$ as $\hat{c} \to 0$.

The macro balance equation for the economy is

$$C + \dot{K} = Kf(\hat{c}),$$

or, $$g_k^s = f(\hat{c}) - (\hat{c})^{1/(1-\alpha)}. \tag{3.33}$$

The effect of a once for all rise in the labour force is captured by reintroducing the parameter $\bar{L}$ in the production function to give

$$C + \dot{K} = f(\hat{c}\,\bar{L}) - (\hat{c})^{1/(1-\alpha)}. \tag{3.34}$$

Thus, a rise $\bar{L}$ increases g^k for each $\hat{c}$. As before, the economy is in balanced growth equilibrium if $g_c^d = g_k^s = g$.

Equation (3.33) implies that $g_k^s = 0$ at $\hat{c} = 0$. Further, given the properties of f and the strict convexity of $(\hat{c})^{1/(1-\alpha)}$, the function g_k^s is a strictly concave function of $\hat{c}$, increasing with $\hat{c}$, reaching a unique maximum g^* at some $\hat{c}^*$ and then falling monotonically to reach 0 at some $\hat{c} = \bar{\hat{c}} > 0$. Thus, for any given K, a rise in C has two opposing effects on g_k^s. First, it reduces the g_k^s rate due to reduced savings. Secondly, it increases g_k^s due to increased productivity. Up to a certain stage (i.e., $\hat{c}^*$), the second effect dominates. Beyond this, the productivity effect becomes too weak on account of diminishing returns and is ultimately wiped out by the first effect.

Given the monotone relationship between r and $\hat{c}$ noted earlier, it follows that $g_k^s = 0$ at $r = 0$, rises with r, reaching the unique maximum g^* at some r^* (corresponding to $\hat{c}^*$) and then falling monotonically to reach 0 again at some $r = \bar{r} > 0$ (corresponding to $\bar{c}$). Let us refer to this latter relationship as

$$g_k^s = \phi(r). \tag{3.35}$$

Equations (3.32) and (3.33) imply that a rise in $\bar{L}$ causes an upward shift in $\phi(r)$. The function $\phi(r)$ may not be concave however, since (3.32) implies that the shape of $\phi(r)$ depends on $f'''(\hat{c})$.

For equilibrium, (3.30) and (3.35) require

$$\frac{r - \rho}{\theta} = \phi(r). \tag{3.36}$$

Assume $\rho < \bar{r}$ to avoid a zero growth rate. In (3.36), the $LHS = 0$ and the $RHS > 0$ at $r = \rho$, while at $r = \bar{r}$, the opposite is the case. Thus, from continuity, there exists a strictly positive equilibrium pair (g_ρ^*, r_ρ^*) solving (3.36). The model does not call for an out of steady state analysis. Given any initial K_0, it is always feasible for the economy to choose the "correct" $C(0)$. To see this, let $\hat{c}_\rho^*$ stand for the value of $\hat{c}$ at g_ρ^*. Then, (3.33) shows that choosing $C(0) = K_0 \left(f(\hat{c}_\rho^*) - g_\rho^* \right)$ and maintaining the growth rate g_ρ^* keeps the economy on the balanced growth path forever.

For the Cobb-Douglas case (3.28),

$$r = \left(\frac{\partial Y}{\partial K} \right)_{K^\alpha \, C^{1-\alpha} = constant}$$

$$= a \, \beta \, \hat{c}^{1-\beta} \tag{3.37}$$

and

$$\frac{\partial r}{\partial \hat{c}} = a \, \beta \, \hat{c}^{-\beta} > 0. \tag{3.38}$$

Further, using (3.37), equation (3.33) is replaced by

$$g_k^s = A \, r^{1-\alpha} - B \, r^{(1-\alpha)/(1-\beta)}, \tag{3.39}$$

where $A = a^{\alpha}/\beta^{1-\alpha}$ and $B = (1/(a\ \beta))^{(1-\alpha)/(1-\beta)}$. It is easy to verify that $g_k^s > o$ if $r \in (0,\ a^{(1-\beta\ \alpha)/(\beta(1-\alpha))})$. Regarding the shape of $\phi(r)$, i.e., g_k^s as a function of r, differentiate twice to get

$$\frac{\partial^2\ g^k}{\partial\ r^2} = -(1-\alpha)\left\{A\ r^{-(1+\alpha)} + \frac{(\beta-\alpha)\ B}{(1-\alpha)^2}\ r^{2\beta-(1+\alpha)}\right\}.$$

(3.40)

The sign of the second derivative is negative if $\beta > \alpha$. In this case, ϕ is strictly concave, which, along with the linearity of $(r-\rho)/\theta$, implies that g^* is unique. When, $\beta < \alpha$, the function is convex in the region $((\alpha-\beta)\ B/(1-\beta)^2)\ r^{2\ \beta} > A$, i.e., say for $r > \hat{r}$, where $\hat{r}$ solves $((\alpha-\beta)\ B/(1-\beta)^2)\ r^{2\ \beta} = A$. As already argued, however, $\phi(r)$ reaches a unique maximum at r^*. This means, and as Figure 3.4 shows, that $\hat{r} \geq r^*$. Once again therefore, we have a unique equilibrium.

As Figure 3.4 also demonstrates, depending on the initial equilibrium, a rise in the Representative Household's discount parameter could actually lead to a rise in the equilibrium growth rate. The intuition underlying the result is as follows. A rise in ρ implies a rise in preference for current consumption over growth. The improved consumption raises labour productivity and causes the growth rate to rise despite lower propensity to save. Of course, after a certain point, due to diminishing returns, the productivity rise is too weak to compensate for the fall in saving and the growth rate falls.

Finally, recalling that $\phi(r)$ rises with $\bar{L}$, it follows that a rise in $\bar{L}$ raises the equilibrium growth rate, somewhat in the spirit of Romer (1990) and d'Autume and Michel (1993). The results arrived at are summarised as follows:

PROPOSITION **3.6** *For the Cobb-Douglas production function case, a unique, positive and endogenously determined equilibrium balanced growth rate exists if the discount rate is not too high. A society with a high discount rate may grow faster than one with a low discount rate. A rise in the labour force raises the growth rate of the system.*

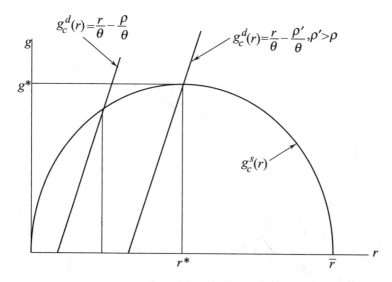

Figure 3.4

The shape of $\phi(r)$ is unclear, however, when f does not have the simple Cobb-Douglas form. In particular, it is not immediately obvious whether or not convexities occur in the region $[0, r^*]$. If there are non-convexities in this interval, non-uniqueness of (g_ρ^*, r_ρ^*) cannot be ruled out. Non-uniqueness, will bring along with it the possibility of a low-level equilibrium growth rate trap. See Figure 3.5. In this case, for the same values of the parameters (such as K_0, ρ, θ and the parameters of the production function), the lower growth rate g^* will be associated with a lower r^*, hence $\hat{c}^*$. The implication is that it is *feasible* to push up the equilibrium growth rate by raising C_0, thereby raising r^* and $\hat{c}^*$, which are then maintained forever.

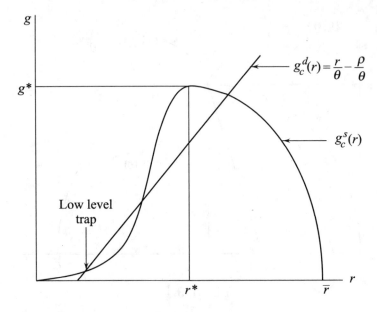

$$g_c^d(r) = \frac{r}{\theta} - \frac{\rho}{\theta}$$

$$g_c^s(r)$$

Figure 3.5

According to the development economists referred to earlier, a worker's capacity to work depends on the level of nutrition he or she enjoys. Ray (1998) notes "... the relationship that exists between a person's nutritional status and his capacity to do sustained work ..." and studies "... how this relationship creates a vicious cycle in the labour market: poverty leading to under-nutrition, hence inability to work, which feeds back on the incidence of poverty." The main emphasis in this line of work, however, is on the issue of equilibrium unemployment and efficiency wage arising from an exogenously presumed labour supply function. A higher wage rate permits higher nutritional standards and labour supply, whereas below a minimum wage rate, the supply drops to dramatically low levels. Our result differs from these studies in at least three respects. First, instead of arising out of an individual worker's response to incentive wages, it depends entirely on the suggested *consumption externality*. Secondly, it is concerned with the issue of sustainable growth rather than the static question of unemployment and efficiency wages. Finally, in the development models, the results depend on the special assumptions about the behaviour of the labour supply curve. In our case too, convexity (of the ϕ function) plays a role in creating the potential for a low level trap, but the convexity is endogenously generated, despite standard assumptions about production and welfare functions.

We end this section by emphasising a fact about Figure 3.1. It is deliberately drawn to show that there may be values of the parameters characterising the welfare function (such as ρ') for which the Private Economy chooses the maximal growth rate g^*. This observation will have a bearing on the next section.

3.3.2 Equilibrium: Command Economy vs. Private Economy

Along a steady state path, $C(t) = C(0) \, e^{g \, t}$, where g is the growth rate for the marketless Command Economy. Substituting this in (2.1) and utilising (2.24), the aggregate utility is given by

$$U = \frac{C_0^{1-\theta}}{(1-\theta)(\rho + (\theta - 1)g)}, \qquad (3.41)$$

which is well-defined under the standard **Assumption:** $\rho + (\theta - 1)g > 0$. For $\theta > 1$, the assumption is automatically satisfied for all $g > 0$. When $\theta < 1$, it amounts to a restriction on the maximum sustainable rate of steady growth, which, in view of equation (3.33), reduces to a restriction on the technology alone. (For example, in the Cobb-Douglas case, the assumption constrains the range of permissible values of α and or β.)

The social planner maximises (3.41) subject to (3.33) (with

g_k^s substituted by g). Equation (3.41) is rewritten as

$$U = \frac{K_0^{1-\theta}}{1-\theta} \frac{\hat{c}_0^{(1-\theta)/(1-\alpha)}}{\rho + (\theta-1)g}, \tag{3.42}$$

which the planner maximises subject to

$$g = f(\hat{c}_0) - (\hat{c}_0)^{1/(1-\alpha)}. \tag{3.43}$$

Since $\hat{c}$ (as well as g) are constants along the steady state, we may replace $\hat{c}_0$ by $\hat{c}$ in (3.42) and (3.43). The planner's problem reduces to a static optimisation exercise of choosing the best pair $(\hat{c}, g)$ subject to (3.43). Substituting (3.43) into (3.42) we obtain

$$U = \frac{K_0^{1-\theta}}{1-\theta} \frac{\hat{c}^{(1-\theta)/(1-\alpha)}}{\rho + (\theta-1)(f(\hat{c}) - \hat{c}^{1/(1-\alpha)})}. \tag{3.44}$$

Differentiating (3.44) *wrt* $\hat{c}$,

$$\frac{d\,U}{d\,\hat{c}} = \{K_0^{1-\theta} \frac{1}{(\rho + (\theta-1))^2}\{\frac{1}{1-\alpha} \hat{c}^{(1-\theta)/(1-\alpha)-1}$$

$$\times (\rho + (\theta-1)g) + \hat{c}^{(1-\theta)/(1-\alpha)}$$

$$\times (f'(\hat{c}) - \frac{1}{1-\alpha} \hat{c}^{\alpha/(1-\alpha)})\}.$$

$$\tag{3.45}$$

By virtue of the assumption that $\rho + (\theta-1)g > 0$ and the earlier observation that g in (3.33) attains a unique optimum at g^*, the *RHS* of (3.45) is strictly positive for all pairs $(\hat{c}, g)$ such that $\hat{c} \le \hat{c}^*$ and $g \le g^*$. On the other hand, (3.44) is a continuous function of $\hat{c}$ over the compact interval $[0, \bar{\hat{c}}]$. Since, $\bar{\hat{c}} > \hat{c}^*$, it follows that $\exists$ a $\hat{c} = \hat{c}^{**}$, $\hat{c}^{**} > \hat{c}^*$, maximising W. Denote the corresponding g for the Command Economy problem by g^{**} and the value of W by W^{**}. Since, $\hat{c}^{**} > \hat{c}^*$, we have $g^{**} < g^*$. The intuition underlying the result is as follows. The planner, being omniscient, is aware of the utility trade-off between g and $\hat{c}$. He has full knowledge of the technological trade-off between the two variables also. Since the social optimum equates the marginal rate of substitution with the rate of technical substitution, the planner will never choose a growth rate in the region where the technological relationship between g and $\hat{c}$ is complementary. In other words, he will exhaust all possibilities of growth improvement through consumption and settle for an equilibrium in a phase where the productivity effect of consumption increase is too weak to counter the negative effect of a savings rate reduction.

An interesting result may now be noted. We ended the previous section by showing that it was possible for the Command Economy to attain the growth rate g^*. Since $g^* > g^{**}$, we conclude that the Private Economy *might* grow faster than the Command Economy.

It is possible to derive a sufficient condition under which the Command Economy optimum growth rate is unique and positive. Using (3.42), the level curves in the $\hat{c} - g$ plane are downward sloping, since

$$\frac{dg}{d\hat{c}} = -\frac{1}{1-\alpha}\,\frac{\rho + (\theta - 1)g}{\hat{c}} < 0. \qquad (3.46)$$

The inequality (3.46) shows that the level curves of the planner's utility function become steeper as ρ rises, thus leading to a lower rate of growth and higher consumption, both intuitively obvious results. In general, the level curves need not be convex. This is seen from

$$\frac{d^2 g}{d\hat{c}^2} = \frac{1}{(1-\alpha)^2}\,\frac{\theta(\rho + (\theta - 1)\,g)}{\hat{c}^2}\,\frac{\theta - \alpha}{1-\alpha}. \qquad (3.47)$$

Equation (3.47) shows that the level curves will be strictly convex or linear if $\theta \geq \alpha$, i.e., provided the learning by doing effect is not overly strong. Since (3.43) defines g as a function of $\hat{c}$, say $g = \psi(\hat{c})$, the planner will choose a nonzero rate of growth if the slope of the level curve W passing through the point $\bar{\hat{c}}$ in Figure 3.3 is less than that of $\psi(\hat{c})$. This leads to the imposition of the condition

$$\rho < (1-\alpha)\bar{\hat{c}}\,\{\frac{(\bar{\hat{c}})^{\alpha/(1-\alpha)}}{1-\alpha} - f'(\bar{\hat{c}})\}, \qquad (3.48)$$

where $[f'(\bar{\hat{c}}) - (\bar{\hat{c}})^{\alpha/(1-\alpha)}/(1-\alpha)] < 0$ is the slope of ψ at $\bar{\hat{c}}$. The restriction implies that the planner does not employ a discount rate that is so high that positive growth is avoided. When (3.48) is satisfied, the socially optimum growth rate is positive. Moreover, g^{**} is unique if $\theta \geq \alpha$, since the function $\psi(\hat{c})$ is strictly concave and the level curves of W are convex. As in the case of the Market economy, the Command Economy too does not admit any transitional dynamics. Also, an increase in $\bar{L}$ increases g^{**}, but as Figure 3.6 suggests, the value of $\hat{c}^{**}$ may fall.

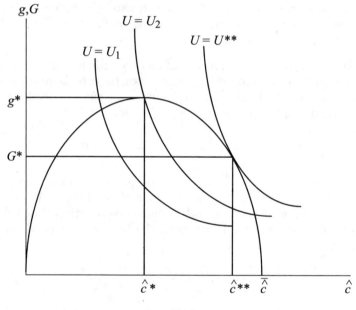

Figure 3.6

PROPOSITION **3.7** (i) *The Command Economy chooses an optimal growth rate that is smaller than the maximum* *feasible growth rate for the economy. Moreover, this growth rate might fall short of the Private Economy growth rate; (ii) the Command Economy growth rate is unique and positive if the intertemporal elasticity of substitution for the utility function and the discount parameter are not too large; (iii) a rise in the discount rate leads to a lower rate of growth and a higher value of consumption per unit of capital; a higher value of the labour force will raise the rate of growth, but the associated consumption per unit of capital may be smaller.*

3.3.3   Public Policy: Decentralising the Command Solution

We have already noted that a rise in C may lead to a rise in the Private Economy's growth rate. However, it is not clear how such an increase may be implemented. Even if implementable, the corresponding growth rate may not be socially optimal. In this section therefore, we ask if the government can design a tax-subsidy programme to sustain the Command Economy steady state within the market structure. The result to be proved is similar to the Second Fundamental Theorem of Welfare Economics, which establishes the existence of taxes, subsidies and prices which, if adopted, sustain a social optimum. Our result extends that theorem to an economy in dynamic steady state equilibrium.

The government is assumed to levy a proportional income tax on capital income or offer a subsidy. Let (τ) denote the rate of tax (> 0) or subsidy (< 0). It uses the tax proceeds to purchase consumer goods from the market and freely distribute them back to the household in a lump sum manner. Alternatively, it gives a proportional subsidy to capital by imposing a lump sum consumption tax on the Household. The decentralisation procedure has the following features:

1. At time point $t = 0$, the government announces a rate of interest r_m, a wage rate w_m and a tax or subsidy rate τ_m to the Household and asks it to maximise its welfare function subject to

$$C_p(t) + \dot{K}(t) = (1 - \tau_m)\, r_m\, K(t) + w_m \qquad (3.49)$$

in the class of steady growth paths, where $C_p(t)$ represents the Household's private consumption choice. 2. The government supplements the Household's chosen consumption path $C_p(t)$ by a lump sum subsidy or imposes a lump sum tax on $C_p(t)$. 3. The values of r_m, w_m and τ_m can be so selected that if the Household accepts them parametrically, then it will choose the growth rate g^{**} of Section 4. Further, the procedure will lead, after netting in/out the subsidy/tax, to the same aggregate consumption path for the Household as the one followed by the Command Economy. We now proceed to prove the following

PROPOSITION **3.8** *The Command Economy steady state path is decentralisable through proportional capital taxation* (resp. subsidisation) *and lump sum consumption subsidy* (resp. tax) *and specifying the interest and wage rates parametrically.*

The proof of this proposition is relegated to the Appendix.

3.4   Some Related Models

We end up this chapter with a discussion of two more models that have a bearing on the discussion carried out so far. The first of the exercises to be outlined in this section is due to Barro (1990) and Barro & Sala-i-Martin (2004), who considered a model that was formally similar to the d'Autume-Michel model above, though it had a different interpretation. Instead of viewing technical progress as the engine of growth, Barro (and Sala-i-Martin) studied the role of public inputs, say freely provided infrastructure, in the determination of the rate of growth of the economy. The public input is financed through taxation and the tax rate fixes the market rate of interest by fixing the ratio of per capita private and public inputs, i.e. factor intensities. As in Section 3.2.7, the supply rate of growth for the Private Economy is infinitely elastic, so that the rate of growth is determined by its intersection with the demand rate curve. The author(s) proceed to analyse the effect of tax changes on the rate of growth.

The second growth model that we shall describe in this section is the so-called AK-Model of growth corresponding to economies characterised by Leontief type fixed coefficient technologies. This model is also capable of giving rise to an endogenous rate of growth determined by the rate of saving chosen by the system. Besides, its stability properties stand in contrast with apparently similar models studied in this chapter. One such model was the d'Autume-Michel exercise. The model involves a fixed $K/K\bar{L}$ ratio, though this feature should not be mistaken with an AK technology. The fixed $K/K\bar{L}$ ratio in this model results from optimal choice of techniques as in any other neoclassical set up involving smooth substitutability. This is clearly borne out by Figure 3.3. We have noted that the d'Autume-Michel model does not admit out of steady state analysis at all. As such, there is no question of studying the stability of the growth path yielded by the model. A typical AK-model on the other hand admits out of steady state behaviour and a growth path that converges over time to the steady state equilibrium.

3.5   Growth with a Public Input

We proceed now to Barro & Sala-i-Martin (2004), who studied the role of public inputs in growth.[26] We visualise identical household producers indexed by i, each endowed with the production function

$$Y_i = A \, L_i^{1-\alpha} \, K_i^\alpha \, \Gamma^{1-\alpha}, \qquad (3.50)$$

where A is a constant, Y_i, L_i and K_i have standard meanings and Γ stands for the aggregate *flow* of a public input supplied free of user cost by the government. As is obvious from (3.50), Γ has the classic features of a public good, non-rivalry and non-excludability. For concreteness, we may refer to Γ as infrastructure.

---

[26]The treatment of this section is influenced strongly by Barro & Sala-i-Martin (2004). Also, most of the results are closely related to Barro (1990), where public inputs are accorded the status of private rather than public goods.

3.5.1   The Private Economy

As with the preceding models of the chapter, L_i will be assumed to be a constant and normalised to unity. However, the reader should note that the size of L_i will have a positive comparative statics effect on the rate of growth of the system as in those same models. The public input is provided out of tax revenue generated by a proportional tax $\tau \in [0,1]$ imposed on aggregate output $Y = \sum Y_i = N\, Y_i$, assuming that there are N identical firms in the economy. Under these conditions, the aggregate output is

$$Y = NAK_i^{\alpha}\Gamma^{1-\alpha}. \tag{3.51}$$

Thus,

$$\Gamma = \tau\, Y,$$

$$= (\tau\, N\, A)^{1/\alpha}\, K_i, \text{ using (3.50).} \tag{3.52}$$

Equations (3.51) and (3.52) show that Y/Γ and Γ/K_i are fixed for fixed τ. Firms maximise $(1-\tau)\, Y_i - r\, K_i - w$, so that the market rate of interest equals

$$r = (1-\tau)\, \alpha\, A\, K_i^{\alpha-1}\, \Gamma^{1-\alpha}$$

$$= (1-\tau)\, \alpha\, A\, \left(\frac{\Gamma}{K_i}\right)^{1-\alpha}. \tag{3.53}$$

It follows from (3.52) that τ determines r independent of the rate at which the economy grows. Thus, appealing to arguments similar to those used in Section 3.2.6, the $g_c^s(r)$ function is perfectly elastic at a level determined by τ.[27] Solving for r as a function of τ from (3.53), the equilibrium rate of growth for the system is found then by substituting the value of r in the expression for g_c^d. The latter is calculated by maximising the aggregate utility[28] of any representative household subject to

---

[27]Students should note the similarity with the d'Autume-Michel model.
[28]For the utility integral to be well-defined, the familiar condition $\rho + (\theta - 1)g > 0$ needs to be imposed.

$$c_i + \dot{K}_i = r\, K_i + w.$$

Proceeding as before, $g_c^d(r)$ is given by (2.44). Equating with $g_c^s(r)$, the equilibrium growth rate is

$$g = \frac{r - \rho}{\theta}$$

$$= \frac{(1 - \tau)\, A\, \alpha\, (\Gamma/K_i)^{1-\alpha} - \rho}{\theta}. \tag{3.54}$$

Substituting (3.52), the equilibrium rate of growth g is given by

$$g = \frac{\alpha\, A^{1/\alpha}\, N^{1-\alpha/\alpha}\, (1 - \tau)\, \tau^{1-\alpha/\alpha} - \rho}{\theta} \tag{3.55}$$

The equilibrium rate of growth g is responsive now to policy specifications, viz. the choice of the tax rate τ, which is equivalent to choosing the size of the government Γ/Y. Hence, it is important to specify the value of τ optimally. Two alternative policy objectives suggest themselves, maximisation of the growth rate and maximisation of welfare. We take these up in turn.

Growth Rate vs. Welfare Maximisation in a Private Economy

Noting that $1/\tau = N\, A\, (K_i/\Gamma)^\alpha$, a rise in the tax rate has two opposing effects on the growth rate. First, by lowering K_i/Γ (See (3.53)), it raises the marginal productivity of capital and hence affects the growth rate positively. This effect is captured by the term $\tau^{1-\alpha/\alpha}$ in (3.55). Secondly, as of given K_i and Γ, a higher τ lowers the net return from investment in capital accumulation, as shown by the expression $(1 - \tau)$ in (3.55). For low levels of the tax rate, the first effect dominates, while the second effect takes over at higher rates. It is easy to check by differentiating (3.55) with respect to τ that the growth maximising tax rate is $\tau^* = 1 - \alpha$. Consequently, the maximum rate of growth for the Private Economy is

$$g^* = \frac{\alpha\, (A^{1/\alpha}\, N^{1-\alpha/\alpha}\, \alpha\, (1 - \alpha)^{1-\alpha/\alpha}) - \rho}{\theta}. \tag{3.56}$$

At this value of τ, the size of the government is $\Gamma/Y = 1 - \alpha$, which has the implication that it satisfies a natural condition for efficient resource allocation at each point of time. To appreciate this fact, differentiate Y in (3.51) with respect to Γ and use $\Gamma/Y = 1 - \alpha$ to get

$$\frac{\partial Y}{\partial \Gamma} = (1 - \alpha)\, A\, N\, K_i^{\alpha}\, \Gamma^{-\alpha}$$

$$= (1 - \alpha)\, \frac{Y}{\Gamma}, \quad \text{using (3.50)}$$

$$= 1. \tag{3.57}$$

Thus, the instantaneous marginal benefit of a unit of Γ is unity.[29] On the other hand, the instantaneous social marginal cost of a unit of Γ is measured by a unit withdrawal of Y from consumption and/or capital formation. Comparing with (3.57), we see that the marginal social cost and return are equated, thereby guaranteeing the aforementioned static efficiency condition.

Despite the distortion introduced by the proportional tax rate therefore, the growth maximising tax rate satisfies an efficiency property, given the assumed Cobb-Douglas form of the technology. This leads us to expect that the growth maximising tax rate may have other optimality properties too. To verify this intuition, we move on to the alternative policy objective for the government, viz. maximisation of welfare. Under balanced growth, $c_i(t) = c_{i0}\, e^{g\, t}$. Consequently, using

$$c_i + \dot{K}_i = (1 - \tau)\, Y_I,$$

$$c_i(t) = K_{i0}\, e^{g\, t} \left(\frac{(1 - \tau)Y_i(t)}{K_i(t)} - g \right). \tag{3.58}$$

---

[29]It is important to note that the marginal benefit has no intertemporal connotation. If Γ were an accumulable input, then an extra unit of Γ would raise marginal productivity forever, as was the case in our discussion of (2.9) in Chapter 2. In the present exercise, however, Γ is a pure flow that is instantaneously used up. We shall present a different view of the nature of infrastructure in Section 4.5.

Before proceeding to the optimality result, note by substituting $Y_i/K_i = A\,(\Gamma/K_i)^{1-\alpha}$ in (3.54) that $(1-\tau)Y_i/K_i - g$ in (3.58) equals $(\theta - \alpha)\,g/\alpha + \rho/\alpha$. Hence, we see that the Command Economy is in perpetual balanced growth equilibrium. No out of balanced growth dynamics is warranted by the model.

Next, integrating the welfare function, note that along a balanced growth path, the household's welfare equals (except for a neglected constant term)

$$U = \frac{c_{i0}^{1-\theta}}{1-\theta}\,\frac{1}{\rho - (1-\theta)g}. \tag{3.59}$$

Moreover, substituting for $(1-\tau)Y_i/K_i - g$ in (3.58), it follows that

$$c_{i0} = K_{i0}\left(\frac{\rho}{\alpha} - \left(1 - \frac{\theta}{\alpha}\right)g\right).$$

Substituting for c_{i0} in (3.59),

$$U = \frac{K_{i0}^{1-\theta}}{1-\theta}\,\frac{(\rho/\alpha - (1-\theta/\alpha)g)^{1-\theta}}{\rho - (1-\theta)g}. \tag{3.60}$$

Differentiating with respect to g and using

$$\frac{\rho}{\alpha} - \left(1 - \frac{\theta}{\alpha}\right)g > \rho - (1-\theta)g > 0,$$

we conclude that U is increasing in g. This means that, as conjectured, a growth rate maximising tax rate is also welfare maximising in the Private Economy.[30]

PROPOSITION **3.9** *A perpetually maintained proportional tax rate on output determines the steady state growth rate for the infrastructure driven Private Economy. A balanced growth rate maximising tax rate exists. For the Cobb-Douglas production structure, a growth rate maximising tax rate maximises the aggregate welfare for the Representative Household. Given the constant tax rate, the economy does not exhibit out of balanced growth dynamics.*

---

[30]Barro (1990) shows that this result does not hold for a general production function.

3.5.2   Command vs. Private Economy

As with our earlier exercises, we proceed now to isolate the external effects in the Private Economy. This calls for a reintroduction of the Command Economy. The social planner would view the aggregate production function as

$$Y = \sum Y_i$$

$$= A \left(\frac{\Gamma}{K_i} \right)^{1-\alpha} (N\, K_i). \qquad (3.61)$$

Two facts should be noted about this representation of the function. First, along any balanced growth path, Γ/K_i is a constant. Since the omniscient planner is aware of this fact, he will calculate the *social* marginal product of capital as $\partial Y/\partial(NK_i) = A\,(\Gamma/K_i)^{1-\alpha}$. Thus, the social marginal product of K_i exceeds the private marginal product $\alpha\,A\,(\Gamma/K_i)^{1-\alpha}$. Secondly, the former is only a gross measure of productivity of capital. For, the constancy of Γ/Y implies that a unit increase of Y requires Γ to be increased by Γ/Y units. Thus, out of each unit of extra Y brought forth by increased K_i, the planner must divert a fraction Γ/Y towards the maintenance of Γ/Y. Next, use (3.51) to express $A\,(\Gamma/K_i)^{1-\alpha}$ as $A^{1/\alpha}\,N^{1-\alpha/\alpha}\,(\Gamma/Y)^{1-\alpha/\alpha}$. Taking these facts into account, the equilibrium rate of growth for the Command Economy is

$$G = \frac{A^{1/\alpha}\,N^{1-\alpha/\alpha}\,(1-\Gamma/Y)(\Gamma/Y)^{1-\alpha/\alpha} - \rho}{\theta}, \qquad (3.62)$$

if Γ/Y is the size of the government. Recall now the efficiency condition $\Gamma = (1-\alpha)\,Y$, which the planner would necessarily satisfy. Using this knowledge, we conclude that the Command Economy growth rate is

$$G^* = \frac{A^{1/\alpha}\,N^{1-\alpha/\alpha}\,\alpha\,(1-\alpha)^{1-\alpha/\alpha} - \rho}{\theta}, \qquad (3.63)$$

As expected, $G^* > g^*$. One may explain this phenomenon by the fact that the planner, being aware of the constancy of

Γ/Y, internalises the *social* marginal productivity of capital, which the private entrepreneur cannot. The result is that the gross marginal product of capital for the social planner equals its average productivity $A (\Gamma/K_i)^{1-\alpha}$, whereas for the private entrepreneur, it equals the marginal product $\alpha A (\Gamma/K_i)^{1-\alpha}$. Under concavity, the former exceeds the later.[31]

It is important to find out if there is any other tax regime that can sustain G^* within the market framework. Barro & Sala-i-Martin show that a lump sum tax on the household achieves the objective. Suppose then that the sole intervention by the government in the market economy takes the form of a lump sum tax equal to Δ at each point of time. Then, the household's budget constraint reduces to

$$c_i + \Delta_i + \dot{K}_i = Y_i.$$

Since the entire income Y_i accrues to the household, Δ_i may also be viewed as a lump sum consumption tax (of the type considered in the decentralisation proposition of the last section). There is no wedge now between the value of the firm's output and the household's income. Thus, the demand rate of growth is given by

$$g_{lm}^d = \frac{\partial Y_i/\partial K_i - \rho}{\theta},$$

$$= \frac{\alpha A (\Gamma/K_i)^{1-\alpha} - \rho}{\theta},$$

where the subscript "*lm*" indicates that the tax is lump sum. We have already seen (while deriving (3.62)) that $A (\Gamma/K_i)^{1-\alpha} = A^{1/\alpha} N^{1-\alpha/\alpha} (\Gamma/Y)^{1-\alpha/\alpha}$. Hence, setting $\sum \Delta_i = \Gamma = (1 - \alpha) Y$, the expression for g_{lm}^d reduces to G^*.

PROPOSITION **3.10** *The Command Economy grows faster than the Market Economy. The growth rate for the Command Economy can be decentralised by means of a lump sum tax.*

---

[31]It may be shown now that the welfare maximising tax rate for the Command Economy also equals $1 - \alpha$.

3.6 Growth, Public Input and Congestion

Barro & Sala-i-Martin (2004) extend their model of the previous section to consider the possibility that the available infrastructure might cause congestion as aggregate output rises relative to a fixed level of infrastructure. The congestion might show up as aggregate output Y rises with increases in K_i in the face of a given level of Γ. In this case, the rise in output will be constrained by the scarcity of Γ relative to Y. A production function that captures this property is

$$Y_i = A \ K_i \ f \left(\frac{\Gamma}{Y} \right), \qquad (3.64)$$

where $f' > 0$, $f'' < 0$ and $Y = \sum Y_i$. The functional form implies the property noted above. As K_i rises, output Y_i rises linearly as of given Γ/Y. However, Y increases with Y_i, which depresses Y_i unless Γ increases.

3.6.1 The Private Economy: Proportional Tax

With reference to the previous exercises, it is straightforward to see that the Private Economy's growth rate is

$$g = \frac{A \ (1 - \tau) \ f(\tau) - \rho}{\theta}, \qquad (3.65)$$

where τ stands for the proportional tax rate, or, what amounts to the same thing, the size of the government Γ/Y and the market rate of interest equals the private marginal product of capital $Af(\tau)$. If the government chooses a tax rate to maximise the rate of growth of the Private Economy, then the optimal tax rate τ^* satisfies

$$f(\tau) = (1 - \tau) \ f'(\tau). \qquad (3.66)$$

Condition (3.66) in turn implies that the natural condition of static efficiency, viz. $\partial Y/\partial \Gamma = 1$ is satisfied. To check this, note that

$$\frac{\partial Y}{\partial \Gamma} = A\,K\,\frac{f'(\tau)}{Y}\left\{1 - \tau\,\frac{\partial Y}{\partial \Gamma}\right\},$$

$K = NK_i$. Using (3.64), and solving,

$$\frac{\partial Y}{\partial \Gamma} = \frac{f'(\tau)}{f(\tau) + \tau\,f'(\tau)},$$

which, under condition (3.66), yields $\partial Y/\partial \Gamma = 1$.

3.6.2 Command Economy Optimum

Given any size of the government Γ/Y, the planner would, using arguments for the no congestion case, choose the growth rate

$$G = \frac{A\,(1 - \Gamma/Y)\,f(\Gamma/Y) - \rho}{\theta}. \tag{3.67}$$

A minimal condition of optimality that the planner would want to satisfy is $\partial Y/\partial \Gamma = 1$. On the other hand, this would mean that the optimal value of Γ/Y for the Command Economy is the solution τ^* to (3.66). That is, the Command Economy will choose the growth rate of the Command Economy corresponding to the optimal proportional tax rate. The interesting feature of this result (which depends crucially on the fact that (3.64) is linear in K_i for fixed Γ/Y) is that the proportional tax distorted growth rate for the Command Economy is the best growth rate from the Command Economy's point of view also.

Indeed, quite opposite to the no congestion model, the Command Economy growth rate is not decentralisable with a lump sum tax. Under a lump sum tax, the Command Economy will grow at the rate

$$g_{lm}^d = \frac{A\,f(\Gamma/Y) - \rho}{\theta}.$$

If Γ/Y is chosen to satisfy the efficiency condition, the economy will grow at a rate that is higher than the efficiency generating rate chosen by the Command Economy. In other words, a lump sum tax will make the economy grow at an excessively high rate if it has to satisfy the condition of efficient resource allocation. Alternatively, with a lump sum tax, the Command Economy *might* succeed in growing at the Command Economy's optimal growth rate, but in order to do so, it must choose a value of Γ/Y that violates the static efficiency condition.

3.7   A Fixed Coefficient AK-Model

The equilibrium growth paths of the d'Autume-Michel and similar models necessarily satisfy the condition of balanced growth. Along the growth paths, the factor ratios are constants although the assumed production structures allow for smooth substitution. The factor prices assume appropriate values to ensure the constancy of factor intensities. As opposed to this an AK-Model is one for which the production function has the form $Y = AK$ where A is a positive constant. It corresponds to Leontief production structure and *does not permit any substitution at all*.[32] The latter has the form

$$Y = min \{AK, BL\}, \qquad (3.68)$$

where A and B are positive constants representing output per unit of capital and labour respectively. As is well known, the isoquants pertaining to the production function are right-angled corners. The wage-rental ratio in the market economy is indeterminate since the marginal rate of technical substitution is undefined at the corner of an isoquant. See Figure 3.7.

The production function pertaining to the Command Economy of the d'Autume-Michel model has an apparent similarity with the AK model. It may be interpreted to have this form with $A = \bar{L}f(1/\bar{L})$. The same observation holds for Frankel's

---

[32]In view of the rigid choice of the factor ratio in the d'Autume-Michel type models, they are often referred to as AK-Models, but this is strictly speaking an erroneous practice.

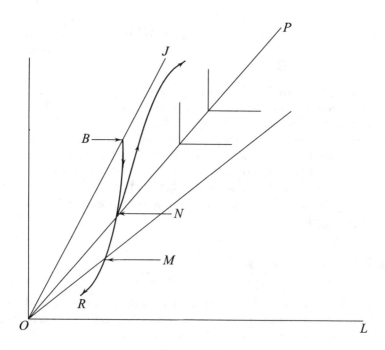

Figure 3.7

model with $A = f(1)$ and for (3.61) with $(\Gamma/K_i)^{1-\alpha} = constant$. Despite the formal similarities, however, these models are intrinsically different from the classic example of an AK-Model. Quite obviously, these models admitted smooth substitution along the isoquants, which the Leontief model does not. Consequently, whether one uses the epithet AK to describe them or not, the production functions for these models are distinctly different from (3.68). This shows up clearly in the fact that, as opposed to the models of the last two sections, the present model may not lead to long run growth with full employment. To appreciate the point, note first of all that actual employment of capital and labour must lie on the ray OP through the origin (Figure 3.7). However, the initial availability of capital and labour may be a point such as M at which only capital can be fully employed and labour is a surplus. At this point, we have $K/L < B/A$.

The AK model is the simplest of production systems that allow endogenous determination of the growth rate. To illustrate this fact in as elementary a manner as possible, we shall ignore the optimisation exercise carried out by H and assume that the savings propensity is a constant s. The choice of s will be seen to fix the rate of growth of the system in a straightforward manner. Assume, to begin with, that $K/L < B/A$ and that $\dot{L}/L = n > 0$. Then, output and investment are given respectively by

$$Y = AK \tag{3.69}$$

and

$$\dot{K} = sAK, \tag{3.70}$$

which immediately demonstrate the link between s and the rate of growth. Two possibilities arise depending on whether $sA > n$ or $sA < n$.

Case 1: $sA > n$. Then $g_k = \dot{K}/K = sA > n \Rightarrow K/L$ rises with time. (See the thick upward pointing path starting at M.) Denote the employment of labour by $\tilde{L}$. Along the ray OP, $\tilde{L}$ grows at the same rate as capital. Hence, $\tilde{L}/L$ rises till $\tilde{L} = L$ at some finite point of time t_0. At t_0, unemployment of labour disappears and the economy is on OP, say at the point N. Since $g_k > n$ all along the path MN, the capital-population ratio is rising at N. At N, we have $K/L = B/A$. Thus, $K/L > B/A$ for $t > t_0$ and labour is the limitational factor. The production function changes to[33]

$$Y = BL \tag{3.71}$$

and

---

[33]Note that the terminology AK may be questionable at this juncture and one might be tempted to describe the model as BL rather than AK. A probable reason underlying the paradoxical nomenclature could be that the AK model was one of the earliest models employed in the Theory of Planning to study programmes of economic development for labour surplus, capital scarce economies.

$$\dot{K} = sBL. \tag{3.72}$$

For $t > t_0$, the rate of growth of capital $\dot{K}/K = sBL/K$ and since $\dot{K}/K > n$, the ratio L/K must be falling. Thus, $\dot{K}/K$ falls towards n. In the meantime, K/L has risen further towards a ray such as OJ. Since $\dot{K}/K$ approaches n in the limit, it follows that the capital-population ratio converges to the ray OJ (say) in the long run. Notice, however, that there is capital unemployment on the ray OJ. Actual employment of capital, $\tilde{K}$, and labour continues to lie on OP, with $\tilde{K}$ and L growing at the same rate n. In the long run, K grows at the same rate as n also. So, $\tilde{K}/K$ approaches a constant less than unity over time. Thus, we have a situation of balanced growth with a constant fraction of capital unemployed in the long run. Of course, the situation considered is unrealistic. Once the point N is reached, one expects the savings rate to be lowered to maintain growth with full employment of both factors.

Case 2: $sA < n$. If the initial capital-population ratio is at a point such as M again, then $g_k < n$ and K/L falls towards zero. Since $\dot{\tilde{L}}/\tilde{L} = \dot{K}/K$, it follows that $\tilde{L}/L$ falls towards zero as well. If the initial capital-population ratio is higher at a point such as B, we have $K/L > B/A$ and L is limitational. In this case, $\dot{K}/K = sBL/K < sA$. Hence, g_k is still less than n and the same conclusion follows. The thick path BMR captures the situation.

As opposed to the economy with Leontief technology, the Command economies of the previous two sections do not allow for unemployment. The corresponding Private economies too have growth with full employment. In fact, for the Private economies, profit maximising entrepreneurs choose optimal factor intensities by maximising profits.

Appendix 3.1

Proof of Proposition 3.8 Given r_m, τ_m, the household's demand rate of growth is

$$g_c^d(r_m, \tau_m) = \frac{(1 - \tau_m)r_m - \rho}{\theta}, \tag{A3.1.1}$$

which, we may write for convenience as

$$r_m = \frac{\theta \, g_c^d}{1 - \tau_m} + \frac{\rho}{1 - \tau_m}. \tag{A3.1.2}$$

Consider now the marginal productivity of capital corresponding to the C/K ratio chosen by the planner, viz. $\hat{c}^{**}$, which equals $\hat{c}_0^{**}$ of Section 3.3.2. If this ratio were to prevail in the free market, then the rate of interest would equal $f(\hat{c}^{**}) - (1 - \alpha)\hat{c}^{**}f'(\hat{c}^{**})$, the private marginal productivity of capital. Choose r_m equal to this value. Similarly, choose w_m to be the marginal product of labour at $\hat{c}^{**}$. Let τ_m be the tax (resp. subsidy) rate such that

$$r_m = \frac{\theta \, G^*}{1 - \tau_m} + \frac{\rho}{1 - \tau_m}, \tag{A3.1.3}$$

where G^* is the rate of growth of the Command Economy. The household's demand rate of growth corresponding to r_m will therefore be G^*. Using (3.49), we may write

$$C_p(t) + \dot{K}(t) \;=\; (1 - \tau_m) \, r_m K(t)$$

$$+ w_m,$$

$$= \; r_m K(t) + w_m$$

$$- \tau_m \, r_m K(t),$$

or,

$$C_p(t) + \dot{K}(t) + \tau_m r_m K(t) = r_m K(t) + w_m. \tag{A3.1.4}$$

For $t = 0$ in particular, this reduces to

$$C_{p0} + \dot{K}_0 + \tau_m r_m K_0 = r_m K_0 + w_m, \qquad \text{(A3.1.5)}$$

Let $C_{g0} = C_0^{**} - C_{p0}$, where C_0^{**} stands for aggregate consumption at $t = 0$ in the Command Economy. We break up the analysis into two cases depending on the sign of C_{g0}. Case 1: $C_{g0} > 0$. In this case, the government subsidises the household by augmenting C_{p0}. Two questions arise here. First, is the government's budget balanced? Second, is the aggregate consumption $C_{p0} + C_{g0}$ technologically feasible? To answer the first question, observe that an aggregate consumption C_0^{**} at $t = 0$ entails an aggregate output of $Y_0^{**} = F(K_0, K_0^\alpha (C_0^{**})^{1-\alpha})$ $= K_0 f(\hat{c}^{**})$. Moreover, by choice of r_m and w_m and using linear homogeneity, we have $r_m K_0 + w_m = Y_0^{**}$. Dividing out (A3.1.5) by K_0,

$$\frac{C_{p0}}{K_0} + \tau_m r_m + G^* = f(\hat{c}^{**}). \qquad \text{(A3.1.6)}$$

Next, the fact that $\hat{c}^{**}$ satisfies (3.43) implies

$$\tau_m r_m = (\hat{c}^{**})^{1/(1-\alpha)} - \frac{C_{p0}}{K_0}$$

$$= \frac{C_0^{**} - C_{p0}}{K_0},$$

since, by definition, $\hat{c}^{**} = ((C/K)^*)^{1-\alpha}$. Hence, the choice of $C_{g0} = C_0^{**} - C_{p0}$ balances the government's budget. Since the economy is in steady state, the same argument applies for all $t > 0$ also.

Given that the government's budget is balanced, (A3.1.5) yields

$$Y_0^{**} = C_{p0} + C_{g0} + \dot{K}_0$$

$$= C_0^{**} + \dot{K}_0$$

$$= C_0^{**} + G^* K_0, \qquad \text{(A3.1.7)}$$

where Y^{**} is aggregate output. By assumption, however, G^*K_0 equals the investment carried out by the social planner at $t = 0$. Hence, $C_{p0} + C_{g0}$ as defined above is feasible. Case 2: $C_{g0} < 0$. The same argument applies *mutatis mutandis*. The algebra is identical though the interpretation is different. In the present case, capital will be subsidised, thus raising C_{p0} to a technologically infeasible level. The lump sum consumption tax will restore feasibility while satisfying the government's budget constraint exactly.

Chapter 4

Technical Progress as a Conscious Economic Activity-I

4.1 Resource Allocation for Technological Advancement

By now, we are reasonably familiar with economic models of growth for which the balanced growth rates are determined by endogenous forces. Chapter 2 taught us why the only sustainable rate of growth of per capita GDP would be identically the same as the rate of technical progress in the long run. The conclusion was unsatisfactory inasmuch as the Solow model had little to offer by way of explaining the nature of technical progress itself. This did not reduce the importance of the Solow exercise, since it contained a valuable insight on the role of diminishing returns in connecting up the rate of capital accumulation with the rate of growth of the effective labour force. Chapter 3 was a preliminary attempt to build up a theory of technical progress by appealing to Arrow's learning by doing hypothesis. As we saw, capital accumulation was by itself expected to have a labour enriching effect. Between two societies, one that had a larger stock of physical capital was likely to be characterised by a more efficient labour force. While this gave rise to a theory of Harrod-neutral technical progress, it suffered from the drawback that it assigned to physical capital accumulation a primary status, of which technical progress turned out to be a passive by-product. Casual empiricism suggests, on the other hand, that causality runs in the reverse direction. Usually, conscious and costly efforts devoted to the discovery of novel methods of production lead to the construction of a piece of physical machinery or equipment in which the new technology is embedded.

In plain terms, changes in the variable A measuring technical progress might appear to be the end point of a consciously driven discovery process, which in turn dictates the choice of the physical capital accumulation path. Since any *discovery* involves a deliberate effort (i.e., the shouldering of economic costs) on the part of a potential *discoverer*, technological progress should strictly speaking be thought of as a productive activity geared towards the harnessing of scarce economic resources needed to *produce* $\dot{A}$. The present chapter and the one that follows immediately will be concerned with adding flesh to this bare skeleton of an idea. We shall spin alternative stories to guide the theoretical construction of models that recognise technical progress as a conscious economic activity.

There are two major differences between the two chapters. The first relates to the concrete form we shall imagine the discovery process to assume. The present chapter will mostly interpret it to mean labour skills acquired through the use of resources diverted away from the production of consumption or physical capital goods. Acquisition of novel skills by individuals (by spending time, a vital economic resource, in educating themselves) constitutes an awakening of dormant abilities and should count as self-discovery, a transformation of unskilled manpower to a skilled work force or *human capital*. The next chapter will view technical progress as a process of knowledge creation (or discovery once again) through R & D. This will introduce a distinction between physical and knowledge (as opposed to human) capital.[1]

The second difference arises from the fact that all the models described in these two chapters will be concerned with the specification of *technologies for technological progress*. A fundamental question that comes up in this context is whether there are technological limits to technical progress itself. In other words, is the rate of technical change producible by rational economic agents constrained by technological factors? Some (though not all) of the models in this chapter will view technical progress as being ultimately bounded by factors. The next one will present a more optimistic view of the matter and argue that bounds on technical progress arise, not due to technological reasons, but on account of scarcity of specialised resources which may conceivably be removed over time.[2]

We shall formalise human capital in this chapter in different ways. One way, to be introduced in Section 4.3, will be to broaden the definition of physical capital and interpret it as a composite of physical and human capital. An alternative approach shall be to look at the value of AL at any point of time t as the prevailing stock of human capital and changes in it considered investment in this form of capital. (Sections 4.2 and 4.4.) Finally, as was the case in the last chapter, where we noted a formal similarity between the Arrow type models of technical change and Barro's work on infrastructure led growth, Section 4.5 will draw parallels between human capital and infrastructure creation in the present chapter also. A common feature shared by all the models of this chapter is that they incorporate two production sectors as opposed to the single commodity framework adopted in the last three chapters

---

[1]The last chapter presented the Romer (1986) model, which was a preliminary attempt at conceptualising knowledge capital. The next chapter will carry this idea forward by viewing knowledge capital as a vitally important ingredient for the creation of an array of specialised inputs that improve the technology. An alternative paradigm will imagine knowledge as adding variety to the menu of commodities consumed by the household, thereby adding directly to utility.

[2]Recall from Chapter 3 that the d'Autume-Michel as well as parts of the Dasgupta-Marjit models had the latter characteristic. A rise in the stock of the labour force led to improvements in the equilibrium growth rate.

(with the sole exception of the Romer (1986) model). The broadened scope of technology in the present chapter will occasionally bring with it two state variables corresponding to two accumulable factors of production. It will also add to the number of control variables. (Note that Romer (1986) was a two sector economy, but there was a single state variable (K) and a single control variable (c).) The appearance of several control and state variables call for extensions of the scope of optimisation techniques developed in Chapter 2. Consequently, the necessary tools for the purpose will need to be forged in this chapter. (See Sections 4.2.2 and 4.2.3.)

4.2   A Two-sector Model of Growth: Rebelo-I

We shall begin with Rebelo's (1991) contributions to the area. To motivate his work, let us go back to the Solow model which demonstrated that there were two essential barriers to endogenising the growth rate: (a) diminishing returns to factors of production and (b) an exogenously specified growth rate of the composite factor AL. Rebelo shows that it is the *simultaneous* presence of both conditions that rules out endogeneity. That is, the growth rate can be endogenously determined provided any one of the two conditions is dispensed with. We shall illustrate this by means of two models. The first satisfies (a) but not (b) and the second retains (b) at the cost of a partial removal of (a). The two exercises will establish a trade off between the two Solow conditions from the point of view of endogenous growth theory and illustrate in a transparent manner the barest structural needs of an endogenous growth model.

As already indicated, we will move out of the single sector scenario of the previous chapters for both exercises. Rebelo's first model requires us to take this step since one must now specify an additional technology for "producing" the factor whose growth was left to exogenous factors in the Solow model. As far as the second model goes, one of the sectors considered has an AK structure of the type discussed in the last chapter, while the other involves a Solow technology as well as an exogenously given factor supply. Despite the latter, the AK forces dominate, thereby de-linking the growth rate from exogenous factors. Thus, the two sectors in the second Rebelo model are required to emphasise the power of the AK assumptions. The present section describes Rebelo's first model.[3]

4.2.1 Description of the Economy

There are two producible commodities, of which the first is similar to the Solow commodity that may be either consumed by the household or invested for physical capital formation. (Notice that Romer (1986) had a similar sector, but did not permit one to one transformation of the investment good into physical capital.) The second represents an additional investment good, used to build up stocks of other forms of capital. Let us denote physical capital by K as before. The second capital good, T, may be identified as human capital or the stock of skills embodied in the available labour force.[4]

The technology for the first sector is given by:

$$Y = C + \dot{K} = A(\nu\, K)^{\gamma}(u\, T)^{1-\gamma}, \qquad (4.1)$$

where ν and u stand for the shares of K and T employed in the Y-sector. Given that human capital is embodied in labourers, the factor T should have a form similar to Solow's AL, where A may be interpreted as education per worker. The technology for producing Y resembles the Solow production function, since $T = AL$. In what follows, however, we shall continue to abstract from growth in L (in line with some of the exercises in Chapter 3) and concentrate attention entirely on the growth of education. This serves to trace back the source of growth to endogenous factors determining the dynamics of T.

---

[3]For a general treatment of two sector endogenous growth, see Bond *et al* (1996).

[4]Section 4.5 will deal with a similar model, but instead of interpreting the second good as human capital, it will look upon it as infrastructure.

The second sector, to be referred to as the *T*-sector, will be viewed as producing a commodity that may be used only to add to the existing stock of *T*. Since *T* is human capital, the product of the *T* sector may be interpreted as new education and/or research output that helps to augment *T*. Accordingly, the output of the *T* sector will be denoted by $\dot{T}$ and the technology given by

$$\dot{T} = B((1-\nu)K)^{\beta}((1-u)T)^{1-\beta}, \tag{4.2}$$

where $1 - \nu$ and $1 - u$ are the shares of K and T employed in this sector. The important characteristic of the *T*-sector lies in the recognition it accords to the fact that human capital is an indispensable resource in the production of human capital. (The shares in the two sectors for each factor input add up to unity, i.e., either the market or a planner ensures that all resources are fully employed at each instant of time.)

The fact that we are ignoring the separation of T into A and L, forces us to define all relevant rates of growth in absolute rather than per capita terms. Thus, in what follows, $g_K = \dot{K}/K$, $g_T = \dot{T}/T$ and $g_C = \dot{C}/C$.[5]

4.2.2 Balanced Growth in Two-sector Economies

We shall mostly restrict our analysis to balanced growth paths alone. However, the study of balanced growth paths in the presence of two state variables requires an extension of the definition employed in earlier chapters. Since T replaces AL, the first natural requirement to impose for balanced growth is that

$$\frac{\dot{K}}{K} = \frac{\dot{T}}{T}$$

i.e., $\qquad \dfrac{K}{T} = constant.$ \hfill (4.3)

---

[5]Strictly speaking, we are concerned here with the growth of C/L. However, L being a constant, it is enough to concentrate on the growth of C alone.

Both sectors employ K and T, however. Hence, we shall impose the above requirement on each sector in isolation also. That is, a second requirement for balanced growth in the current two-sector framework will be

$$\frac{\nu\,K}{u\,T} = constant \qquad (4.4)$$

and $\qquad \dfrac{(1-\nu)\,K}{(1-u)\,T} = constant. \qquad (4.5)$

4.2.3 Private and Command Economies

Private accumulation of T is best viewed as an activity carried out by the household as part of its optimisation exercise. In other words, we shall imagine that agent H decides on the allocation of the stock of human capital it owns for its own augmentation. The decision cannot be separated from the simultaneous choice of the share of T to be employed in the Y-sector. The logical implication is that production decisions in the Y-sector must also be thought of as a part of the household's optimisation exercise. So conceived, the Private Economy will not distinguish between H and B and turn into a representative household firm.[6] In our previous exercises, the planner was viewed as solving an overall optimisation exercise and we did not distinguish between supply and demand rates of growth. In the present problem, the household's behaviour is identical with that of the planner. Hence, we have to separate out different parts of the planner's exercise to isolate demand from supply.[7]

The household solves the problem

$$\text{Maximise} \int_0^\infty \frac{C^{1-\theta}-1}{1-\theta} e^{-\rho\,t} dt$$

subject to 4.1 and 4.2.

---

[6]Note that the Romer (1986) model was treated similarly in the last chapter. As opposed to that exercise however, there are no externalities in Rebelo's model.

[7]See Barro (1990) for another example of the household firm structure.

Since this way of viewing the Private Economy amounts to removing the distinction between the Private and Command Economies, the two economies will end up with the same optimal paths *by definition*.

Unless essential, we shall drop the time argument attached to variables for notational simplicity. Denoting the prices of K and T, measured in utils, by ξ and η respectively, profit maximisation requires that the values of marginal products of each type of capital be equalised across sectors:

$$\xi \, \gamma \, A \, (\nu \, K)^{\gamma-1} \, (u \, T)^{1-\gamma} \;=\; \eta \, \beta \, B \, ((1-\nu) \, K)^{\beta-1}$$

$$\times ((1-u) \, T)^{1-\beta}, \qquad (4.6)$$

$$\xi \, (1-\gamma) \, A \, (\nu \, K)^{\gamma} \, (u \, T)^{-\gamma} \;=\; \eta \, (1-\beta) \, B \, ((1-\nu) \, K)^{\beta}$$

$$\times ((1-u) \, T)^{-\beta}. \qquad (4.7)$$

Dividing (4.6) by (4.7),

$$\frac{\gamma}{1-\gamma} \frac{u \, T}{\nu \, K} = \frac{\beta}{1-\beta} \frac{(1-u) \, T}{(1-\nu) \, K}. \qquad (4.8)$$

We do not know as yet the equilibrium values of $uT/\nu K$ or $(1-u)T/(1-\nu)K$. Consequently, the market rate of interest in unknown. However, under the assumption of balanced growth, viz. (4.3) and (4.5), the rate of interest is a constant, since it depends on factor ratios under constant returns to scale. Since $\dot{T}/T$ and $(1-\nu)K/(1-u)T$ are constants,

$$\frac{\dot{T}}{T} = g_T^s = B \, \left(\frac{(1-\nu)K}{(1-u)T} \right)^{\beta} (1-u) \qquad (4.9)$$

implies u is a constant. Hence, according to (4.8), ν is a constant also. Consider now the macro identity

$$\frac{C}{K} + \frac{\dot{K}}{K} = A \, \nu \, \left(\frac{uT}{\nu K} \right)^{1-\gamma}.$$

Under balanced growth, ν as well as the factor intensity on the RHS and $g_K^s = \dot{K}/K$ on the LHS are constants. Hence, $g_C^s = \dot{C}/C = g_K^s =$ constant. Thus, g_C^s is perfectly horizontal at the equilibrium value of r.

To solve for the demand rate of growth, let $V(K(t), T(t))$ stand for the optimal level of aggregate utility obtainable during (t, ∞) starting from $(K(t), T(t))$. Along an optimal accumulation path, $\partial V/\partial K$ and $\partial V/\partial T$ must equal the prices of $K(t)$ and $T(t)$, viz., $\xi(t)$ and $\eta(t)$. Equation (A2.1.6) continues to hold with essential changes in details. We reproduce this below:

$$V(K(t), T(t)) \cong max_{C(t)} \{h\, u(C(t))$$
$$+ V(K(t+h), T(t+h))\}. \quad (4.10)$$

For an optimum *wrt* C (assuming reversible investment),

$$\frac{h\, \partial u(C(t))}{\partial C(t)} + \frac{\partial V(K(t+h), T(t+h))}{\partial C(t)} = 0, \quad (4.11)$$

where

$$\frac{\partial V(K(t+h), T(t+h))}{\partial C(t)} = \frac{\partial V(K(t+h), T(t+h))}{\partial K(t+h)}$$
$$\times \frac{\partial K(t+h)}{\partial C(t)}$$
$$+ \frac{\partial V(K(t+h), T(t+h))}{\partial T(t+h)}$$
$$\times \frac{\partial T(t+h)}{\partial C(t)}. \quad (4.12)$$

Linearising,

$$K(t+h) \cong K(t) + h\, \dot{K}(t),$$

$$T(t+h) \cong T(t) + h\, \dot{T}(t).$$

Using the facts that $\dot{K}(t) = A(\nu\, K(t))^{\gamma}(u\, T(t))^{1-\gamma} - C(t)$ and $T(t)$ is independent of $C(t)$, (4.12) reduces to

$$\frac{\partial V(K(t+h), T(t+h))}{\partial C(t)} \;=\; -h\,\xi(t+h)$$

$$=\; -\xi(t)\left(h + h^2\,\frac{\dot{\xi}(t)}{\xi(t)}\right)$$

$$\cong\; -h\,\xi(t) \text{ (for small } h).$$

Equations (4.11) now implies that

$$C^{-\theta} = \xi \tag{4.13}$$

at each point of time. Equation (4.13) corresponds to static optimality.

We move over now to dynamic optimality conditions. The social cost of a unit of investment in K at t is $\xi(t)$. The social return to the investment at any $s > t$, given the optimal values of ν and u, is $\xi(s)\partial Y(s)/\partial K(s) + \eta(s)\partial\dot{T}/\partial K(s)$.[8] In order for the investment to break even, the discounted present value of the stream of returns will equal $\xi(t)$. Thus,

$$\xi(t) = \int_t^{\infty} \left\{\xi(s)\frac{\partial Y(s)}{\partial K(s)} + \eta(s)\frac{\partial\dot{T}(s)}{\partial K(s)}\right\} e^{-\rho(s-t)}ds, \tag{4.14}$$

or, taking account of the explicit forms of the production functions,

$$\xi(t) = \int_t^{\infty} \{\gamma\nu A(\nu K)^{\gamma-1}(uT)^{1-\gamma}\xi(s)$$
$$+ \beta(1-\nu)B((1-\nu)K)^{\beta-1}(uT)^{1-\beta}\eta(s)\} e^{-\rho(s-t)}ds. \tag{4.15}$$

---

[8]Note that we agreed in Chapter 1 to drop the depreciation parameter Chapter 3 onwards.

The time derivative of (4.15) yields, using (4.6),

$$
\begin{aligned}
\dot{\xi}(t) &= -\gamma\nu A(\nu K)^{\gamma-1}(uT)^{1-\gamma}\xi(t) \\
&\quad -\beta(1-\nu)B((1-\nu)K)^{\beta-1}((1-u)T)^{1-\beta}\eta(t) + \rho\xi(t) \\
&= -\gamma A(\nu K)^{\gamma-1}(uT)^{1-\gamma}\xi(t) + \rho\,\xi(t). \tag{4.16}
\end{aligned}
$$

Equations (4.13) and (4.16) are easily manipulated to yield the demand rate of growth, viz. (2.44).

To determine the equilibrium growth rate, we must find the equilibrium value of $r = r^*$. The solution involves several steps. Let us first use (4.7) and the parallels of (4.15) and (4.16) for η to get

$$
\begin{aligned}
\dot{\eta}(t) &= -(1-\gamma)uA(\nu K)^{\gamma}(uT)^{-\gamma}\xi(t) - (1-\beta)(1-u)B \\
&\quad \times((1-\nu)K)^{\beta}((1-u)T)^{-\beta}\eta(t) + \rho \\
&= -(1-\beta)B((1-\nu)K)^{\beta}((1-u)T)^{-\beta}\eta(t) + \rho\,\eta(t).
\end{aligned}
\tag{4.17}
$$

Equations (4.16) and (4.17) constitute a two sector counterpart of (2.11) of Chapter 2. Substituting (4.6) in (4.15), we get

$$
\xi(t) = \int_t^\infty \gamma A(\nu K)^{\gamma-1}(uT)^{1-\gamma}\xi(s)\, e^{-\rho(s-t)}ds. \tag{4.18}
$$

Under balanced growth, $\gamma A(\nu K)^{\gamma-1}(uT)^{1-\gamma} = constant$. Thus, for $\xi(t)$ to be well-defined

$$
e^{-\rho t}\,\xi(t) \to 0 \text{ as } t \to \infty. \tag{4.19}
$$

A parallel argument shows that

$$
e^{-\rho t}\,\eta(t) \to 0 \text{ as } t \to \infty. \tag{4.20}
$$

Finally, differentiating (4.6) and recalling that factor intensities are constant along a balanced growth path, it follows that

$\dot{\xi}/\xi = \dot{\eta}/\eta$. Using this in conjunction with (4.16) and (4.17), we see that

$$\gamma \; A \; \left(\frac{u \; T}{\nu \; K}\right)^{1-\gamma} = (1 - \beta) \; B \; \left(\frac{(1 - u) \; T}{(1 - \nu) \; K}\right)^{-\beta} \qquad (4.21)$$

is satisfied. Equations (4.8) and (4.21) may be solved for the factor intensity levels $u \; T/\nu \; K$ and $(1 - u) \; T/(1 - \nu) \; K$ in balanced growth equilibrium. This determines the constant equilibrium value of r^*. Substituting for r^* in (2.44), we obtain the equilibrium rate of growth g^* for the Private Economy.[9]

We may now utilise (4.9) to solve for u. Next, ν is found using the equilibrium value of $uT/\nu K$. Plugging in the equilibrium values of u, ν and $g_T^s = g^*$ in (4.9), an equilibrium value of T/K follows. There is no guarantee of course that the arbitrarily given initial value of T_0/K_0 would equal the balanced growth equilibrium value of T/K. This gives rise to a stability problem somewhat similar to the one faced by the original Solow model. As will be recalled, in that model, balanced growth fixed the value of K/AL. However, the initial value K_0/A_0L_0 being specified in an ad hoc manner, it was necessary to argue that any equilibrium path starting from K_0/A_0L_0 would converge to the balanced growth value of K/AL.[10] The stability analysis for the Rebelo I model will be more complicated than the one developed for the Solow model, since the economy is now characterised by two sectors of production rather than one. This book will not concern itself with stability problems in general, though it is a serious issue and cannot be ignored altogether. Consequently, the Appendix to this chapter will present a local stability analysis for a two-sector model of growth based on the economy described in Section 4.5. Readers interested in the stability properties of the Rebelo I model will find a clear analysis in Chapter 5 of Barro & Sala-i-Martin (2003).

---

[9]By definition of balanced growth, $g_C^s = g_K^s = g_T^s$. Therefore, (4.9) implies that g_C^s takes values in the set $(0, B((1 - \nu)K/(1 - u)T)^\beta)$. This puts some obvious restrictions on the parameters of the model.

[10]Chapter 3 presented examples of models that avoided this problem altogether.

PROPOSITION **4.1** *The two-sector Rebelo model of growth with physical and human capital allows for the endogenous determination of the balanced rate of growth of the economy. The balanced growth equilibrium has associated with it a fixed value of the ratio of physical and human capital stocks. Consequently, the model calls for out of balanced growth dynamics.*

4.2.4   The Hamiltonian Approach

We may represent the above results in compact form by referring to the Hamiltonian function

$$\mathcal{H}(C, \nu, u, \xi.\eta, K, T) = u(C) + \xi \dot{K} + \eta \dot{T}.$$

For a path $\{C, \nu, u, \xi, \eta, K, T\}_0^\infty$ to be optimal, it is necessary that

$$\frac{\partial \mathcal{H}(C, \nu, u, \xi, \eta, K, T)}{\partial C} = 0,$$

$$\frac{\partial \mathcal{H}(C, \nu, u, \xi, \eta, K, T)}{\partial \nu} = 0,$$

$$\frac{\partial \mathcal{H}(C, \nu, u, \xi, \eta, K, T)}{\partial u} = 0,$$

$$\frac{\partial \mathcal{H}(C, \nu, u, \xi, \eta, K, T)}{\partial \xi} = \dot{K},$$

$$\frac{\partial \mathcal{H}(C, \nu, u, \xi, \eta, K, T)}{\partial \eta} = \dot{T}. \tag{4.22}$$

Equations (4.16) and (4.17) are rewritten

$$\dot{\xi} = -\frac{\partial \mathcal{H}}{\partial K} + \rho \xi \quad \text{and}$$

$$\dot{\eta} = -\frac{\partial \mathcal{H}}{\partial T} + \rho \eta. \tag{4.23}$$

Finally, the two transversality conditions (4.19) and (4.20) are satisfied.

4.3   A Two-sector Model of Growth: Rebelo-II

4.3.1   Description of the Economy

The earliest version of a neoclassical two-sector growth model which Rebelo's second model resembles goes back to Uzawa (1961, 1963). It draws a physical distinction between the consumption good C and investment good $\dot{K}$.[11] Rebelo retains this contrast but replaces Uzawa's technology for producing the investment good by an AK production function.

The factors of production are divided up into technologically reproducible and non-reproducible groups, say, K and L. The former is a composite of physical and human capital, while the latter will be referred to as unskilled labour, or simply labour. The non-reproducibility of L ($=\bar{L}$, say) implies the existence of diminishing returns to the variable factor K. As already noted, Rebelo establishes the possibility of endogenous growth despite this fact. The two sectors produce respectively an investment good (I) (which is qualitatively the same as the composite of physical and human capital) and a consumption good (C). Since labour is explicitly brought back, we may once again speak of per capita consumption c. However, $L = \bar{L}$ implies c is (effectively) identical with C. The investment good is produced by the non-sector specific composite capital good (K) using an AK technology

$$I = b(1 - \nu)K, \qquad (4.24)$$

where b is a technological constant and $1 - \nu$ the endogenously determined share of capital used for producing I. The linearity

---

[11]Retracing our steps back to the Solow model, the one for one transformation of saving into investment might appear to be too narrow a representation of the production of capital goods. In Uzawa's framework, the traditional macro separation of GDP between consumption and saving is replaced by a division of resources allocated for consumption and investment goods production. The most general multi-sector model of economic growth goes back to von Neumann (1945-46). The reader should try and compare this approach with Romer (1986).

of the production function for I, hence the absence of diminishing returns, may be explained as follows. Diminishing returns is caused by a disproportionate use of one or more factors relative to others. Thus, in the Solow model, diminishing returns to capital in producing Y could arise when increasing quantities of capital were combined with a fixed amount of labour. In the Rebelo model on the other hand, K has already been interpreted as a combined factor of production. Thus, (4.24) represents the production of a *vector* of human and physical capital (symbolised by I) by means of yet another *vector* of human and physical capital (symbolised by K), where the ratio of human to physical capital is a constant and identically the same for I and K.[12] Diminishing returns will not arise under the circumstances, since the two factors are being employed in the same proportion. The consumption good is produced by a Cobb-Douglas technology using K and $\bar{L}$:

$$C = B(\nu K)^\gamma \bar{L}^{1-\gamma}, \qquad (4.25)$$

where B is a constant. As before, we shall be concerned with determining the balanced growth rate of the economy. Since there is a single capital good, but two sectors which use it, the definition of balanced growth reduces to the requirement that

$$\frac{\dot{K}}{K} = constant$$

and

$$\frac{(\nu \dot{K})}{\nu K} = constant,$$

$$\text{i.e., } \nu = constant, \qquad (4.26)$$

since $\nu \in [0, 1]$.

4.3.2 The Private Economy

In the absence of (4.25), i.e., if the model had a single sector with (4.24) as the technology, the supply curve would be in-

---

[12]Of course, the last section has already demonstrated that it is possible to analytically separate out physical and human capital.

finitely elastic at the level b.[13] On the other hand, if (4.25) represented an *aggregate* production function as in Solow, the supply curve would be perfectly inelastic, passing through a point determined by the exogenously given rate of growth of natural resources (zero, in Rebelo's case, since $L = \bar{L}$). The simultaneous existence of the two sectors in Rebelo, however, leads to a supply curve that lies in between the two extremes.

Under competition, profit maximising firms will ensure that capital is allocated across sectors to equate the (value of) its marginal productivity for every t. In other words,

$$p\, b = \gamma B(\nu K)^{\gamma-1}\bar{L}^{1-\gamma}, \tag{4.27}$$

where p represents the price of K relative to C. Dividing both sides of (4.27) by p, we see that although the marginal productivity of K falls in the C-sector, its value measured in units of K remains a constant. For this to happen, $1/p$ rises (i.e., p declines) in the same proportion as the fall in the marginal product of K in the C- sector, which helps avoid the depressing effects of diminishing returns. Differentiation of (4.27) (given a constant ν) yields

$$g_p = \frac{\dot{p}}{p} = (\gamma - 1)g_K^s, \tag{4.28}$$

where g_K^s is the supply rate of growth of K, since the derivation of this rate of growth of K does not involve any demand side arguments. The RHS of (4.28) represents the rate of fall of marginal productivity in the C-sector. This is a constant under balanced growth, i.e., when g_K^s is a constant. Thus, g_p is a constant under balanced growth. Equation (4.25) implies that g_C^s satisfies

$$g_C^s = \gamma g_K^s,$$

which, using (4.28), implies

$$g_C^s = \frac{\gamma}{\gamma - 1}\, g_p.$$

[13]This is typical for the AK technology and follows from the fact that the marginal productivity of K, which equals the rate of interest, is a constant b irrespective of the level of K. We saw an instance of this phenomenon in Section 3.2.6.

It is possible to reduce g_C^s to a function of the rate of interest. To do so, we must evoke a second no arbitrage condition signifying equilibrium asset holding by the household. Notice that this means appealing to household equilibrium conditions to derive the supply rate of growth. This amounts to mixing up supply and demand factors. However, as shown below, the no arbitrage condition requires knowledge of market parameters alone and, to that extent, can be internalised by the firms.

Going over to the said condition now, the household should be indifferent between holding capital assets in the two sectors. Denote the rate of return at s from holding a unit of capital employed in the C-sector by $r_C(s)$. (Note that the ultimate objective being to derive the balanced growth path, we assume ν to be a constant.) On the other hand, the own rate of return in the I-sector is b. In order to be indifferent between assets in the two sectors, the Household should satisfy a condition parallel to (2.13). Hence, using the arguments used to derive (2.13),[14] we have

$$\dot{p}(t) = -b\,p(t) + r_C(t)\,p(t). \tag{4.29}$$

Dividing out by $p(t)$, we obtain

$$r_C(t) = b + g_p(t). \tag{4.30}$$

Substituting this in the expression for g_C^s, we end up with

$$g_C^s = g_C^s(r_C) = \frac{\gamma(b - r_C)}{1 - \gamma}. \tag{4.31}$$

---

[14]A unit of investment in either sector at time t costs $p(t)$. A unit of investment in the I-sector at t leads to a stream of returns $p(s)b \ \forall \ s > t$. For the investment to break even, the discounted present value of the stream must equal $p(t)$ and the discount rate used for the purpose stands for the *rate* of return to a unit of investment in the I- sector. The latter rate must be equal to $r_C(s)$ for the household to be indifferent between investing in the two sectors. Thus, the second no arbitrage condition boils down to

$$p(t) = \int_t^\infty p(s)\,b\,e^{-\int_t^s r_C(x)dx}ds,$$

which, differentiated with respect to t, yields (4.29).

This downward falling function of r_C is the Rebelo supply curve for C.

As far as the demand rate of growth is concerned, the household maximises

$$\int_0^\infty u(C(t))\, e^{-\rho\, t} dt$$

subject to

$$C + pI = r_C K + w\bar{L}.$$

We may solve this problem using the Hamiltonian function

$$\mathcal{H} = u(C) + \xi\, \frac{r_C K + w\bar{L} - C}{p}.$$

The necessary conditions of optimum are

$$C^{-\theta} = \frac{\xi}{p}$$

and

$$\dot{\xi} \;=\; -\frac{\partial \mathcal{H}}{\partial K} + \rho\xi$$

$$=\; -\frac{\xi r_C}{p} + \rho\xi.$$

The last two equations along with (4.27) and (4.30) imply (2.44). The equilibrium value of g_C, say g_C^*, is determined as before by the intersection of the demand and the supply rate curves. Thus,

$$g_C^* = \frac{\gamma(b - \rho)}{1 - \gamma(1 - \theta)}. \tag{4.32}$$

Also, using $g_C^s = \gamma\, g_K^s$,

$$g_K^* = \frac{(b - \rho)}{1 - \gamma(1 - \theta)}. \tag{4.33}$$

The determination of equilibrium is shown in Figure 4.1 below. It is easy to see from the diagram that the condition for a positive rate of equilibrium growth is $b > \rho$. Writing $Y = C + pI$, the equilibrium rate of growth of Y is $g_Y^* = g_C^* = \gamma g_K^*$.

The variable ν showing the allocation of K between the two sectors was left indeterminate. This is found from (4.24) which shows that the supply rate of growth of capital satisfies

$$g_K^s = \frac{\dot{K}}{K} = b\,(1 - \nu).$$

Unlike Rebelo I, the present model does not admit any out of steady state dynamics. To see this, observe that substitution of the equilibrium value of ν and K_0 in (4.27) yields the initial value of C_0 uniquely. Starting from this value and with K growing at the rate g_K^*, consumption grows at the equilibrium balanced rate g_C^* forever.

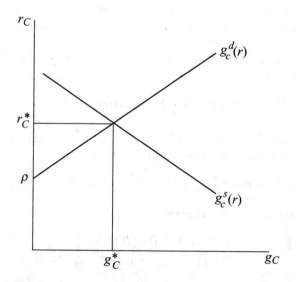

Figure 4.1

Rebelo's results may be summarised as follow:

PROPOSITION **4.2** *Even in the presence of strong diminishing returns in parts of the economy, steady state capital
accumulation is possible at an* **endogenously** *chosen rate
so long as there is a subsector of the economy which produces capital goods by using capital goods alone and there
are perfectly functioning asset markets. All other sectors
into which the capital good enters as an input and where
production is carried out under diminishing returns, ad-
just to this rate of growth through a continuous fall in the
relative price of capital goods. The model does not admit
out of steady state dynamics.*

The astute reader will not fail to note that the equilibrium rates
of growth in (4.32) and (4.33) do not depend on the level of the
fixed factor $\bar{L}$. This is a shortcoming of the Rebelo II exercise,
for one would intuitively expect $\bar{L}$ to act a shift variable, whose
increase boosts the rate of growth of the system. The idea of
a shift variable affecting the rate of growth plays a major role
in the growth models of the following two chapters. Recent
research has looked deeply into this aspect of growth models
and Dinopoulos & Sener (2003) offers a lucid summary.

4.3.3 The Command Economy

Denote the shadow price $\partial V/\partial K$ of K by ξ. There is a single
control variable ν for the problem. As before,

$$V(K(t)) \cong max_{(\nu_{t,t+h})} \{h\ u(C(t)) + V(K(t+h))\} \quad (4.34)$$

An optimum *wrt* ν requires

$$\frac{h\ \partial u(C(t))}{\partial \nu(t)} + \frac{\partial V(K(t+h))}{\partial \nu(t)} = 0, \quad (4.35)$$

where

$$\frac{\partial V(K(t+h))}{\partial \nu(t)} = \frac{\partial V(K(t+h))}{\partial K(t+h)} \cdot \frac{\partial K(t+h)}{\partial \nu(t)} \quad (4.36)$$

Linearising,
$$K(t + h) \cong K(t) + h \, \dot{K}(t).$$
Using (4.24), (4.36) reduces to

$$\frac{\partial V(K(t + h))}{\partial \nu(t)} = - \, \xi(t) \, h \, b \, K.$$

Also, (4.25) shows that $h \, \partial u(C)/\partial \nu = h \, u'(C) \, B \, \gamma \, (\nu \, K)^{\gamma - 1} K \, \bar{L}^{1-\gamma}$. Thus, (4.35) gives

$$u'(C) \, B \, \gamma \, (\nu \, K)^{\gamma - 1} \, \bar{L}^{1-\gamma} = \xi \, b. \tag{4.37}$$

As far as the dynamic restriction on ξ goes, the social cost at t of a unit of investment at t is ξ. The discounted present value of the stream of returns is

$$\int_t^\infty \{ \nu \, u'(C) \, B \, \gamma \, (\nu \, K)^{\gamma - 1} \, \bar{L}^{1-\gamma}$$

$$(1 - \nu)\xi b \} \, e^{-\rho(s-t)} ds = \int_t^\infty \xi b e^{-\rho(s-t)} ds,$$

given (4.37). Equating cost and benefit and differentiating, we get

$$\dot{\xi} = -\xi \, b + \xi \, \rho.$$

Thus,

$$\frac{\dot{\xi}}{\xi} = - \, b + \rho. \tag{4.38}$$

Differentiating (4.37) *wrt* to t and using (4.38),

$$-\theta \, \frac{\dot{C}}{C} + (\gamma - 1) \, \left(\frac{\dot{\nu}}{\nu} + \frac{\dot{K}}{K} \right) = - \, b + \rho.$$

Under balanced growth, ν is a constant. Equation (4.25) implies $\dot{K}/K = (1/\gamma) \, \dot{C}/C$ as before. Substituting this into the last equation, we obtain the rate of growth of C to be identically the same as (4.32). This establishes that in balanced growth equilibrium, the Private Economy succeeds in attaining the Command Economy growth path. Hence, the socially optimal growth path is decentralisable, as was the case in Proposition 4.1. The derivation of the results of this section with reference to the Hamiltonian function is left as an exercise.

A drawback of this model arises from the AK specification of (4.24). It is easy to see that the rate of growth of K for the system is bounded above by b, a technological parameter. The model to be considered in the next section suffers from a similar restriction. Chapter 5 will present attempts to solve this problem, though we have come across simple structures in the previous chapter also which link the ultimate limitation on the growth rate to scarce resources alone.[15]

4.4 Human Capital Formation: The Uzawa-Lucas Approach

4.4.1 Description of the Economy

To the extent that Rebelo I and Rebelo II typify two alternative approaches to modelling human capital accumulation (or, more generally, consciously generated technical progress), one expects to come across models that occupy an intermediate position between them. Two such exercises go back to Uzawa (1965) and Lucas (1988). To appreciate these contributions, let us return to Rebelo I but retain the AK aspect of Rebelo II by replacing (4.2) of Rebelo I by (4.24):

$$\dot{T} = b(1 - \phi)T, \qquad (4.39)$$

where $1 - \phi$ stands for the share of human capital engaged in producing additions to its own stock. (Instead of justifying the AK structure of (4.39) by appealing to a composite factor as in Rebelo II, we are merely *assuming* a linear technology.) However, human capital has other uses, as in Rebelo

---

[15]It will be a worthwhile effort on the part of the reader to try and discover the factors explaining bounds on the growth rate for the remaining models of the present chapter.

I. Hence, a fraction ϕ of T is employed in producing the final good Y. The other input into that process is physical capital K, which, unlike Rebelo I, has no role to play in producing T. The production function for Y is given by

$$Y = B(K)^{\gamma}(\phi T)^{1-\gamma}. \tag{4.40}$$

Under balanced growth, the model will satisfy (4.26). With these specifications, we may proceed now to analyse the balanced growth equilibria of the relevant Private and Command Economies.

4.4.2 Uzawa: The Private Economy

To begin with we shall present the basic outlines of the Uzawa approach.[16] The household's optimisation problem is assumed to be similar to that of Section 4.2.3. From (4.39), the own rate of return for T is b. On the other hand, the real rate of interest r (on K) is

$$r = \gamma B(K)^{\gamma-1}(\phi T)^{1-\gamma}. \tag{4.41}$$

Let p stand for the price of T relative to Y. Then, an equation similar to (4.27) must be satisfied. This is given by

$$b = \frac{(1-\gamma)BK^{\gamma}(\phi T)^{-\gamma}}{p}. \tag{4.42}$$

By virtue of the equality between g_K^s and g_T^s and the constancy of ϕ under balanced growth, it follows that $g_p = 0$. Hence, the no arbitrage condition relating to household's asset holdings turns out to be

$$r = b \tag{4.43}$$

and the supply curve is horizontal at the level $r = b$. Intersection with the demand curve now determines the equilibrium rate of growth for the Uzawa model. Since there are no externalities, the Private Economy's behaviour does not differ from that of the Command Economy.

---

[16]This is a simplified version of the Uzawa paper and differs from it in details.

4.4.3   Lucas: The Private Economy

The above idea may be pushed further to elucidate Lucas (1988). The latter introduces an Arrovian touch of externality to the Uzawa model by recognising the fact that the production of human capital would normally generate a positive spillover for society as a whole, but in particular on simultaneously operated production processes, such as the technology for producing Y. For example, interactions with educated members of the population outside the workplace could lead to better utilisation of all resources. Thus, the production function for Y is written

$$Y = BK^{\gamma}(\phi T)^{1-\gamma}T^{\alpha}, \qquad (4.44)$$

where T^{α} stands for the external effect. The accumulation of human capital continues to be governed by (4.39). Defining r to be the real rate of interest as above, it follows that

$$r = \gamma B(K)^{\gamma-1}(\phi T)^{1-\gamma}T^{\alpha}. \qquad (4.45)$$

Under balanced growth, differentiation of (4.45) gives

$$g_T^s = \frac{1-\gamma}{1+\alpha-\gamma}g_K^s. \qquad (4.46)$$

The basic macro identity requires

$$\frac{C}{K} + \frac{\dot{K}}{K} = B(K)^{\gamma-1}(\phi T)^{1-\gamma}T^{\alpha}.$$

The constancy of the *RHS* under balanced growth implies as before that C and K grow at the same rate. In other words,

$$g_C^s = g_K^s. \qquad (4.47)$$

In a *private* economy, entrepreneurs would ignore the externality caused by T^{α} in computing the marginal product of T in the Y-sector. Thus, for such an economy, the equality of the values of marginal products of T leads to

$$p\,b = (1-\gamma)BK^{\gamma}\phi^{-\gamma}T^{\alpha-\gamma}, \qquad (4.48)$$

which, on differentiation and substitution from (4.46) and (4.47) yields

$$g_p = \frac{\alpha}{1 - \gamma + \alpha} \, g_C^s. \tag{4.49}$$

As in Rebelo II, r and b must be related according to

$$r = b + g_p.$$

Substituting this in (4.49), the equation for the supply rate of growth follows. Thus,

$$g_C^s(r) = \frac{(1 - \gamma + \alpha)}{\alpha}(r - b).$$

Combining with the demand rate of growth,[17] the equilibrium rate of growth of C turns out to be

$$g_C^* = \frac{(1 + \alpha - \gamma)(b - \rho)}{\theta(1 + \alpha - \gamma) - \alpha}. \tag{4.50}$$

Finally, using (4.46), it follows that

$$g_T^* = \frac{(1 - \gamma)(b - \rho)}{\theta(1 + \alpha - \gamma) - \alpha}. \tag{4.51}$$

To the extent that $1 \geq \phi \geq 0$, equation (4.39) implies, like Rebelo II, that the maximum rate of growth of human capital possible in the Lucas model is given by b. This in turn puts an upper bound on g_C also, viz., $b \, (1 + \alpha - \gamma)/(1 - \gamma)$, since $g_C = ((1 + \alpha - \gamma)/(1 - \gamma))g_T$.

The demand and supply curves as well as the equilibrium rates of interest and growth are depicted in Figure 4.2. The supply curve is drawn under the assumption of a positive externality. In case the latter is negative, the curve *could* be downward sloping.[18] A possible set of sufficient conditions for

---

[17]It will be useful for the reader to derive the expression for the demand rate for this model.

[18]Balanced growth equilibrium, as in the case of Rebelo I, fixes the value of K/T, thus bringing up the question of stability of the equilibrium path. The issue has been analysed by Arnold (1997) and Xie (1994).

positive solutions to exist is

(i) The curve $g_C^s(r)$ in Figure 4.2 is flatter than the curve $g_C^d(r)$, i.e., $\alpha/(1 + \alpha - \gamma) < \theta$;
and
(ii) the intercept of $g_C^s(r)$ on the r axis in Figure 4.2 > intercept of $g_C^d(r)$, i.e., $b > \rho$.

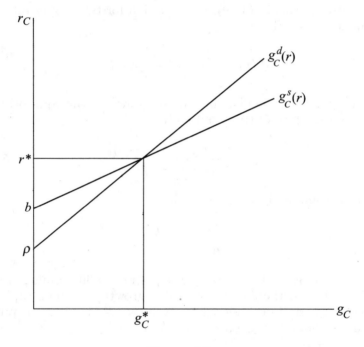

Figure 4.2

4.4.4   Lucas: The Command Economy

Our discussion of the Rebelo I model treated the Private Economy problem from the Command Economy perspective. We reverse that procedure now and present the planner's exercise as one solved by a Private Economy that is aware of all externalities. Since the planner will internalise the effect of T^α in (4.44), the production function for Y is given by

$$Y = BK^\gamma(\phi T^{(1+\alpha-\gamma)/(1-\gamma)})^{1-\gamma}.$$

or alternatively, as

$$Y = BK^\gamma(\phi T')^{1-\gamma}, \qquad (4.52)$$

where $T' \equiv T^{(1+\alpha-\gamma)/(1-\gamma)}$. The substitution of T by T' in the production function, thus reducing it to one free of external effects, merely expresses the fact that the planner takes account of the social productivity of T rather than its private productivity as in (4.44). Given this change, the planner's technology for producing Y is formally equivalent to that of a private producer faced with (4.52) rather than (4.44).

To complete the model, one needs to specify the technology for producing $\dot{T}'$. This is done by differentiating T' with respect to t and using (4.39) to get

$$\dot{T}' = \frac{1+\alpha-\gamma}{1-\gamma} \, b \, (1-\phi)T'. \qquad (4.53)$$

Equations (4.52) and (4.53) accord to the Command Economy exactly the same structure as the Uzawa economy described by (4.39) and (4.40) above. The conclusions that applied to

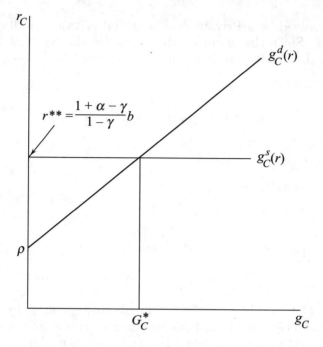

Figure 4.3

that economy, must hold here also. The planner will compute
the real rate of interest r as

$$r^{**} = \frac{1 + \alpha - \gamma}{1 - \gamma}\, b, \qquad (4.54)$$

which is the exact counterpart of (4.43). Thus, in the Command Economy, the supply curve is horizontal[19] at the level
$r = [(1+\alpha-\gamma)/(1-\gamma)]b$. The equilibrium is depicted in Figure
4.3.

It is easy to see that (4.46) and (4.47) are satisfied by
the Command Economy also. Using this fact, the equilibrium

---

[19]There is now no change in the relative price. The Command Economy
is aware of the true social productivity of T'. As a result, the marginal
product of T' is unchanging along the balanced growth path.

growth rates of C and T workout to

$$G_C^* = \theta^{-1} \left(\frac{b(1 + \alpha - \gamma)}{1 - \gamma} - \rho \right) \qquad (4.55)$$

and[20]

$$G_T^* = \theta^{-1} (b - \frac{\rho(1 - \gamma)}{1 + \alpha - \gamma}). \qquad (4.56)$$

A sufficient condition for a positive solution to G_C^* to exist now is that

$$r^{**} = b \left(\frac{1 + \alpha - \gamma}{1 - \gamma} \right) > \rho.$$

In order to compare the two rates

$$g_T^* = \frac{(1 - \gamma)(b - \rho)}{\theta(1 + \alpha - \gamma) - \alpha}$$

and

$$G_T^* = \frac{(1 - \gamma)(b - \rho) + b\alpha}{\theta(1 + \alpha - \gamma)},$$

note first that meaningful solution to the two problems require that both rates be bounded above by b. Imposing this restriction on g_T^* and G_T^* by turn, we can easily see that in each case the following common inequality is satisfied:

$$\theta \geq 1 - \frac{(1 - \gamma) \rho}{(1 + \alpha - \gamma) b}.$$

This inequality may also be written as

$$\theta b (1 + \alpha - \gamma) - (1 - \gamma)(b - \rho) \geq \alpha b. \qquad (4.57)$$

Noting now that

$$G_T^* - g_T^* = \frac{\alpha\{\theta b (1 + \alpha - \gamma) - (1 - \gamma)(b - \rho)\} - \alpha^2 b}{\theta(1 + \alpha - \gamma)\{\theta(1 + \alpha - \gamma) - \alpha\}},$$

it follows that human capital accumulation will be faster for the Command Economy than in the Private Economy whenever

---

[20]The derivation of G_T^* uses (4.46)

(4.57) is satisfied as a strict inequality.[21] Using this conclusion
along with (4.46) and (4.47), it follows that

$$G_C^* > g_C^*,$$

$$G_K^* > g_K^*.$$

Thus, as with previous models, the existence of positive externalities implies further that the rates of growth of C and K for
the Command Economy are higher than those of the Private
Economy

Lucas' results are summarised as

PROPOSITION **4.3** *In a model of endogenous human capital
formation along with accumulation of physical capital, the
growth rate of the system is endogenously determined by
the parameters of the preference function and technology.
In the presence of a positive spillover effect generated by
human capital formation, the equilibrium rates of growth
of consumption, physical capital as well as human capital for the Command Economy dominate those for the
Private Economy.*

We end this section by noting that the present chapter has
recognised a form a savings that is fundamentally different
from the Solow notion in that it takes the form of allocating resources away from the production of final goods for the
sake of human capital. It is this form of savings that plays a
vital role in determining the rate of growth of the economy.
We shall come across this idea of savings repeatedly in the rest
of the book.

4.5   A Model of Infrastructure
Accumulation

Inadequate accumulation of human capital poses one constraint
for economic growth and development.   For developing

---

[21]For meaningful solutions, the strict inequality alone must hold, or else
the Y-sector produces nothing.

economies, infrastructure creation[22] constitutes an equally important input into the growth process. Inadequate availability of infrastructure, such as roadways, irrigation facilities, telecommunications, power generation, educational institutions and so on, inhibits the process of capital accumulation. Scarcity of infrastructure leads to rapid diminishing returns from capital accumulation. The consequent low rate of return acts as a disincentive to private capital accumulation and results in a low rate of growth for the economy. Thus, any appreciable rise in the sustainable growth rate for an economy calls for simultaneous development of infrastructure.

Entrepreneurs in poorer economies, however, are unlikely to participate in infrastructure development. First of all, infrastructure by its very nature, is a bulky commodity. An airplane is large, but the airport that caters to it is a much larger investment, since it needs to attend to several large aircraft twenty four hours a day, seven days a week. The same observation applies to highways, to power generating plants etc. The finances necessary to develop such big objects are unlikely to be available to private business, especially so in developing societies. Yet another difficulty associated with such massive investments is that the waiting time involved for the projects to yield returns may be very long. These impediments in the way of private investments naturally creates room for the government to participate in infrastructure development and/or provision.

Infrastructure, by its very nature, has an element of non-rivalry built into it. Given its largeness, several users are expected to use its services simultaneously. It may not be a pure public good, however, since it could well be excludable (such as the services of an airport enjoyed by airliners, cable television, highways with a toll, user cost based internet services, telephone networks etc.). Infrastructure goods and services may vary of course from one another in terms of the degrees of non-rivalry as well as non-excludability, so that a prototype may not be easy to distinguish. For analytical clarity, we assume

---

[22]The material of this section is based on Dasgupta (1999, 2001). Readers interested in the details of the results discussed here are referred to the original papers.

that a single type of infrastructure distinguishes the economy. Its services are nonrival and excludable.

Section 3.5 presented an attempt to link infrastructure and the growth rate, where infrastructure assumed the form of a publicly provided input service. It was a pure flow and its rate of growth a flow rate. As opposed to this, the examples quoted above suggest that an economy is endowed with *stocks* of infrastructure, out of which the services flow into the different productive activities.[23] If so, infrastructure should qualify as an accumulable input, whose rate of growth is governed (in the spirit of the Rebelo I model) by a technology that is independent of the one producing the consumption and physical capital good. The present section will follow this approach.

The first of the two sectors of the Rebelo type two sector economy that follows produces Y, a Solow type private good which may be consumed (C) or accumulated as physical capital (K). Production of Y requires the services of K and infrastructure whose stock as well as service flows are denoted by Γ. The second sector accumulates infrastructure, once again with the help of physical capital and infrastructure services. The output of the second sector is therefore denoted $\dot{\Gamma}$.

Allowing for an instantaneous rate of growth of Γ (similar to that of private capital) implies that we ignore the bulkiness of infrastructure mentioned earlier. The abstraction is guided by the fact that we view infrastructure to be fully utilised at any point of time in a developing economy. Thus, for sustainable growth to be feasible, infrastructure must grow simultaneously with physical capital in balanced growth equilibrium.[24]

As already hinted above, the production system to be considered is *mixed*, with the first sector behaving competitively and the second operating on a non-profit basis under the control of the state.[25] There is a user charge levied on the private

---

[23] See World Development Report, 1994, Futagami *et al* (1993).

[24] The out of steady state dynamics considered in the Appendix to this chapter will, however, allow for differing growth rates of infrastructure and private capital also.

[25] In principle of course, a nonrival but excludable commodity could be produced privately also. The bulk of infrastructure, however, that

sector for the services of infrastructure. However, the flow of these services purchased by the private sector, being nonrival, are available for consumption by the public sector also. The public sector has free use of these for accumulation of infrastructural stocks. The latter activity, as noted above, calls for the use of privately supplied inputs too, viz., K services, which are purchased out of government revenues, partly generated by the sale of infrastructural services. We shall be judging the efficiency properties of the Mixed Economy with reference to the Command Economy.[26]

4.5.1 Description of the Economy

Like Rebelo II, we shall assume K to represent a composite of physical and human capital. Unlike Rebelo II, however, capital formation involves a one to one transformation of savings out of Y-sector income. The technological specification for the model mimics Rebelo I except for the replacement of T by Γ and the recognition of Γ-services as nonrival. The technology for Y is given by

$$Y = AK_y^\alpha \Gamma^{1-\alpha}, \ 0 < \alpha < 1, \qquad (4.58)$$

where $K_y =$ flow of capital services used to produce Y and A is parametrically specified. Unlike K_y, the factor Γ carries no

normally supports the process of economic growth continues to be the realm of the state in developing economies. We may regard this as a structural feature of developing economies.

[26] An alternative treatment of infrastructure as a stock may be found in Futagami, Morita and Shibata (1993). This work, which is interesting in its own right, differs from the present one in several respects. Noteworthy amongst these are that it does not (a) deal with nonrival infrastructure, (b) concern itself with the allocation of private inputs between final goods production and infrastructure accumulation and (c) compare the relative performances of the Mixed and the Command Economies in steady state. The main thrust of this work lies in out of balanced growth dynamics. In particular, they establish that for the Cobb-Douglas economy, an out of balanced growth path dominates, welfare wise, the growth rate maximising balanced growth path. It will be recalled from the Barro-Sala-i-Martin exercise of Chapter 3 that in an economy characterised by flow infrastructure and one that did not admit out of balanced growth behaviour, the growth rate maximising balanced growth path was also the optimal path for the Private Economy. See Proposition 3.9.

subscript, since the same quantum of the service is enjoyed by both sectors. Our attention will be restricted to growth paths consistent with a full utilisation of the available nonrival infrastructure in *both* sectors, a natural assumption for a model concerned with infrastructural constraints on growth. Thus, the technology for $\dot{\Gamma}$, the change in the *stock* of Γ, is

$$\dot{\Gamma} = BK_\Gamma^\beta \Gamma^{1-\beta}, \ 0 < \beta < 1, \tag{4.59}$$

where the meaning of K_Γ is self-evident and B is parametrically specified.[27]

4.5.2 A Mixed Economy

The Y-sector maximises profit in a competitive environment. It is charged a price q by the Government per unit flow of Γ consumed and r by the Household per unit flow of capital services consumed. Both q and r are fixed in balanced growth equilibrium.[28] Further, there is a proportional tax τ on rental income the proceeds from which are passed on entirely to the Γ-sector.

Profit maximisation gives rise to demands for K and Γ services by the Y-sector. The former is added to the demand for K services by the Γ-sector to yield the aggregate demand for K. The rental r on K is determined as in the Solow model. To accumulate infrastructure, the Γ-sector pays H the competitive rental and K-services are purchased from the proceeds of the sale of Γ services to the Y-sector and the tax on rental. This determines the Γ-sector's demand for K.

As in the case of K, the aggregate of Γ-services available is also supplied inelastically at each point of time. Its price q is determined by equating this supply to the demand for it by the

---

[27] Thus, $K_y = \nu K$ and $K_\Gamma = (1 - \nu)K$ in the notation of Sections 4.2 and 4.3. We are opting for the change in the interest of a lighter notation structure. The older notation will be restored back in Section 4.5.4, which will discuss the Command Economy.

[28] The reader should test his/her understanding by explaining this observation.

Y-sector, the only sector that pays for Γ-services. Thus, total consumption of Γ-services in the economy must be bounded above by the consumption of the Y-sector. Given its nonrival nature then, the aggregate demand for Γ will be the same as the demand by the Y-sector.[29]

For the Y-sector to behave competitively, the ratio of marginal products of the factors should equal their price ratio. This means

$$\frac{q}{r} = \frac{A(1-\alpha)(K_y/\Gamma)^\alpha}{A\alpha(K_y/\Gamma)^{\alpha-1}} = \frac{1-\alpha}{\alpha}\frac{K_y}{\Gamma}$$

or, alternatively,

$$K_y = \frac{\alpha}{1-\alpha}\,\Gamma\,\frac{q}{r}. \tag{4.60}$$

Given the inelastically supplied value of Γ, equation (4.60) defines the competitive sector's demand for K as a function of q/r when all Γ is used up. The Γ-sector employment of K is governed by a budget constraint, viz.,

$$rK_\Gamma = q\Gamma + \tau\,rK. \tag{4.61}$$

Hence, the demand for K by the Γ-sector is

$$K_\Gamma = \frac{q}{r}\,\Gamma + \tau K. \tag{4.62}$$

Using $K = K_y + K_\Gamma$, aggregate demand for K is then

$$K_y + K_\Gamma = \frac{1}{1-\tau}\left[\frac{\alpha}{1-\alpha} + 1\right]\Gamma\,\frac{q}{r}. \tag{4.63}$$

---

[29]Infrastructure being a productive service that causes bottlenecks for any developing economy, the Γ-sector is best understood to be nonsatiated in its use. In other words, the Γ-sector will use up the *entire* supply of nonrival Γ at each point of time.

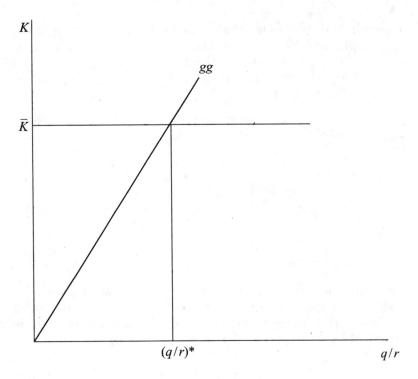

Figure 4.4

Equation (4.63) gives the locus of $(K_y + K_\Gamma, q/r)$ combinations consistent with the full employment of Γ by the Y-sector. The curve representing this relationship in the $(K, q/r)$ plane will be called the gg curve. The static equilibrium value of

the relative price q/r is determined by the intersection of the $\Gamma\Gamma$ curve and the inelastic supply curve of K. This is shown in Figure 4.4 under the assumption that the supply of $K = \bar{K}$. The equilibrium relative price is shown by $(q/r)^*$. The demand for K falls with a fall in τ, thereby raising the value of $(q/r)^*$.

PROPOSITION **4.4** *At any given point of time, each possible specification of the tax rate and the stocks of capital and infrastructure gives rise to a unique positive value of* *the relative returns to their services such that the market for capital services is in equilibrium and the services of infrastructure fully utilised.*

Given the equilibrium price ratio established by Proposition 4.4, the ratio K_y/Γ employed in the Y-sector is known from equation (4.60). Since the technology displays constant returns to scale, the marginal productivity of each factor is known for this sector. For competitive behaviour, it is necessary that q and r be chosen equal to the respective marginal productivities. Thus,

$$q = A(1 - \alpha)(\frac{K_y}{\Gamma})^\alpha \qquad (4.64)$$

and

$$r = A\alpha(\frac{K_y}{\Gamma})^{\alpha-1}. \qquad (4.65)$$

Equation (4.63) shows that a rise in K/Γ increases the equilibrium q/r. In fact, $q/r \to \infty$ as $K/\Gamma \to \infty$ and $q/r \to 0$ as $K/\Gamma \to 0$. Hence, combining (4.60) and (4.64), q satisfies

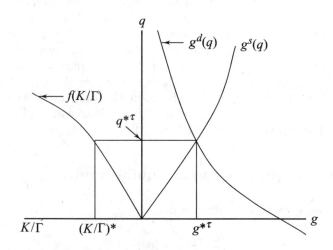

Figure 4.5

a similar property. Thus, $q \to \infty$ as $K/\Gamma \to \infty$ and $q \to 0$ as $K/\Gamma \to 0$. We shall denote this monotonic relationship between the market clearing q and K/Γ by $q = f(K/\Gamma)$. (See Figure 4.5, left hand panel.) Notice that under the Cobb-Douglas framework assumed, there is another restriction on the model. This arises from the fact that the share of each factor in the Y-sector output must be a constant under competitive conditions. Thus,

$$rK_y = \alpha Y \qquad (4.66)$$

and

$$q\Gamma = (1 - \alpha)Y.$$

According to the Γ-sector's budget constraint, however, $r\,K_\Gamma = q\,\Gamma + \tau\,rK$, so that

$$r\,K_\Gamma = (1-\alpha)\,Y + \tau\,r\,(K_y + K_\Gamma) = (1-\alpha)\,Y + \tau\,\alpha\,Y + \tau\,r\,K_\Gamma. \qquad (4.67)$$

Dividing out (4.67) by (4.66), we see that

$$\frac{K_\Gamma}{K_y} = \left(\frac{1}{1-\tau}\right)\left(\frac{1-\alpha}{\alpha}\right) + \left(\frac{\tau}{1-\tau}\right) \qquad (4.68)$$

It should be noted that the allocative rule represented by (4.68) is inefficient. This follows from two facts. First, as is evident from equation (4.61), the Γ-sector does not equate the marginal product of K to its market rate of return r. Secondly, the Y-sector equates the price q of Γ to its *private* rather than *social* marginal product. The latter is higher than the former given the nonrivalry of Γ. Thus, on the one hand, the rival commodity fails to satisfy a marginal condition and on the other, the nonrival commodity satisfies the wrong one.

4.5.3 Balanced Growth Equilibrium

Balanced growth equilibrium involves:

$$\frac{K}{\Gamma} = \text{constant},$$

$$\frac{K_y}{K_\Gamma} = \text{constant}.$$

(The above imply K_y/Γ and C/K are constants along a balanced growth path.)

The variable q has two different roles to play in the model. First, as shown in the previous section, each specification of K/Γ leads to a market clearing value of q. Alternatively, each q corresponds to *some* unique value of K/Γ. (Left panel of Figure 4.5.) This may be referred to as the *static* role of q. Second, as will soon be established, for any given τ, $\exists$ a value of q equating g_C^s to g_C^d. This constitutes the *dynamic* role of q.

For each τ, both g_C^d and g_C^s are functions of q. To see this, substitute (4.68) in (4.64) to get

$$
\frac{K_\Gamma}{\Gamma} = \frac{1}{1-\tau}\left[\frac{q^{1/\alpha}}{A\alpha(A(1-\alpha))^{1-\alpha/\alpha}} + \tau\,(\frac{q}{A(1-\alpha)})^{1/\alpha}\right].
$$

(4.69)

From (4.59) and (4.69), the supply rate of growth turns out to be

$$
\begin{aligned}
g^s(q) &= \frac{\dot{\Gamma}}{\Gamma} \\
&= B(\frac{K_\Gamma}{\Gamma})^\beta
\end{aligned}
$$

(4.70)

$$
= B\left[\frac{1}{1-\tau}\left[\frac{q^{1/\alpha}}{A\alpha(A(1-\alpha))^{1-\alpha/\alpha}} +\tau(\frac{q}{A(1-\alpha)})^{1/\alpha}\right]\right]^\beta.
$$

(4.71)

Note that (4.68) is satisfied along the $g_C^s(q)$ curve. This follows since (4.71) is derived using (4.62) and the marginal productivity conditions for the Y-sector. Obviously, g_C^s is a monotone increasing function of q. Moreover, $g_C^s(q) \rightarrow 0$ as $q \rightarrow$

0 and $g_C^s(q) \to \infty$ as $q \to \infty$. (See right hand panel of Figure 4.5.) Finally, (4.71) shows that $g_C^s(q)$ is monotone increasing in τ. The intuition behind these results lies in the fact that with a rise in revenue, more infrastructural accumulation is feasible.

The household optimisation exercise yields the demand rate of growth

$$
\begin{aligned}
g_C^d(q) \;&=\; \frac{\dot{C}}{C} \\[2mm]
&=\; \frac{(1-\tau)r - \rho}{\theta} \tag{4.72} \\[2mm]
&=\; \frac{(1-\tau)A\alpha(K_y/\Gamma)^{\alpha-1} - \rho}{\theta} \tag{4.73} \\[2mm]
&=\; \frac{(1-\tau)A\alpha(q/A(1-\alpha))^{(\alpha-1)/\alpha} - \rho}{\theta}. \tag{4.74}
\end{aligned}
$$

Unlike $g_C^s(q)$, the demand rate of growth does not necessarily satisfy (4.62). Consequently, (4.68) need not hold at all points lying on $g^d(q)$. The demand rate of growth g_C^d is monotone decreasing in q, with $g^d(q) \to \infty$ as $q \to 0$ and $g^d(q) < 0$ for q large enough . This monotone relationship follows from the fact that with a rise in q, the K_y/Γ ratio employed by the profit maximising Y-sector rises, thereby reducing the marginal productivity of capital and along with it, the demand rate of growth. (See right hand panel of Figure 4.5.) Further, $g_C^d(q)$ decreases with τ. The intuition for this result is straightforward also. The effective return from a postponement of consumption decreases with a rise in the tax rate. This has a dampening effect on the household's desire to grow.

Given these properties of g_C^d, g_C^s, there is, corresponding to each value of $\tau \in [0,1)$, a unique value of q such that $g_C^d = g_C^s$. At this value of q, both functions satisfy (4.68). This establishes the dynamic role of q anticipated above. Denote the equilibrium (g,q) pair by $(g^{*\tau}, q^{*\tau})$. Since the demand rate falls and the supply rate rises with a rise in the tax rate, it is intuitively obvious that $q^{*\tau}$ is monotone decreasing in τ.

(Shifting curves in the right hand side of Figure 4.5 reveals this clearly.)

These observations are summarised in

PROPOSITION **4.5** *For the Mixed Economy, each possible value of the proportional tax rate is associated with unique positive steady state values of the rate of growth, infrastructural price and aggregate capital-infrastructure ratio. The equilibrium value of the infrastructural price falls as the tax rate rises.*

The model then works as follows. Any value of τ gives rise to an equilibrium value $q^{*\tau}$ of q. The function f^{-1} finds the unique ratio K/Γ, say $(K/\Gamma)^*_\tau$, that simultaneously makes $q^{*\tau}$ a static equilibrium price also. In other words, *had the economy started out with the ratio* $(K/\Gamma)^*_\tau$, then it would remain there indefinitely with K and Γ growing at the rate $g^{*\tau}$, *provided* that q is also held fixed at $q^{*\tau}$ forever.

For reasons discussed in Chapter 3, the triplet $(g^{*\tau}, q^{*\tau}, (K/\Gamma)^*_\tau)$ established by Proposition 4.5 corresponds to a true optimum for the household if

$$\rho > (1 - \theta)g^{*\tau}. \tag{4.75}$$

The condition will be satisfied if A and B are not too large.

It is not clear what the effect of a higher τ would be on $g^{*\tau}$. It might rise or fall, depending on the relative magnitudes of the shifts in the demand and supply functions. We proceed now to investigate this question by representing the equilibrium of Proposition 4.5 in an alternative manner. Inverting (4.73), we have

$$\frac{K_y}{\Gamma} = \left(\frac{g_C^d \theta + \rho}{(1 - \tau)A\alpha} \right)^{1/(\alpha - 1)} \tag{4.76}$$

On the other hand, (4.70) yields

$$\frac{K_\Gamma}{\Gamma} = \left(\frac{g_C^s}{B} \right)^{1/\beta} \tag{4.77}$$

Writing the common value of g_C^d and g_C^s as g, division of (4.77) by (4.76) gives rise to

$$\frac{K_\Gamma}{K_y} = \left(\frac{g}{B}\right)^{(1/\beta)} \left(\frac{g\theta + \rho}{(1-\tau)A\alpha}\right)^{1/(1-\alpha)} \qquad (4.78)$$

Equation (4.78) gives the relative allocation of capital between the two sectors necessary to maintain the equality of the demand and the supply rates at the level g. Let us call this the *necessary* ratio. From Proposition 4.5, we know that each τ will correspond to a particular g only. Hence, equation (4.78) will not be meaningful for arbitrary choices of (g, τ) pairs. To find the right pairs, we recall that equation (4.68) gives the constraint exogenously imposed on (K_Γ / K_y) by the Γ-sector's budget constraint. The equilibrium g corresponding to τ must be the one that equates the *necessary* ratio to the exogenous ratio. Taking this into account, the equilibrium condition turns out to be

$$(\frac{g}{B})^{1/\beta} \left(\frac{\theta g + \rho}{\alpha A}\right)^{1/(1-\alpha)} = (1-\tau)^{\alpha/(1-\alpha)} \left[\frac{1-\alpha}{\alpha} + \tau\right].$$
$$(4.79)$$

Figure 4.6 shows the alternative representation of the equilibrium for the Mixed Economy. The LHS of (4.79) can be shown to be a strictly convex and increasing function of g. Also, the function vanishes at $g = 0$. Given that the RHS is a positive constant for each τ, the conclusion of Proposition 4.5 on the existence of a unique value of $g^{*\tau}$ is confirmed. Further, it is quite obvious from Figure 4.6 that $g^{*\tau}$ is not too large when A and B are small. The RHS of (4.79) falls with a rise in τ, a fact easily checked by differentiation. Hence, given the monotone rising property of the LHS with respect to g, it follows that $g^{*\tau}$ falls with a rise in τ. Going back to Figure 4.5, this answers the question raised above about the relative magnitudes of the shifts in g_C^d and g_C^s in response to a rise in τ. Clearly, g_C^d falls relatively more than the rise in g_C^s. Accordingly, we have

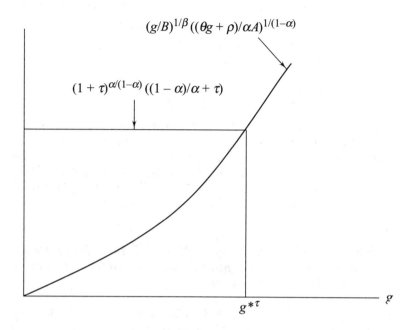

Figure 4.6

PROPOSITION **4.6** *The unique equilibrium value for the steady state growth rate falls with a rise in the tax rate.*

Following Barro & Sala-i-Martin (Section 3.5 above), a further task before the Government is to find a τ that leads to the best of the balanced growth paths. We proceed now to a search for this optimal value of τ. Using (4.72) and the macro identity

$$C + \dot{K} = (1 - \tau)\, r\, K,$$

it follows that

$$C_t^{*\tau} = \{\rho + (\theta - 1)g^{*\tau}\}K_0 e^{g^{*\tau}t}, \tag{4.80}$$

where the $C_t^{*\tau}$ stands for the Mixed Economy's consumption at tax rate τ. Substituting (4.80) and (2.24) in (2.1), the welfare associated with the choice of τ is

$$U^{*\tau} = \frac{K_0^{1-\theta}}{1-\theta} \frac{1}{(\rho + (\theta-1)g^{*\tau})^\theta} - \frac{\rho}{1-\theta}, \qquad (4.81)$$

where $W^{*\tau}$ represents the welfare in question. Differentiating with respect to $g^{*\tau}$, the RHS is seen to be rising with $g^{*\tau}$. In other words, the welfare of the Mixed Economy rises with the rate of growth and the Household would wish to grow as fast as feasible. Hence, Proposition 4.6 implies that the optimal value of the tax rate in the Mixed Economy is zero. Therefore, we have

PROPOSITION **4.7** *Maximum welfare for the Mixed Economy corresponds to the maximum rate of growth. The optimal profit tax rate is zero.*

We shall denote the maximal, hence optimal, growth rate for the Mixed Economy by g^*. The first part of the Proposition is similar to the result in Section 3.5. Even with stock infrastructure, the Mixed Economy wishes to grow as fast as possible. The result, as before, follows from the fact that for the chosen form of the utility function, society's welfare is an increasing function of the equilibrium rate of growth. We have noted earlier that the growth rate g^* will be attained by the Mixed Economy by means of an inefficient allocation of resources. Hence, it will not represent the best possible growth rate for the economy. On the other hand, the Command Economy of Section 4.4 is concerned with the achievement of the full optimum.

The second part of Proposition 4.7 is reminiscent of Lucas (1990) who found that the socially optimum profit tax rate for a model of human capital accumulation is zero in steady state. To the extent that taxes are distortionary, Lucas' finding in understandable. The difference between our result and his is that the zero tax rate of our model, though welfare maximising for the Mixed Economy, is nevertheless socially suboptimal. The reasons underlying the divergence are the same as those outlined in the last paragraph.

4.5.4 The Command Economy

The planner maximises (2.1) subject to (2.24) and

$$\dot{K} = A(\nu K)^{\alpha} \, \Gamma^{1-\alpha} - C \tag{4.82}$$

and

$$\dot{\Gamma} = B((1 - \nu)K)^{\beta} \, \Gamma^{1-\beta}, \tag{4.83}$$

where ν and $1 - \nu$ are respectively the shares of K in the Y and Γ sectors. To solve the problem, let

$$\mathcal{H} = \frac{C^{1-\theta} - 1}{1 - \theta} + \eta[A(\nu K)^{\alpha}\Gamma^{1-\alpha} - C] + \xi[B((1 - \nu)K)^{\beta}\Gamma^{1-\beta}], \tag{4.84}$$

where η and ξ are the co-state variables associated with the stocks of K and Γ. The balanced growth equilibrium rate of growth for the problem is denoted g^*. The first order optimality conditions are

$$\frac{\partial \mathcal{H}}{\partial C} = 0 \tag{4.85}$$

$$\frac{\partial \mathcal{H}}{\partial \nu} = 0 \tag{4.86}$$

$$\dot{\eta} = -\frac{\partial \mathcal{H}}{\partial K} + \eta\rho \tag{4.87}$$

$$\dot{\xi} = -\frac{\partial \mathcal{H}}{\partial \Gamma} + \xi\rho. \tag{4.88}$$

along with the transversality conditions

$$\eta(t)e^{-\rho t} \to 0 \text{ as } t \to \infty$$

and

$$\xi(t)e^{-\rho t} \to 0 \text{ as } t \to \infty.$$

Manipulating these equations, we obtain

$$\frac{1 - \nu}{\nu} = \frac{1 - \alpha}{\alpha} \frac{\beta G}{\rho + (\theta - (1 - \beta))G} \tag{4.89}$$

and

$$\frac{1-\nu}{\nu} = \left(\frac{G}{B}\right)^{1/\beta} \left(\frac{\theta G + \rho}{\alpha A}\right)^{1/(1-\alpha)}, \qquad (4.90)$$

where G is the balanced growth rate. Equation (4.89) represents the relationship that must hold between indefinitely maintained values of $(1 - \nu)/\nu$ (i.e., K_Γ/K_y) and G if resources are allocated efficiently. This, in other words, is the efficient counterpart of (4.68) in the Mixed Economy. Equation (4.90) yields the value of $(1 - \nu)/\nu$ to be maintained in balanced growth in order for demand and supply side considerations to yield a common value of G. We may look upon (4.89) and (4.90) as the reduced form optimality conditions for the planner's problem. The optimal rate of growth is found by solving these two equations simultaneously for $(1-\nu)/\nu$ and G.

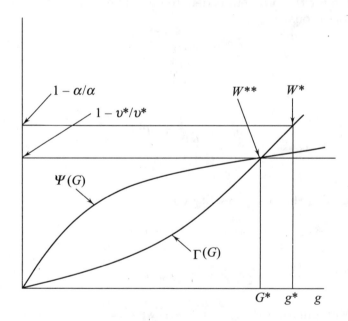

Figure 4.7

Eliminating $(1 - \nu)/\nu$ between (4.89) and (4.90),

$$\left(\frac{G}{B}\right)^{1/\beta} \left(\frac{\theta G + \rho}{\alpha A}\right)^{1/(1-\alpha)} = \frac{1-\alpha}{\alpha} \frac{\beta G}{\rho + (\theta - (1-\beta))G}.$$

$$(4.91)$$

In what follows, the LHS will be represented by the function $\Phi(G)$ and the RHS by $\Psi(G)$. Equation (4.91) has a solution $G = 0$. This solution is ignored. A condition under which a positive solution $G = G^*$ exists is discussed below in Proposition 4.8. A particular case is shown in Figure 4.7.

The function $\Phi(G)$ (viz., the *necessary* ratio) is shown in the diagram by the convex, monotone increasing function. On the other hand, $\Psi(G)$ is an increasing function of G and concave if $\sigma \geq 1 - \beta$ (strictly concave if the inequality is strict). The positive solution G^* to the planner's exercise is represented by the abscissa of the point W^{**} in Figure 4.7 where the two curves intersect. For later reference, denote the ordinate of W^{**} by $1 - \nu^*/\nu^*$. A point such as W^*, which does not fall on both curves, is expected to yield a lower level of welfare compared to W^{**}. The point W^* is chosen to represent the solution to (4.79) when $\tau = 0$. Its co-ordinates are given by the pair $(g^*, 1 - \alpha/\alpha)$. As drawn, $g^* > G^*$ and $1 - \alpha/\alpha > 1 - \nu^*/\nu^*$. The following Proposition, which assumes that $\Psi(G)$ is concave, establishes a condition under which this will be true.

PROPOSITION **4.8** *Suppose a solution exists to the Mixed Economy's problem characterised by a bounded value of the welfare function. Then, there exists a strictly positive solution for the Command Economy's growth rate that is exceeded by the growth rate for the Mixed Economy and for which the Mixed Economy allocates more capital for infrastructure accumulation relative to final good production.*

Proof: (See Figure 4.7.) The function $\Psi(G)$ has the following easily verifiable properties:

$$\Psi'(G) = \frac{1-\alpha}{\alpha} \frac{\beta\rho}{[\rho + (\theta - (1-\beta))G]^2} > 0$$

and
$$\Psi'(G) \to \frac{(1-\alpha)}{\alpha} \frac{\beta}{\rho} > 0 \text{ as } G \to 0.$$

On the other hand, the function $\Phi(G)$ satisfies the property that
$$\Phi'(G) \to 0 \text{ as } G \to 0.$$

Thus, for G arbitrarily close to zero, $\Psi(G) > \Phi(G)$. Again, (4.75) implies that for $G = g^*$,

$$\Psi(G) < \frac{(1-\alpha)}{\alpha}.$$

The continuity of $\Psi(G)$ and $\Phi(G)$ implies now from the Intermediate Value Theorem that $\exists\ G^*$ satisfying (4.91)such that $0 < G^* < g^*$.

The relative magnitudes of K_Γ/K_y under the two systems follow trivially.   ∎

COROLLARY 1 *The solution G^* is unique if $\theta + \beta \geq 1$.*

Proof: The conclusion follows from the fact that $\Psi(G)$ is strictly concave under the given assumption.   ∎

The fact that the Mixed Economy can grow faster than the Command Economy stands in contrast to the Barro and Sala-i-Martin result that the opposite is the case. In their analysis, the Command Economy grows faster since it is able to internalise the social productivity of capital in calculating the demand rate of growth. The reason underlying the reversal of the Barro result in the present paper is discussed in the following section.

4.5.5   Command Solution in the Mixed Economy

We pursue this discussion under the assumption stated in the above corollary. Given that the full command solution is not achievable in the Mixed Economy, is it possible at least to grow at the command rate? The answer is "yes", since according to

(4.79), $g^* \to 0$ as $\tau \to 1$ and $g^* > G^*$ when $\tau = 0$. Hence, by continuity, $\exists$ a $\tau = \bar{\tau} \in (0,1)$ such that $g^{*\bar{\tau}} = G^*$. Thus, the Mixed Economy can *in fact* attain the growth rate of the Command Economy.

PROPOSITION **4.9** *There exists a tax rate for which the equilibrium rate of growth for the Mixed economy is the same as that of the Command Economy.*

From our discussion following (4.68), we know that the Mixed Economy attains $g^{*\bar{\tau}}$ inefficiently. Consequently, it is intuitively obvious why the Command Economy dominates the Mixed Economy in welfare even at the same rate of growth $g^{*\bar{\tau}} = G^*$. In fact, there is no value of τ at which the Mixed Economy dominates the Command Economy.[30]

What, however, makes g^* greater than G^*? From the optimality conditions for the Command Economy and the fact that in the Command Economy

$$C + \dot{K} = A(\nu^* K)^\alpha \Gamma^{1-\alpha},$$

we can easily show that

$$C_t^{**} = \left[\frac{\nu^*}{\alpha} \rho + \left(\frac{\nu^*}{\alpha} \theta - 1 \right) G^* \right] K_0 e^{G^* t}, \qquad (4.92)$$

where C^{**} stands for consumption undertaken by the Command Economy. From Proposition 4.8, we have $1 - \alpha/\alpha > 1 - \nu^*/\nu^*$. This means $\nu^*/\alpha > 1$. Comparing (4.80) and (4.92) now, it is clear that $C_t^{**} > C_t^*$ when $\tau = \bar{\tau}$. In other words, even at the same rate of growth, the Command Economy enjoys a higher level of consumption than the Mixed Economy at each point of time if it starts from the same value of K_0. To make up for the shortfall in the consumption level therefore, the Mixed Economy tries to raise its welfare by maximising the rate of growth, i.e., it chooses $\tau = 0$ and grows at the rate $g^* > g^{*\bar{\tau}} = G^*$. Although $g^* > G^*$, however, the negative *level* effect dominates the positive *growth* effect. This happens because the Mixed Economy attains *any* rate of growth inefficiently.

---

[30]Dasgupta (1999) contains a proof of this result.

4.5.6 Public Policy: Decentralising the Command Solution

As in Sections 3.3.3 and 3.4.3, we proceed to discuss the possibility of attaining the Command Equilibrium as a market solution supported by taxes and subsidies.[31] However, the presence of a nonrival good modifies the theorem to say that the socially optimal allocation is achievable as a *Lindahl*, rather than a competitive equilibrium. Further, we are concerned here with infrastructure as an accumulable stock. Consequently, the pricing problem breaks up into two parts, First, an appropriate price has to be found for infrastructural stocks. Secondly, Lindahl prices need to be worked out for the nonrival services of infrastructure.

The Decentralised Economy is assumed to be made up of four agents, viz., the representative Household, two aggregative firms and the Government. The first three agents have well-defined objective functions which they maximise at parametrically specified prices. The Government provides the initial stock of Γ and finances its accumulation over time from the revenue generated by the sale of Γ-services to the firms. The Household has a dynastic structure and maximises (2.1) subject to (2.24) and an instantaneous budget constraint. Its budgetary resources fall into two parts. First, it has an income, $rK(t)$ from private capital holdings, where r stands for the rate of interest on K, held constant over time. Secondly, it receives a subsidy equal to $\Delta(t)$ from the Government at each t. The amount of the subsidy, which is beyond the control of the Household, will be specified later. Hence, the Household's budget Constraint is

$$C(t) + \dot{K}(t) = rK(t) + \Delta(t), \qquad (4.93)$$

where $K(0) = K_0$ has the same value as the initial capital stock for the Command Economy. Firm I produces Y and is assumed to maximise the instantaneous profit function

$$\Pi^1 = AK_y^{\alpha}\Gamma^{1-\alpha} - rK_y - \sigma\phi\Gamma, \qquad (4.94)$$

---

[31]This section is based on Dasgupta (2001).

where $\sigma\phi$, $1 \geq \sigma \geq 0$, represents the Lindahl price charged per unit use of Γ-services by Firm I. Commodity Y is treated as the numéraire. Firm II "produces" $\dot{\Gamma}$ by maximising instantaneous profits given by

$$\Pi^2 = \mu B K_\Gamma^\beta \Gamma^{1-\beta} - r K_\Gamma - (1-\sigma)\phi\Gamma, \qquad (4.95)$$

where μ is the price per unit charged by Firm II for its product, viz., $\dot{\Gamma}$ and $(1-\sigma)\phi\Gamma$ is the Lindahl price of the Γ-service for Firm II.[32]

The Government accumulates Γ by purchasing $\dot{\Gamma}$ from Firm II.[33] The net revenue accruing to the Government on the infrastructural account is the difference between its sales revenue from infrastructural services and its investment cost for creating additional infrastructure. By definition of ϕ and μ, the Government's revenue and expenditure at each t are

$$\phi\Gamma \qquad (4.96)$$

and

$$\mu B K_\Gamma^\beta \Gamma^{1-\beta}. \qquad (4.97)$$

Thus, the Government has a net revenue from infrastructure accumulation and sale equal to

$$D = \phi\Gamma - \mu B K_\Gamma^\beta \Gamma^{1-\beta}. \qquad (4.98)$$

This completes the description of the decentralised economy.

We proceed now to discuss in succession two different issues concerning the Decentralised Economy. First, we analyse the allocational efficiency of the steady growth path chosen by it. In this context, Proposition 4.10 below demonstrates the existence of a price-subsidy scheme for the Decentralised Economy that supports the first best growth path. By the very construction of the subsidy, the Government's budget will be seen to be balanced. Secondly, we compute the rate of return

---

[32]It may be noted that while $\sigma\phi$ or $(1-\sigma)\phi$ are the prices charged for the flow of Γ-services, the price μ applies to the *stock* of Γ.

[33]Without loss of generality, Firm II could be operated by the Government itself, in which case the relevant prices are used for book-keeping.

to the Government from its investment in infrastructure at the chosen prices. Proposition 4.11 proves that this is identically the same as the rate of return on private capital.˙The property may be viewed as a *sine qua non* for the social optimality of investment projects. Both propositions are proved in Appendix 4.2.

PROPOSITION **4.10** *There exist time dependent values of the Household subsidy and time invariant values of the rate of interest, the price of the output of Firm II and firm specific prices for the use of infrastructural services such that the Decentralised Economy chooses identically the same growth path as the Command Economy. Moreover, along this growth path, the Government maintains a balanced budget.*

PROPOSITION **4.11** *The present value of the infinite stream of net returns to the Government, discounted at the rate of interest on private capital, is exactly equal to the imputed value of initial investment in the infrastructural stock.*

This concludes our discussion of one class of models that make it possible for private economic forces to determine the rate of long run growth of an economy. The models relied on human capital accumulation or infrastructure development to function as the engine of growth. We move on now to a class of models which go one step further and consider the most abstract form of capital, knowledge, and its accumulation. The remaining two chapters will present some of the classic works on knowledge driven growth.

Appendix 4.1: Transitional Dynamics for the Mixed Economy

The discussion of transitional dynamics will be restricted to the case where $\tau = 0$, i.e., when the tax rate is optimal. Define

$$k = \frac{K}{\Gamma} \quad \text{and} \quad c = \frac{C}{K}.$$

Using (1.3), (4.58), (4.59), (4.60), (4.62) and (4.63),

$$\frac{\dot{k}}{k} = A\alpha^\alpha k^{\alpha-1} - B((1-\alpha)k)^\beta - c. \tag{A4.1.1}$$

Again, from (4.72), (4.65), (1.3) and (4.60),

$$\frac{\dot{c}}{c} = \frac{1-\theta}{\theta}A\alpha^\alpha k^{\alpha-1} - \frac{\rho}{\theta} + c. \tag{A4.1.2}$$

This system of differential equations describes the transitional dynamics of the Mixed economy. To study its properties, we shall first establish the existence of a unique equilibrium or stationary state for this system. The latter would simultaneously solve

$$c = A\alpha^\alpha k^{\alpha-1} - B((1-\alpha)k)^\beta \tag{A4.1.3}$$

and

$$c = -\left(\frac{1-\theta}{\theta}\right)A\alpha^\alpha k^{\alpha-1} + \frac{\rho}{\theta}. \tag{A4.1.4}$$

Eliminating c, the stationary value of k is a solution to

$$\frac{1}{\theta}A\alpha^\alpha k^{\alpha-1} = B((1-\alpha)k)^\beta + \frac{\rho}{\theta}.$$

It is easy to see that this equation has a unique positive solution k^*. The corresponding unique value for c^* is found from either (A4.1.3) or (A4.1.4). The sign of c^* is discussed below.

In order to study the local stability of the dynamic system, we may rewrite (A4.1.1) and (A4.1.2) as

$$\dot{k} = (A\alpha^\alpha k^{\alpha-1} - B((1-\alpha)k)^\beta - c)k$$
$$\dot{c} = \left(\frac{1-\theta}{\theta}A\alpha^\alpha k^{\alpha-1} - \frac{\rho}{\theta} + c\right)c.$$

Linear approximation around (k^*, c^*) gives

$$\dot{k} = (A\alpha^{1+\alpha}(k^*)^{\alpha-1} - B(1+\beta)((1-\alpha)k^*)^\beta - c^*)$$
$$(k - k^*) - k^*(c - c^*)$$

$$\dot{c} = (((1-\theta)/\theta)A(\alpha-1)\alpha^{\alpha}(k^*)^{\alpha-2}c^*)(k-k^*)$$
$$-(((1-\theta)/\theta)A\alpha^{\alpha}(k^*)^{\alpha-1} - (\rho/\theta) + 2c^*)(c-c^*).$$

$$(A4.1.5)$$

Using (A4.1.3) and (A4.1.4), the determinant corresponding to the simultaneous equation system (A4.1.5) simplifies to

$$(\alpha - (1+\beta))g^*c^* + (\alpha - 1)\frac{\rho}{\theta} < 0,$$

where $g^* = g_C^d(q^*) = g_C^s(q^*) = B((1-\alpha)k^*)^{\beta}$. The sign of the determinant establishes that the equilibrium is a saddle

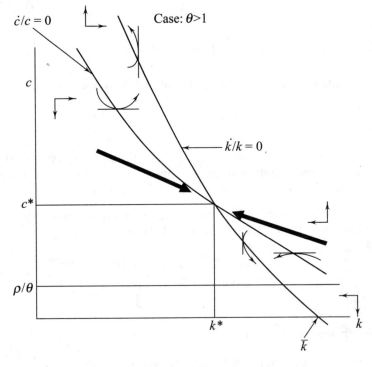

Figure 4.8

point.[34] In other words, for each possible choice of the initial value $k(0)$ of k in a small neighbourhood of k^*, $\exists$ a choice of the initial value of c in a corresponding small neighbourhood of c^*, such that the system (A4.1.5) converges to (k^*, c^*).

The phase diagrams below, pertaining to the two cases $\theta > 1$ and $\theta < 1$, reveal the dynamics more clearly.

Case 1: $\theta > 1$ Subtracting (A4.1.4) from (A4.1.3), it is easily seen that the difference is strictly positive for $k \cong 0$. Further, along (A4.1.3), c is monotone decreasing in k, $c \to \infty$ as $k \to 0$ and $c \to -\infty$ as $k \to \infty$. Similarly, from (A4.1.4), c is monotone decreasing in k, $c \to \infty$ as $k \to 0$ and $c \to \rho/\theta$ as $k \to \infty$. Clearly, $c^* > \rho/\theta > 0$. The stable path is indicated by the thick arrowheads. See Figure 4.8.

Case 2: $\theta < 1$ The situation is depicted in Figure 4.9. The intersection of the two curves occurs in the positive orthant. To see this, suppose that the reverse is the case. Let $\bar{k}$ denote the value of k for which $c = 0$ in (A4.1.3). By assumption, $k^* > \bar{k}$. Substituting this value in (A4.1.4),

$$-\frac{1-\theta}{\theta}B((1-\alpha)\bar{k})^\beta + \frac{\rho}{\theta} < 0.$$

From (4.59), (4.62) and (4.63), the expression that $B((1-\alpha)\bar{k})^\beta$ represents the value of g^s corresponding to $\bar{k}$. Since $k^* > \bar{k}$, it follows that $g^* > B((1 - \alpha)\bar{k})^\beta$, where $g^* = (B(1 - \alpha)k^*)^\beta$. Then

$$-\frac{1-\theta}{\theta}g^* + \frac{\rho}{\theta} < -\frac{1-\theta}{\theta}B((1-\alpha)\bar{k})^\beta + \frac{\rho}{\theta} < 0,$$

or,

$$\rho + (\theta - 1)g^* < 0,$$

which violates (4.75).

---

[34]See Chiang (1984), Chapter 18 for a lucid discussion on the matter.

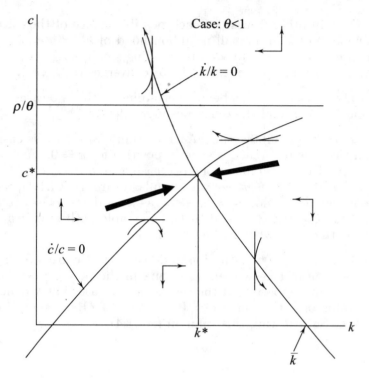

Figure 4.9

Appendix 4.2: Decentralisation of the Command Economy

Proof of Proposition 4.10.[35]

We shall assume that $\theta + \beta > 1$. Choose

$$r = r^* = \alpha A(\nu^* K^*)^{\alpha-1}(\Gamma^*)^{1-\alpha}, \qquad (A4.2.1)$$

---

[35]The proof skips a number of details. Readers interested in these are referred to Dasgupta (2001).

where $\alpha A(\nu^* K^*)^{\alpha-1}(\Gamma^*)^{1-\alpha}$ is the marginal product of K along the optimal steady state path of the Command Economy. Since both K and Γ grow at the same rate, r^* is a constant for all t. Similarly, let

$$\mu = \frac{\xi^*(t)}{\eta^*(t)} \quad \forall\, t \qquad (A4.2.2)$$

and

$$\phi = (\theta G^* + \rho)\mu, \qquad (A4.2.3)$$

where ξ^* and η^* are the optimal values of ξ and η for the Command Economy. Given the uniqueness of the optimal path chosen by the Command Economy, it follows that μ and ϕ are well-defined. Differentiate (4.86) and use (4.85) to conclude

$$\frac{\dot{\eta}^*}{\eta^*} = \frac{\dot{\xi}^*}{\xi^*} = -\theta\, G^*.$$

This implies μ is a constant. Hence, ϕ is a constant also.

The Household's optimisation exercise leads to the maximisation of the current value Hamiltonian

$$H^h = \frac{C^{1-\theta}}{1-\theta} + \eta_h(r^* K + \Delta - C), \qquad (A4.2.4)$$

where η_h is the relevant co-state variable associated with (4.93). A set of necessary conditions for the optimum solution to the problem is

$$C^{-\theta} = \eta_h \qquad (A4.2.5)$$

and

$$\dot{\eta}_h = -\eta_h r^* + \eta_h \rho = -\eta_h \alpha A(\nu^* K^*)^{\alpha-1}(\Gamma^*)^{1-\alpha} + \eta_h \rho. \quad (A4.2.6)$$

The equation on the extreme right of (A4.2.6) follows from (A4.2.1).

The instantaneous profit maximisation problems of Firms I and II lead to the following two conditions each:

$$\alpha A K_y^{\alpha-1} \Gamma^{1-\alpha} = r^* \qquad (A4.2.7)$$

$$(1 - \alpha) A K_y^{\alpha} \Gamma^{-\alpha} = \lambda\phi \qquad (A4.2.8)$$

and

$$\mu\beta BK_\Gamma^{\beta-1}\Gamma^{1-\beta} = r^* \qquad (A4.2.9)$$

$$\mu(1-\beta)BK_\Gamma^\beta\Gamma^{-\beta} = (1-\lambda)\phi. \qquad (A4.2.10)$$

Equations (A4.2.7) and (A4.2.9) together imply

$$\alpha AK_y^{\alpha-1}\Gamma^{1-\alpha} = \mu\beta BK_\Gamma^{\beta-1}\Gamma^{1-\beta} = r^*. \qquad (A4.2.11)$$

Similarly, adding (A4.2.8) and (A4.2.10), we obtain

$$(1-\alpha)AK_y^\alpha\Gamma^{-\alpha} + \mu(1-\beta)BK_\Gamma^\beta\Gamma^{-\beta} = \phi. \qquad (A4.2.12)$$

Using (4.85), (4.86) and the definitions of μ and ϕ, (A4.2.11) and (A4.2.12) reduce to

$$\eta^*\alpha AK_y^{\alpha-1}\Gamma^{1-\alpha} = \xi^*\beta BK_\Gamma^{\beta-1}\Gamma^{1-\beta} \qquad (A4.2.13)$$

and

$$\dot{\xi}^* = -(1-\alpha)\eta^* AK_y^\alpha\Gamma^{-\alpha} - (1-\beta)\xi^* BK_\Gamma^\beta\Gamma^{-\beta} + \xi^*\rho. \quad (A4.2.14)$$

Equations (4.86), (5.61) and the definitions of ν^*, K^* and Γ^* imply that $K_y = \nu^*K^*$, $K_\Gamma = (1-\nu^*)K^*$ and $\Gamma = \Gamma^*$ satisfy (A4.2.13) and (A4.2.14).

Going over now to the Household's problem, we may differentiate (A4.2.5) and substitute from (A4.2.6) to obtain

$$\frac{\dot{C}}{C} = \frac{r^* - \rho}{\theta}.$$

From (4.85), (4.86), (4.87) and (A4.2.1), the Household chooses the same growth rate as that of the Command Economy. However, this still does not determine the *level* of $C(t)$. To fix the latter, choose $\Delta(t) = D(t)$ for each t. That is, the subsidy provided to the Household is exactly equal to the net revenue of the Government as defined in (4.98). Hence, the Government's Budget is balanced. Moreover, $D(t) > 0 \; \forall \; t$. For, using

(A4.2.2) and (A4.2.3) and (4.83)

$$\phi\Gamma^* - \mu B((1-\nu^*)K^*)^\beta(\Gamma^*)^{1-\beta} = \mu(\theta G^* + \rho)\Gamma^*$$

$$-B\left(\frac{(1-\nu^*)K^*}{\Gamma^*}\right)^\beta \Gamma^*$$

$$= \mu((\theta-1)G^* + \rho)\Gamma^*$$

$$> 0,$$

$$(A4.2.15)$$

where the last inequality follows from (4.75).

Equations (A4.2.7) through (A4.2.10) imply then that the *RHS* of (4.93) reduces to $Y(t)$. Rewriting (4.93) as

$$\frac{C}{K} + \frac{\dot{K}}{K} = \nu^* A\left(\frac{\nu^* K^*}{\Gamma^*}\right)^{\alpha-1},$$

balanced growth requires C and K to grow at the same rate. In other words, $\dot{K}/K = G^*$. This in turn means that

$$C(t) = K(t)\left(\nu^* A\left(\frac{\nu^* K^*(t)}{\Gamma^*(t)}\right)^{\alpha-1} - G^*\right) \quad \forall\ t.$$

Hence, (4.82) implies that the choice of $C(t)$ by the Household is the same as that for the Command Economy. Equation (4.85) yields

$$C^{-\theta} = \eta.$$

Comparing this with (A4.2.5), we see that $\eta_h(t) = \eta^*(t) \ \forall\ t$.

Collecting the results, it follows that equations (A4.2.5), (A4.2.6), (A4.2.13), and (A4.2.14) describing the evolution of the Decentralised Economy are the same as (4.85), (4.86), (4.87) and (5.61) characterising the Command Economy path. The solution to the Command Economy problem being unique, the Decentralized Economy chooses identically the same path.

Finally, rewriting (A4.2.12) as

$$(1-\alpha)A(\nu^* K^*)^\alpha(\Gamma^*)^{-\alpha} + \mu(1-\beta)B((1-\nu^*)K^*)^\beta(\Gamma^*)^{-\beta} = \phi,$$

$$(A4.2.16)$$

$\exists$ a unique $\lambda^* \in (0, 1)$ with

$$(1 - \alpha)A(\nu^* K^*)^{\alpha}(\Gamma^*)^{-\alpha} = \lambda^* \phi$$
$$\mu(1 - \beta)B((1 - \nu^*)K^*)^{\beta}(\Gamma^*)^{-\beta} = (1 - \lambda^*)\phi.$$

However, ϕ is time invariant. Hence, $\lambda^* \phi$ and $(1 - \lambda^*)\phi$ are also constants over time.

Proof of Proposition 4.11:

With reference to (A4.2.15), the discounted present value of the infinite stream of surpluses at $t = 0$ may be written

$$\int_0^{\infty} \mu((\theta - 1)G^* + \rho)\Gamma^*(t)e^{-r^* t}dt. \qquad (A4.2.17)$$

Noting that $\Gamma^*(t) = \Gamma^*(0)e^{G^* t}$, equation (A4.2.17) reduces to

$$\mu((\theta - 1)G^* + \rho)$$

$$\times \Gamma^*(0)\int_0^{\infty} e^{(G^* - r^*)t}dt \;\; = \;\; \mu((\theta - 1)G^* + \rho) \times$$

$$\Gamma^*(0)\int_0^{\infty} e^{(G^*(1-\theta)-\rho)t}dt$$

$$(\text{ using (4.85) through}$$

$$(5.61) \text{ and (A4.2.1) })$$

$$= \;\; \mu\Gamma^*(0) \qquad \blacksquare$$

Chapter 5

Technical Progress as a Conscious Economic Activity-II

5.1 Resource Allocation for Technological Advancement

Chapter 4 developed models to show how human capital formation might influence the growth rate of an economy. We move on now to our next theme, the link between economic growth and knowledge accumulation. In other words, this chapter will view knowledge itself as a form of capital. In Solow's aggregative growth model, diminishing returns implied that increases in physical capital relative to effective labour lead to declining growth rates of output and physical capital itself till, in the long run, capital and effective labour grow at equal rates, or, what comes to the same thing, per capita capital, output etc. grow at the same rate as the exogenously specified rate of growth of technology. In the language of supply and demand, the supply rate of growth turns out to be perfectly inelastic to interest rate changes, thereby making the equilibrium growth rate impervious to changes in demand forces.

Chapter 3 suggested ways of separating the growth rate of capital from exogenous factors by introducing either learning by doing induced changes in effective factor supply (Arrow, d'Autume & Michel, Frankel, Romer) or allowing for growth in endogenously provided infrastructure (Barro & Sala-i-Martin). In these cases too, diminishing returns ensured the equality of the rates of growth of physical capital and effective labour or infrastructure (when a balanced growth path exists). However, the rates of growth of the latter were not exogenously specified. Supply side considerations nailed down the equilibrium rate of interest, or alternatively, the marginal productivity of capital, independently of the economy's rate of growth. Consequently, Solow's zero elastic supply curve was replaced by one that was infinitely elastic and changes in demand parameters began to influence the equilibrium rate of growth even in the absence of supply shifts.

Both Chapter 2 and Chapter 3, however, were concerned with extreme forms of the supply curve. Accordingly, Chapter 4 considered more moderately behaved supply responses. This involved the introduction of two sectors of production, the first of which produced final goods as in Solow, while the second was concerned exclusively with the activity of accumulation and determined the supply rate of growth as a function of the factor intensity ruling in that sector. The latter changed with variations in factor prices, in particular the rate of interest. Consequently, the supply rate of growth was neither infinitely elastic nor perfectly inelastic.

Rebelo II and the Lucas models represented particularly clear versions of the new approach. The distinctive feature of these models lay in the AK feature of the second sector. We justified this assumption in the Rebelo II case by interpreting K as a mixture of physical and human capital. As far as Lucas was concerned, no defence was provided for the assumption at all. In both cases, however, the AK assumption led to an upper bound on the economy's achievable rate of growth. We choose this fact as a point of departure and move on to the next stage of our investigation.

An often ignored, though vitally important, factor of production is the stock of knowledge at the disposal of any society.[1] Knowledge in this context refers of course to familiarity with productive techniques, in particular the latest advances in that area. Countries that have discovered better ways of carrying out production are obviously better equipped to break through growth barriers. Moreover, at any point of time, the total knowledge in existence resembles a *stock*. Quite obviously, like any other stock, knowledge too grows over time. Consequently, it has features similar to capital. Unlike other forms of capital though, the stock of knowledge can grow in two different ways. First, it grows through dissemination across persons, i.e., the learners. Second, it grows in the shape of new knowledge, when improved upon through research. We may refer to these two forms of knowledge generation as quantitative and qualitative expansion respectively.

Technologically speaking, both forms of knowledge enhancement involve two basic factors of production, the existing stock of knowledge (as incorporated in the pages of a book for example) and labour. As far as quantitative expansion goes, the application of human effort to master it is not likely to give rise to diminishing returns. The reason for this lies in the fact that the body of knowledge incorporated in the book counts as knowledge only if the latter is studied by a student. Two students (with similar capability) studying the book produce then twice as much knowledge. Three students multiply the knowledge threefold. Viewed this way, the technology for knowledge *dissemination* would appear to display constant returns to labour as of a fixed pool of knowledge. That is to say, the technology is endowed with an AK structure.[2]

Moving over now to the second aspect of knowledge accumulation, i.e., qualitative expansion, it would appear that no clear boundary separates it from quantitative expansion. The

---

[1]Romer (1986) may be the earliest model to recognise this feature of knowledge.

[2]Note that this channel of knowledge expansion is not clearly distinguishable from growth in human capital. Although Lucas analysed the matter, existing knowledge did not play any role in the creation of new human capital. As such, the assumption of a linear technology for human capital accumulation had an ad hocness about it.

understanding that the reading of a book generates may not be limited to the exact content of the book studied. Each individual reading the book is likely to interpret it in his own way and each new way of understanding existing phenomenon counts as new knowledge. Of course, full-fledged knowledge creation involves more than application of labour on a given volume of knowledge. Indeed, a series of discoveries, hence new bits of knowledge or intermediate products, separate the starting point of a research endeavour from its destination. However, this fact is likely to be suppressed in any vertically integrated representation of the knowledge technology. As a result, from the point of view of technology specification, there may be little to distinguish between the two forms of knowledge expansion.

Thus, Romer (1990) and Grossman & Helpman (1991-b) assume the creation of new knowledge to be linear in the use of human capital (or labour in general) as of a given stock of knowledge. However, with respect to the use of human capital and existing knowledge taken together, the technology is taken to display increasing returns. The linearity assumption lends justification to the AK format, so long as the stock of knowledge in use is held fixed. At the same time, the replacement of the technology of human capital creation by the one for new knowledge creation rids the model economy of the earlier noted undesirable feature of the Rebelo II and Lucas models, viz. the technological upper bound on the achievable growth rate (See Chapter 4). As will be apparent from the following sections, the rate of growth of knowledge accumulation will, in principle, be unbounded above. The existing *level* of human capital will put temporary bounds on this growth rate. But a growth in human capital will relax the bound. In other words, Romer and Grossman & Helpman trace back the bound on economic growth to scarcity of resources rather than to a technological constraint.

For Romer, each new addition to the knowledge stock helps to produce a novel input which in turn helps to raise the productivity in the final goods sector. By contrast, Grossman & Helpman build models to highlight the role played by knowledge capital in giving rise to consumption variety. The first part of the present chapter will discuss Romer's work. This will be followed up by a presentation of a model of brand proliferation due to Grossman & Helpman.

5.2 Description of the Romer Economy

Technological progress in Romer's model shows up in the form of specialised inputs used for producing final goods.[3] The production function is given by

$$Y = T_y^\alpha \int_0^A x(i)^{1-\alpha} di, \qquad (5.1)$$

where T_y represents human capital employed in producing Y, $x(i)$ the quantity of the ith variety of specialised input used in the production of Y and A the cardinality of a continuum of existing varieties. Specialised inputs are indexed according to the chronological order of their appearance. The proximate object of research is the ith design or idea[4], whose concrete embodiment is the input $x(i)$. Progress in research, i.e., knowledge accumulation, implies an increase in the value of A and along with it, an expansion in the size of the set of ideas as well as that of the set of specialised inputs.

That (5.1) captures the notion of specialisation may be appreciated from the following considerations. Assuming all $x(i)$'s to be used at the same level, say x, the production function reduces to

$$Y = T_y^\alpha A x^{1-\alpha}. \qquad (5.2)$$

Given x, the marginal return to variety is measured by

$$\frac{\partial Y}{\partial A} = T_y^\alpha x^{1-\alpha}.$$

In other words, there are constant returns to variety, given the level of $x(i)$. As opposed to this, the marginal return to

---

[3]Following an idea of Ethier (1982), the function is a reinterpretation of the Dixit-Stiglitz (1977) preference function for variety.

[4]The words "design", "idea", "knowledge" etc. will be used synonymously in what follows.

an increase in x, given that variety is fixed at A, behaves as follows:

$$\frac{\partial Y}{\partial x} = T_y^\alpha A(1 - \alpha)x^{-\alpha} > 0$$

$$\frac{\partial^2 Y}{\partial x^2} = T_y^\alpha A(-\alpha)(1 - \alpha)x^{-\alpha-1} < 0.$$

Thus, given A, there are decreasing returns to a mere increase in the quantity in which the different inputs are employed. In other words, specialisation offsets the tendency for diminishing returns associated with an intensive use of existing inputs.

The production of $x(i)$ is thought of as a two stage (but not necessarily vertically integrated) process. The lower stage consists of the creation of a design, i.e., the task of "hitting an idea". Human capital is an essential input in this process and calls for a once for all payment to the inventor. At the higher stage, non-specialised or raw capital (Solow's K) is converted to specialised $x(i)$ by means of a fixed coefficient production function, each unit of $x(i)$ requiring ζ units of raw capital.

5.2.1   The Private Economy

When used for producing new designs, the design for a specialised input is nonexcludable, since it can be copied relatively costlessly. It is also nonrival, since two research processes based on the *same* idea can be simultaneously operated. Unlike rival inputs, there is no sense in which the two processes can be viewed as employing two *pieces* of the same idea. Being both nonrival and non-excludable, a design has the required characteristics of a pure public good. Consequently, all existing designs may be freely employed by competing researchers to produce new designs or knowledge.

Free availability of knowledge, however, could act as a disincentive for research as a privately organised activity. Romer's Private economy resolves the difficulty by adopting a monopolistically competitive market structure backed by patent laws. There are two ways in which an existing design may be utilised.

First, as already explained, any idea can be utilised to create newer ideas through further research. Second, it may be used to produce the specialised input based on it. The patent laws inhibit free access to a design by a non-patent holder in the second of these activities. However, the laws cannot preclude the free use of an existing idea to churn out new ones. In other words, a patent accords to the product of invention the status of a *partially* excludable commodity. The total body of knowledge incorporated in the stock of existing ideas (of size A) is a free input into new research, but the use of each individual design is excludable in producing the corresponding input.

Social Accounts for the Romer Model			
Sector	Output	Input	Market Structure
Final Goods	Y	T_y, $x(i)$, $i \in (0, A]$	Competitive
Intermediate Goods	$x(i)$, $i \in (0, A]$	K, i^{th} design, $i \in (0, A]$	Monopoly
Research	$\dot{A}$	T_A, A	Competitive

As the above scheme demonstrates, the economy consists of three parts: a perfectly competitive sector producing Y; for each i, a monopolist producing $x(i)$ by means of a non-sector specific capital good K, which (as in Solow) is physically the same as Y; and a competitive sector producing research ideas or designs with the aid of human capital T_A and the stock A of "ideas".

The household H faces the instantaneous budget constraint

$$C(t) + \dot{A}(t) = W_T + r\ \mathcal{A}(t),$$

where W_T represents aggregate wages of human capital[5] and

---

[5]Note the difference between Rebelo II and the present model as far as the returns to human capital goes.

$\mathcal{A}(t)$ stands for the aggregate value of assets held by H. More precisely, $\mathcal{A}(t)$ stands for the aggregate value of equity (or, shares in profits of monopoly firms) and $K(t)$ at each t. In equilibrium, H must be supposed to be indifferent between the two forms of assets. Hence, r is the common rate of return from the two types of assets. Subject to the above constraint, H maximises

$$\int_0^\infty \frac{C^{1-\theta} - 1}{1 - \theta} e^{-\rho\, t} dt.$$

As before, the exercise gives rise to the standard demand curve, i.e.,

$$g_C^d(r) = \frac{r - \rho}{\theta},$$

The equations characterising the production sectors will be derived under the assumption that the economy satisfies standard market equilibrium conditions at each t. In particular, the following should be satisfied:

(i) $\mathcal{A}(t) = P_A\, A(t) + K(t)\ \forall\ t$, where P_A is the price of a unit of A;
(ii) demand for $x(i) =$ supply of $x(i) = x\ \forall\ i$;
(iii) sectoral as well as the aggregate demands for human capital equal their supplies.

The final good Y being produced under perfect competition, the wage rate w_T^y of human capital in this sector equals its marginal product:

$$w_T^y = \alpha T_y^{\alpha-1} \int_0^A x(i)^{1-\alpha} di \qquad (5.3)$$

In what follows, Y will act as the numéraire. The inverse derived demand function for the input $x(i)$ is

$$p(i) = (1 - \alpha) T_y^\alpha x(i)^{-\alpha} \qquad (5.4)$$

where $p(i)$ is the price paid per unit use of $x(i)$.

The raw capital congealed in $x(i)$ is borrowed from H. If $x(i)$ is infinitely lived, there is an interest cost per period to be incurred by its producer for infinite time. Alternatively, $x(i)$ could also be looked upon as a consumable input, reproduced in each period. In this case too, there is an infinite stream of interest payments.[6] A patent holder of the ith idea is the monopolist supplier of $x(i)$ who earns an infinite stream of profits. The stream is discounted using the prevailing market rate of interest r on K, which is viewed as the minimal acceptable return on investment. This is justified, as already argued above, by the fact that H must be indifferent between ownership rights over K and ownership rights over monopoly firms in equilibrium. Potential monopolists compete for difference between the present value of the stream and the once for all payment for the design. This raises or depresses the price of the design, till the cost is equalised with the benefit.

The instantaneous profit of a monopoly producer of $x(i)$ is given by

$$\pi(i) = p(i)x(i) - r\zeta x(i), \qquad (5.5)$$

where $\zeta x(i)$ is borrowed from the households. Using (5.4), hence the second of the equilibrium conditions noted above, the maximisation of (5.5) yields an expression for $p(i)$ that depends only on r for each i:

$$p = p(i) = \frac{r\zeta}{1 - \alpha}. \qquad (5.6)$$

Combining this with (5.4), $x(i)$ is also dependent on r only. This value of $x(i)$ will be denoted simply by x. Hence, (5.3) reduces to

$$w_T^y = \alpha T_y^{\alpha-1} A x^{1-\alpha}. \qquad (5.7)$$

The value of $\pi(i)$ is also dependent on r alone:

$$\pi = px - r\zeta x = \frac{r\zeta}{1 - \alpha} x - r\zeta x = \alpha px \qquad (5.8)$$

---

[6]The input $x(i)$ does not undergo obsolescence in Romer. Given the nature of the production function, there will always be positive demand for it by the competitive producers of Y. Obsolescence related problems are recognised by Aghion and Howitt (1992) and Young. Chapter 6 will investigate these problems.

and the infinite stream of π, discounted at the market rate of interest, equals

$$
\int_0^\infty e^{-rt}\pi dt = \frac{\pi}{r}
$$

$$
= \frac{\alpha p x}{r}
$$

$$
= \frac{\alpha(1-\alpha)T_y^\alpha x^{1-\alpha}}{r}. \tag{5.9}
$$

Since P_A is none other than the investment in research by prospective monopolists competing for the right to produce $x(i)$, no arbitrage requires that in equilibrium it be equal to the discounted infinite stream of monopoly profits in (5.9). Hence,

$$
P_A = \frac{\alpha(1-\alpha)T_y^\alpha x^{1-\alpha}}{r}. \tag{5.10}
$$

This, along with a second no arbitrage condition to be specified below, will yield the supply rate of balanced growth for the Romer economy.

The technology for research is given by

$$
\dot{A} = aAT_A \tag{5.11}
$$

where a is a positive constant and T_A the human capital employed in producing new ideas (i.e., $\dot{A}$). The production function captures the idea discussed in the introductory section. Given A, production of new knowledge is linearly related to T_A, though there are increasing returns to simultaneous variations in A and T_A. On the other hand, the sector is perfectly competitive. Since the production function is homogeneous of degree 2 in A and T_A, payment of factors according to their marginal productivity will over-exhaust the output value. This is avoided however, A being a free input into the research process by the assumption of partial excludability. There is thus no difficulty in paying T_A according to the value of its marginal productivity. The value of the marginal product of T_A is $P_A aA$.

With reference to Sections 4.2.2 and 4.3.1, balanced growth

imposes the following two conditions on the Romer model:

$$\frac{\dot{K}}{K} = \frac{\dot{A}}{A} = \textit{constant}$$

and

$$\frac{T_y}{T_A} = \textit{constant}.$$

Equating the wages of human capital w_T^A in research to the value of its marginal product and using (5.10),

$$w_T^A = P_A a A = \frac{\alpha(1-\alpha)T_y^\alpha x^{1-\alpha}}{r} a A. \qquad (5.12)$$

A second no arbitrage requirement calls for equality of wages received by human capital in the final good sector and the research sector, i.e., $w_T^y = w_T^A = w_T$. Hence, using (5.7) and (5.12) and cancelling terms,

$$T_y = \frac{r}{a(1-\alpha)}. \qquad (5.13)$$

Substituting (5.13) into (5.11) and recalling that $T_y + T_A = \bar{T}$, i.e., the third of the equilibrium conditions listed earlier,

$$\frac{\dot{A}}{A} = a\left(\bar{T} - \frac{r}{a(1-\alpha)}\right). \qquad (5.14)$$

The last step in the derivation of the supply rate function is to identify it with (5.14). Going back to (5.1), at any fixed value of r,

$$
\begin{aligned}
Y &= T_y^\alpha A x^{1-\alpha} \\
&= T_y^\alpha A^\alpha A^{1-\alpha} x^{1-\alpha} \\
&= T_y^\alpha A^\alpha (Ax)^{1-\alpha} \\
&= (AT_y)^\alpha K^{1-\alpha} \frac{1}{\zeta^{1-\alpha}}, \qquad (5.15)
\end{aligned}
$$

where $K = \zeta A x$ is the aggregate value of raw capital embodied in the specialised inputs when the rate of interest is fixed at

r.[7] Now, K/A, being equal to ζx, is a constant given r. Using (5.15),

$$\frac{C}{K} + \frac{\dot{K}}{K} = \frac{1}{\zeta^{1-\alpha}} T_y^\alpha \left(\frac{A}{K}\right)^\alpha.$$ (5.16)

Given r, the value of T_y is fixed. Hence, the RHS of (5.16) is a constant. This implies that the rates of growth of A, C, K and Y are the same in balanced growth. Thus, (5.14) is equivalently rewritten as

$$g_C^s(r) = a\left(\bar{T} - \frac{r}{a(1-\alpha)}\right).$$ (5.17)

As with Rebelo, this is a declining function of r. The intersection $g_C^d(r)$ with $g_C^s(r)$ determines the equilibrium rate of interest (r^*) and rate of growth (g^*) as before. The dynamic equilibrium is shown in Figure 5.1.[8] The diagram clarifies that a positive rate of growth is achievable in equilibrium only if $\bar{T}$ is large enough.[9] Romer argues on the basis of this observation that a minimum size of the stock of human capital is a necessary precondition for growth. The difference between rich nations and the poor may be explained therefore in terms of the differences in the size of human capital in these societies.[10]

---

[7]It is of interest to note that (5.15) reduces the output of Y to a function of K and *augmented human capital* AT_y as opposed to Solow's K and AL.

[8]As should be obvious, the Romer balanced growth equilibrium fixes the value of K/A. Consequently, as with the Rebelo I (1991) and Lucas (1988) models, a detailed analysis of the stability of the balanced growth path is called for. A nontrivial analysis of this issue may be found in Arnold (2000).

[9]To be precise, the condition is $a(1-\alpha)\bar{H} > \rho$.

[10]As is obvious, $\bar{T}$ acts as a shift variable in Romer's model. The remaining models to be presented below in this chapter and the next are characterised by similar shift variables. Since a rise in $\bar{T}$ raises the rate of balanced growth in the economy, Peretto (1998) offered the following criticism against models involving shift variables affecting the rate of growth. With population growing exponentially over time, Romer's model predicts the rate of growth of the economy to rise exponentially over time. The criticism has been handled by later researchers (such as Segerstrom (1998)), who suggested that productivity of research falls with a rise the stock of knowledge. These developments have been neatly summarised in Dinopoulos & Sener (2003).

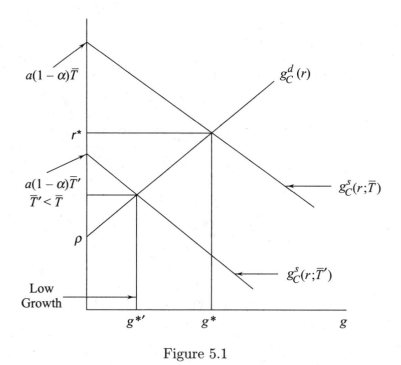

Figure 5.1

Romer's findings for the private economy may now be summarised.

PROPOSITION **5.1** *When technical progress assumes the form of specialised inputs into the productive process, the equilibrium growth rate of an economy can be sustained by a combination of perfectly competitive and monopolistically competitive markets, the latter backed by a legal structure recognising patent rights.*

5.2.2 Inefficiencies in the Private Economy

The existence of a monopoly sector in the Romer model is a potential source of inefficiency in resource allocation. A second reason for inefficiency may be traced back to a possible divergence between the social marginal productivity of knowledge and the price paid by the market for a unit of knowledge. We take these up in turn restricting the discussion to balanced growth equilibrium paths only.

Monopoly and Inefficiency For the purpose of the discussion that follows, we shall express all prices in some abstract unit of account instead of choosing Y as the numéraire good. Under balanced growth, $T_y/x = \lambda$ say $=$ *constant*. Consequently, the total cost of producing Y is

$$C_1(Y) \;=\; w_T^y T_y + pAx$$

$$=\; (w_T^y \lambda + pA)x$$

$$=\; \left(\frac{w_T^y \lambda + pA}{\lambda^\alpha A} \right) Y. \qquad (5.18)$$

The corresponding marginal cost is

$$C_1'(Y) \;=\; \left(\frac{w_H^y \lambda + pA}{\lambda^\alpha A} \right)$$

$$=\; \left(\frac{w_H^y \lambda + (r\zeta/1 - \alpha)A}{\lambda^\alpha A} \right), \qquad (5.19)$$

using (5.6).

Consider now an alternative way of producing Y by vertically integrating the Y-sector with monopolistic intermediate goods sector. In this enlarged Y-sector, the final output may be viewed as being produced by means of T_y and K. We may, however, eliminate T_y by noting that $Y = AT_y^\alpha x^{1-\alpha} = (T_y^\alpha x^{-\alpha}) Ax = \lambda^\alpha Ax$. Since $K = \zeta Ax$, we obtain

$$Y = \left(\frac{\lambda^\alpha}{\zeta} \right) K,$$

which reduces Y to a function of K alone. Using this function, the total K required to produce Y is

$$K = \left(\frac{\zeta}{\lambda^\alpha} \right) Y.$$

Hence, the aggregate cost of producing Y is

$$C_2(Y) = \left(\frac{\zeta r}{\lambda^\alpha} \right) Y, \qquad (5.20)$$

so that the marginal cost is

$$C_2'(Y) = \left(\frac{\zeta r}{\lambda^\alpha} \right). \qquad (5.21)$$

Comparing (5.19) and (5.21), it is clear that in the presence of the monopoly producers of the intermediate good, the marginal cost of producing Y is higher. Since the Y-sector is perfectly competitive, the price q of its product in the chosen unit of account is

$$
\begin{aligned}
q \;&=\; C_1'(Y) \\
&>\; C_2'(Y),
\end{aligned}
$$

where $C_2'(Y)$ may be interpreted as the true marginal cost of producing Y. This explains the monopoly-induced inefficiency in the model.

Divergence between Private and Social Marginal Product of A

Given the balanced growth equilibrium path of A and the fact that $Y = A T_y^\alpha x^{1-\alpha}$ along this path, raising A marginally at any point of time increases the output of Y by $T_y^\alpha x^{1-\alpha}$ forever. Consequently, the social marginal productivity of A is

$$
\begin{aligned}
MP_A^s \;&=\; \int_0^\infty e^{-\rho t} T_y^\alpha x^{1-\alpha} \, dt \\
&=\; \frac{T_y^\alpha x^{1-\alpha}}{\rho}.
\end{aligned}
$$

The market, however, does not ensure this return for a unit of knowledge creation. In fact, knowledge cannot be directly sold to the final users (i.e., Y producers) of the produce of knowledge (i.e., x). Instead, the market pays P_A for a unit of knowledge, where

$$P_A = \int_0^\infty e^{-rt}\pi \, dt$$

$$= \int_0^\infty e^{-rt}\{(1-\alpha)T_y^\alpha x^{1-\alpha} - r\zeta x\} \, dt$$

$$< MP_A^s,$$

We therefore conclude that

PROPOSITION **5.2** *The Private economy for the Romer model is characterised by inefficiencies induced by* (a) *monopoly pricing of intermediate products and* (b) *divergence between the social and private marginal product of knowledge.*

5.2.3   The Command Economy

We end up our discussion of Romer's problem by comparing the Private Economy's growth rate with the Command Economy's growth rate. Given the inefficiencies noted in the last section, we expect the Command economy to correct the inefficiencies and grow faster.

For the purpose of the discussion, we normalise the stock of human capital to unity, i.e., $\bar{T} = 1$. Solving (2.44) and (5.17), the equilibrium balanced growth rate for Romer's Private economy is

$$g^* = \frac{(1-\alpha)a - \rho}{1 - \alpha + \theta}. \tag{5.22}$$

Denote the Command economy balanced growth rate by G^*. Differentiating (5.26) and using $\dot{C}/C = \dot{K}/K = \dot{A}/A$ under balanced growth, we have

$$\frac{\dot{\eta}}{\eta} = \frac{\dot{\xi}}{\xi}$$

$$= -\theta G^*. \tag{5.23}$$

Eliminating $\dot{\eta}/\eta$ from(5.23) and (5.27),

$$G^* = \frac{a - \rho}{\theta}. \tag{5.24}$$

To solve for the Command Economy's growth rate, let δ denote the share of human capital used in the Y-sector. Further, the planner is assumed to produce Y in a vertically integrated fashion by internalising the intermediate good sector. This eliminates the inefficiency caused by the monopoly sector. Thus, the production function for Y reduces to

$$Y = \zeta^{\alpha-1}(A\delta)^{\alpha}K^{1-\alpha}$$

and the planner's optimisation problem is written

$$\text{Maximise } \int_0^{\infty} \frac{C^{1-\theta} - 1}{1 - \theta} e^{-\rho t} dt$$

subject to

$$\dot{K} = \zeta^{\alpha-1}(A\delta)^{\alpha}K^{1-\alpha} - C$$

$$\dot{A} = a(1 - \delta)A.$$

The problem is solved by setting up the Hamiltonian function

$$\mathcal{H} = \frac{C^{1-\theta} - 1}{1 - \theta} + \xi\{\zeta^{\alpha-1}(A\delta)^{\alpha}K^{1-\alpha} - C\} + \eta a(1 - \delta)A$$

and appealing to the conditions set out in Section 4.2.4. Equating the derivative of $\mathcal{H}$ with respect to C to zero and differentiating further, we have

$$-\theta\frac{\dot{C}}{C} = \frac{\dot{\xi}}{\xi}. \tag{5.25}$$

Equating the derivative with respect to δ to zero,

$$\alpha\xi\zeta^{\alpha-1}(A\delta)^{\alpha-1}K^{1-\alpha} = \eta a. \tag{5.26}$$

Finally, the condition governing the evolution of the co-state variable η is

$$\frac{\dot{\eta}}{\eta} = -a + \rho. \qquad (5.27)$$

Comparing (5.22) and (5.24), we conclude $G^* > g^*$. Hence, the intuition stated at the beginning of the section is justified.

PROPOSITION **5.3** *The Command economy for the Romer model corrects for monopoly induced inefficiencies and internalises the intertemporal externalities associated with knowledge capital to achieve a faster balanced growth rate compared to the Private economy.*

This completes our discussion of the Romer model.

5.3   Brand Proliferation: Grossman & Helpman

Romer's work constitutes an important move towards capturing the role of knowledge capital in economic growth. Grossman & Helpman (1991-b) represents another instance of a similar attempt. For Romer, knowledge accumulation was geared towards reducing the cost of producing the final good. Cost reduction was effected through an increase in the variety of inputs used, as of a given level of intensity of each type of input. To appreciate this fact, note that according to the cost function (5.18), the average cost of production falls with a rise in A. This resulted in a sustained quantitative expansion of the output of the final goods sector. As opposed to this, Grossman & Helpman were concerned with a rise in the number of varieties constituting a final goods basket, i.e., product innovation (rather than Romer's process innovation). The ensuing scenario was described as one involving brand proliferation.[11]

---

[11]This is only one type of product innovation considered by the authors. The next chapter will introduce a second type, viz. the quality ladder model involving improvements in the qualities of a well-defined set of commodities.

An enlargement in the size of the "vector" of final products involves the invention of new varieties of goods. With no (Romer like) reduction in cost of production, however, and as of a given size of the labour force, the expansion in the set of goods can take place only at the expense of a reduction in the size of individual components in the basket. For a meaningful growth model, the rise must more than compensate for the fall. Grossman & Helpman ensured this by appealing to the positive impact of increasing variety on utility. As will be argued in the sequel (See Section 5.3.4), aggregate utility will grow if the rate of growth in variety more than balances off the rate of fall in individual components in the consumption basket. The associated growth process must therefore imply a growth in utility, rather than a growth in output as such.

Given the focus on utility enhancement through increase in consumption variety, it is natural that the exercise abstracts from the role of intermediate inputs altogether. There is of course a Romer type Research sector that produces blueprints of new varieties of final goods either with the help of human capital alone, or with human capital and the existing stock of knowledge. The blueprint is then purchased by a patent protected monopolist, who produces the commodity by means of human capital. For neither productive activity is it necessary to employ physical capital. Hence, growth in the Grossman-Helpman economy is driven entirely by the accumulation of knowledge capital. The model, in other words, is an abstraction designed to single out the role of knowledge capital in producing economic growth. We shall present two versions of the model, depending on the nature of technology characterising the Research sector. In one version, technology is a private commodity, to which no one other than the patent holder has access. The second is a Romer type world where the research sector, though not the final goods sector, has free access to the stock of blueprints discovered till date.

At the analytical plane, the model to be presented involves generalisations in two directions. The first one comes up when knowledge is a private commodity. As we shall observe, this rules out the existence of a balanced growth equilibrium. Consequently, we will need to appeal to the notion of a perfect foresight equilibrium, as was the case for the Romer (1986) paper. It is for the case of public knowledge capital, however, that the more interesting of the generalisations show up. The economy in this instance will be capable of exhibiting a balanced growth equilibrium. Yet, the dynamic equilibrium for the case will not be representable as the supply-demand cross of our previous chapters. The underlying reason may be explained as follows. The household's dynamic optimisation exercise will lead it to choose a rate of growth of the commodity basket over time. We noted above that a growth in the basket has at least two components of change: a change in the size of the "vector" and a change in the individual components of the vector. A further complication will come up on account of the fact that we shall be generally concerned with the *value* of the changing basket along the balanced growth path. Thus, a third variable will appear in the shape of a commodity price. Consequently, the demand rate of growth will be a composite of three rates of change, the rate of change of the quantity of each commodity in the basket, the rate of change of the "number of elements" in the basket and the rate of change of the price of each commodity. Like Romer (1990), however, the supply rate of growth will involve the growth in the set of ideas, i.e., the cardinality of the aforementioned basket. Consequently, it will not be possible for us to equate the supply and the demand rates as before.

Put differently, the earlier exercises involved two equations. The first expressed the demand rate of growth of consumption as a function of the rate of interest. The second gave the supply rate of growth of consumption (which was identically the same as the supply rate of growth of ideas in Romer (1990)) as a function of the rate of interest. Equating the supply and the demand rates, we were left with two equations in two variables, the equilibrium growth rate and the rate of interest. Conceptually therefore, the system was solvable. As opposed to this, the model to be presented now will give rise to a composite of demand growth rates. Though the supply side will be less complicated, the resultant system will no longer be a system of two equations in two unknowns. Hence, we shall need to dispense with the simple demand supply device to determine the growth rate of the system. The matter will be elaborated further when the occasion arises below (in Sections 5.3.2 and 5.3.4).

We move on now to a description of the basic details of the economy.

5.3.1 Description of the Economy

We begin with a description of agent H's behaviour, which breaks up into a static and a dynamic part. There is a continuum of imperfectly substitutable commodities consumed at any moment of time. The cardinality of the set of commodities is $A(t)$ at the point of time t. The static problem consists of finding the demand functions of H for each commodity in the basket available at any given t. The amount of the jth type demanded is $x(j)$, with $j \in (0, A(t)]$. Dropping t for convenience and following Dixit & Stiglitz (1977), instantaneous utility (or, felicity) is defined over the composite commodity

$$D = \left(\int_0^A x(j)^\alpha dj \right)^{1/\alpha}, \; 0 < \alpha < 1, \qquad (5.28)$$

so that the elasticity of substitution between any pair of commodities is a constant $\epsilon = 1/(1 - \alpha)$. The instantaneous utility function is $ln\,D$, which the household maximises subject to

$$E = \int_0^A p(j)x(j)dj, \qquad (5.29)$$

where $p(j)$ is the price paid for commodity j.[12] We have so far followed the convention of choosing the output of the final good sector as the numéraire. In the present set up, however, there is an evolving variety of final goods, so that there is no obvious candidate for a numéraire. To preserve symmetry therefore,

---

[12]The choice of the utility function $ln\,D$ may be viewed as a special case of the function $(D^{1-\theta} - 1)/1 - \theta$, obtained by choosing $\theta = 1$. Whether the results reported below generalise to arbitrary positive values of θ need to be verified carefully.

we shall suppose that all price variables for the economy are expressed in some exogenously specified unit of account. The *FOC* for the problem is

$$\frac{x(j)^{\alpha-1}}{x(k)^{\alpha-1}} = \frac{p(j)}{p(k)}. \tag{5.30}$$

Thus, the static demand function is given by

$$
\begin{aligned}
x(j) &= \frac{x(k)}{p(k)^{1/(\alpha-1)}} \, p(j)^{1/(\alpha-1)} \\[2mm]
&= \frac{\int_0^A p(k)x(k)dk}{\int_0^A p(k)p(k)^{-1/(1-\alpha)}dk} \, p(j)^{-1/(1-\alpha)} \\[2mm]
&= \frac{\int_0^A p(k)x(k)dk}{\int_0^A p(k)^{1-\epsilon}dk} \, p(j)^{-\epsilon}. \tag{5.31}
\end{aligned}
$$

The coefficient of $p(j)^{-\epsilon}$ admits an economic interpretation. To do so, we associate with the composite commodity an efficient price p_D by imagining D to be produced with the help of the intermediate products $x(j)$ under perfect competition. Profit from production is

$$p_D \left[\int_0^A x(j)^{\alpha}dj \right]^{1/\alpha} - \int_0^A p(j)x(j)dj.$$

Maximisation of profit yields

$$p_D\left[\int_0^A x(j)^{\alpha}dj\right]^{1-\alpha/\alpha} x(j)^{\alpha-1} = p(j). \tag{5.32}$$

which reduces to identically the same *FOC* as (5.30). Manipulating (5.30), we have

$$\left(\int_0^A x(j)^{\alpha}dj \right)^{(1/\alpha)-1} = \frac{\left(\int_0^A p(j)^{\alpha/(\alpha-1)}dj \right)^{1-\alpha/\alpha}}{p(k)^{-1} \, x(k)^{-(1-\alpha)}}.$$

Using this in (5.32), we get

$$p_D = \left(\int_0^A p(j)^{\alpha/\alpha-1} dj \right)^{-(1-\alpha)/\alpha} \tag{5.33}$$

$$= \left(\int_0^A p(j)^{1-\epsilon} dj \right)^{1/(1-\epsilon)} \tag{5.34}$$

Equations (5.33) and (5.34) are alternative expressions of the efficiency price attached to D. Competitive pricing also implies that $p_D D = \int_0^A p(j)x(j)dj = E$. Hence, (5.31) may be replaced by

$$x(j) = \frac{p_D D}{p_D^{1-\epsilon}} p(j)^{-\epsilon} \tag{5.35}$$

$$= \frac{E}{p_D^{1-\epsilon}} p(j)^{-\epsilon}. \tag{5.36}$$

When the composite good is large compared to any individual component $x(j)$, the demand for the latter may be assumed to be a function of $p(j)$ alone, for $p(j)$ will have negligible influence on D or p_D. Thus, (5.35) and (5.36) can be treated in the standard manner as downward falling functions of $p(j)$ alone. This completes the description of the household's static problem.

The dynamic problem involves characterising the optimal time path of E (alternatively, p_D and D). To do this, we take account of the fact that the household's income flows from two sources. The first is $w\bar{T}$, the income from human capital, where $\bar{T}$ is assumed to be a constant across t. The second is the profit income from ownership of monopoly firms producing the different $x(j)$'s. Denote the aggregate value of shares in firms' profits by $\mathcal{A}$.[13] The dynamic maximisation problem is written

---

[13] In Romer, $\mathcal{A}$ stood for the aggregate value of shares in profits *and* physical capital held by the monopoly firms. The latter disappears in Grossman & Helpman, since physical capital plays no role at all.

$$\text{Maximise} \qquad \int_0^\infty \ln D \, dt$$

$$\text{subject to } \dot{\mathcal{A}} \;=\; w\bar{T} + r\mathcal{A} - p_D D,$$

where r stands for the rate of return, to be called interest, paid on $\mathcal{A}$. The by now standard procedure leads to the following first order condition describing the optimal path of E:

$$\frac{\dot{E}}{E} \;=\; \frac{\dot{D}}{D} + \frac{\dot{p}_D}{p_D}$$

$$\;=\; r - \rho. \tag{5.37}$$

This expression obviously corresponds to the demand rate of growth for the economy. At the cost of repetition, it is worth emphasising that the demand rate of growth subsumes three explicit rates of growth, of x, of A and of p.

As before, the economy must be in equilibrium at each t. Thus, the following should be satisfied:

(i) $\mathcal{A}(t) = p_A A(t) \; \forall t$, where p_A is the value of each monopoly firm;
(ii) demand for $x(j) = $ supply of $x(j) \; \forall \; j$;
(iii) return to human capital in the manufacturing sector $=$ return to human capital in the research sector;
(iv) sector wise as well as aggregate demands for human capital equal supplies at each t.

Keeping these conditions in mind, we proceed to a discussion of each atomistic monopoly firm's instantaneous profit maximisation problem. For all j, production of a unit of $x(j)$ requires a unit of human capital. Thus, the profit function of the jth firm is given by

$$\pi(j) \;=\; p(j)x(j) - wx(j)$$

$$\;=\; \frac{E}{p_D^{1-\epsilon}} \, p(j)^{1-\epsilon} - w \, \frac{E}{p_D^{1-\epsilon}} \, p(j)^{-\epsilon}.$$

Maximisation leads to

$$p(j) \;=\; -\frac{\epsilon}{1-\epsilon}\, w$$

$$\;=\; \frac{w}{\alpha}, \tag{5.38}$$

so that prices of all $x(j)$'s are equal. Substituting for $p(j)$ in $\pi(j)$, we conclude that

$$\pi(j) \;=\; \frac{E}{p_D^{1-\epsilon}}\, p^{-\epsilon}\,(p-w)$$

$$\;=\; \frac{E}{p_D^{1-\epsilon}}\left(\frac{w}{\alpha}\right)^{1-\epsilon}(1-\alpha)$$

$$\;=\; \frac{E}{\int_0^A (w/\alpha)^{1-\epsilon} dj}\left(\frac{w}{\alpha}\right)^{1-\epsilon}(1-\alpha)$$

$$\;=\; \frac{(1-\alpha)\,E}{A}. \tag{5.39}$$

Thus, at any t, the value of an existing monopoly firm is

$$p_A(t) \;=\; \int_t^\infty e^{-\int_t^s r(\tau)d\tau}\,\pi(s)\,ds$$

$$\;=\; \int_t^\infty e^{-\int_t^s r(\tau)d\tau}\,\frac{(1-\alpha)E(s)}{A(s)}\,ds. \tag{5.40}$$

We move on now to alternative descriptions of the research sector. The first treats knowledge as a private commodity, while the second adopts the Romer (1990) viewpoint.

5.3.2 Research without Public Knowledge

The technology for research is given by

$$\dot{A} = a\, T_A, \tag{5.41}$$

where T_A represents human capital employed in research and a is a constant. Like Romer, there is perfect competition in the research sector. Since the value of a unit of A, i.e., the value of $\dot{A}$, is p_A, the research firm's profit is $p_A \dot{A} - wT_A = (p_A a - w) T_A$. Consequently, profit maximisation implies

$$p_A a - w \quad \leq \quad 0, \text{ if } \dot{A} \geq 0$$

$$= \quad 0, \text{ if } \dot{A} > 0. \qquad (5.42)$$

Similar to the Romer (1986) exercise,[14] the model does not allow for a balanced growth equilibrium path. This follows from the third of the market equilibrium conditions, viz., the condition for equilibrium in the market for human capital. To appreciate this, denote the total demand for human capital for producing final goods by T_x. Since all brands carry the same price p and there are A brands, the quantity produced of each brand is E/Ap (from the second equilibrium condition above). Thus, $T_x = A(E/Ap) = E/p$ and the market for human capital is in equilibrium if

$$\bar{T} \quad = \quad T_A + T_x$$

$$= \quad \frac{1}{a} \dot{A} + \frac{E}{p}. \qquad (5.43)$$

If $\dot{A}/A = constant > 0$, as required by balanced growth, then (5.43) will be violated from some finite t onwards. As asserted therefore, the model cannot display balanced growth equilibrium. For the model to work, one must follow Romer (1986) to generalise the condition of dynamic equilibrium.

Definition: For the Grossman-Helpman model, a *perfect foresight* equilibrium path of $\{A(t)\}_0^\infty$ satisfies the condition that it is realised if expected.

We proceed now to characterise the dynamic path followed by the economy in perfect foresight equilibrium. First, let us derive the path governing the behaviour of A. Equations (5.41)

---

[14]See Chapter 3, Section 3.2.9.

and (5.40) imply that the wage rate in the research sector is

$$p_A(t)\, a = \left(\int_t^\infty e^{-\int_t^s r(\tau)d\tau}\, \frac{(1-\alpha)E(s)}{A(s)}\, ds \right) a, \qquad (5.44)$$

if $\dot{A}(t) > 0$. No arbitrage requires the wage rate in the manufacturing sector (given by (5.38)) to be equalised with the wage rate in the research sector. Using $T_x = E/p$, (5.38) and (5.44), the no arbitrage condition is written

$$\alpha\, p(t) \;=\; \frac{\alpha\, E(t)}{T_x(t)}$$

$$\;=\; \left(\int_t^\infty e^{-\int_t^s r(\tau)d\tau}\, \frac{(1-\alpha)E(s)}{A(s)}\, ds \right) a.$$

Hence,

$$T_x(t) = \frac{\alpha}{1-\alpha}\, \frac{E(t)}{\int_t^\infty e^{-\int_t^s r(\tau)d\tau}\, (E(s)/A(s))\, ds}\, \frac{1}{a}. \qquad (5.45)$$

From (5.42), (5.43) and (5.45),

$$T_A(t) \;=\; \frac{1}{a}\, \dot{A}(t)$$

$$\;=\; \bar{T} - T_x(t)$$

$$\;=\; \bar{T} - \frac{\alpha}{1-\alpha}\, \frac{E(t)}{\int_t^\infty e^{-\int_t^s r(\tau)d\tau}\, (E(s)/A(s))\, ds}\, \frac{1}{a}.$$

$$(5.46)$$

The differential equation (5.46) governs the motion of A when all the four conditions of equilibrium stated above are satisfied. For the path to constitute a dynamic equilibrium one needs further that it be consistent with the demand rate of growth of E, viz. (5.37). Accordingly, substituting $E(s) = E(t)\, e^{\int_t^s (r(\tau)-\rho)d\tau}$

in (5.47), we conclude that the dynamic equilibrium path of A must satisfy[15]

$$\frac{1}{a} \, \dot{A}(t) = \bar{T} - \frac{\alpha}{1 - \alpha} \, \frac{1}{\int_t^\infty e^{-\rho(s-t)}(1/A(s)) \, ds} \, \frac{1}{a}. \qquad (5.47)$$

Let us simplify (5.47) by defining a new variable

$$\kappa(t) = \int_t^\infty e^{-\rho(s-t)} \, \frac{1 - \alpha}{A(s)} \, ds, \qquad (5.48)$$

which, from (5.40) expresses p_A in units of E. Then, (5.41) and (5.47) $\Rightarrow$

$$\dot{A} = \begin{cases} a\bar{T} - \alpha/u, & \text{if } \dot{A} > 0 \\ 0 & \text{otherwise .} \end{cases}$$

Note that $\dot{A} > 0 \Rightarrow w = p_A a$, or, $p_A = w/a = \alpha p/a$, from (5.38). On the other hand, (5.43) shows that $p > E/\bar{T}$ when $\dot{A} > 0$. Thus, $p_A = \alpha p/a > \alpha E/a\bar{T}$, or, $\kappa > \alpha/a\bar{T} = \bar{\kappa}$, (say). In other words, $\dot{A} > 0 \Rightarrow \kappa > \bar{\kappa}$. Conversely, let $\kappa > \bar{\kappa}$, or, $p_A > \alpha E/a\bar{T}$. Since, $w \geq p_A a$, we have $\alpha p/a = w/a \geq p_A > \alpha E/a\bar{T}$. Hence, $p > E/\bar{T}$, or, $\dot{A} > 0$. Consequently, $\dot{A} > 0$ *iff* $\kappa > \bar{\kappa}$. Thus, the equation describing the equilibrium dynamics of $\dot{A}$ is finally written

$$\dot{A} = \begin{cases} a\bar{T} - \alpha/\kappa, & \text{if } \kappa > \bar{\kappa} \\ 0 & \text{otherwise .} \end{cases} \qquad (5.49)$$

Since (5.49) involves the variable κ, we need a second differential equation characterising changes in u over time. This is

---

[15]Note that the expression for $\dot{A}(t)$ does not depend upon $r(\tau)$, which cancels out so long as the utility function has the assumed logarithmic form. This prevents the determination of an equilibrium (path for the) rate of interest in the model. Alternatively, dynamic long run equilibrium can hold for any exogenous specification of the interest rate. While we do not fix the rate of interest at any arbitrary level, the Grossman-Helpman approach involves pegging $r = \rho$.

found by differentiating $u\kappa(t)$ in (5.48).[16]

$$\dot{\kappa} = \rho\,\kappa - \frac{1-\alpha}{A}. \tag{5.50}$$

Thus,

$$\dot{\kappa} \;>\; 0 \Leftrightarrow \kappa > \frac{1-\alpha}{A\rho}$$

$$\dot{\kappa} \;=\; 0 \Leftrightarrow \kappa A = \frac{1-\alpha}{\rho}$$

$$\dot{A} \;>\; 0 \Leftrightarrow \kappa > \bar{\kappa}.$$

According to the definition of a perfect foresight equilibrium, note that the path of $\{\kappa(t)\}_0^\infty$ implied by an expected path of $\{A(t)\}_0^\infty$ via (5.48) must be realised, since $\{A(t)\}_0^\infty$, if expected, is realised by definition. The reader is encouraged to infer the nature of the perfect foresight paths by drawing a phase diagram based on the following observations. (Figure 3.1 of Grossman & Helpman (1991), constructed for a choice of numéraire different from ours, will provide further illumination.) There are two cases to consider.

Case 1: $A_0 < \bar{A} = (1-\alpha)/\bar{\kappa}\rho$. If κ_0 is too small, A is ultimately a constant (since $\kappa < \bar{\kappa}$) along this path. If this is a perfect foresight path, then agents are aware that $A(s) = constant \; \forall\, s > t_0$. Hence, by (5.48), they expect $\kappa(s) = constant \; \forall\, s > t_0$. But κ is continually declining along the path. Hence, the expected κ is not realised, a contradiction.

If on the other hand, κ_0 is too large, then both κ and A diverge along a typical path. Hence, $1 - \alpha/A \downarrow 0$. This means, agents must ultimately expect κ to decline, once again a contradiction Thus, a perfect foresight path beginning from $A_0 < \bar{A}$ can only converge to $(\bar{A}, \bar{\kappa})$.

Case 2: $A_0 > \bar{A}$. The only feasible perfect foresight paths in this region stay put on a stationary point vertically above A_0 on the curve defining the locus of points satisfying $\dot{u} = 0$.

---

[16]This qualifies as the Fisher equation.

The phase plane analysis therefore confirms our observation that the economy in question does not exhibit balanced growth.[17]

5.3.3 Efficiency Questions

There are two potential sources of distortions in the model. The first is static in nature and arises from monopoly pricing. The distortion would actually materialise if the monopoly sector had an interface with a (say) competitive manufacturing sector (as in Romer (1990). However, this is not the case in the Grossman & Helpman model. Consequently, monopoly power can cause distortions to the extent that it varies across monopoly firms. As we saw, however, all manufacturing firms enjoyed the same degree of monopoly, viz. $1/\alpha$. This means that the ratio of prices charged by the monopoly firms will uniformly equal the ratio of marginal costs ($w/w = 1$). In other words, no distortion would arise on account of monopoly.

Two other sources of market failure remain, both dynamic in nature. To begin with, entrepreneurs do not internalise the extra utility accruing to H due to the appearance of new variety, as of a given E. Secondly, and once again as of given E, profits ($(1 - \alpha)E/A$) of incumbent entrepreneurs fall as A rises. New entrants fail to internalise this. The external economy and the diseconomy cancel out however, thus eliminating distortions altogether. We show this below.

The aggregate welfare at t may be written as

$$U_t = \int_0^\infty e^{-\rho(s-t)} \ln \left(\frac{E}{p_D}\right) ds, \text{ since } E = p_D D$$

$$= \int_t^\infty e^{-\rho(s-t)} \ln \left(\frac{E}{w}\right) ds - \int_t^\infty e^{-\rho(s-t)} \ln \left(\frac{p_D}{w}\right) ds,$$

$$\tag{5.51}$$

---

[17]The reader is invited to follow Appendix 4.1 and demonstrate the local saddle point property of the long run equilibrium point Q in Figure 5.2.

expressing expenditure and prices in T units. We assume a marginal increase in variety at t, causing a parallel shift in the path of A, thereby leaving $\dot{A}$ unchanged at all $s > t$. Each individual firm's profit in wage unit being $\pi/w = (1-\alpha)(E/w)/A$, aggregate profit is $A\pi/w$. Hence, the effect of a small rise in A is $\pi/w + Ad(\pi/w)/dA$ at all $s > t$. The first term represents the gain to the innovating firm at the margin, while the second represents a fall in the profits of existing firms. The discounted value of the stream of gains is exactly offset by the cost of innovation along the equilibrium path. Hence, there is no net social gain or loss associated with the additional A alone. Thus, the aggregate social effect on profit is $A\, d(\pi/w)/dA = -(1-\alpha)(E/w)/A + (1-\alpha)d(E/w)/dA$.

Consider the macro identity $E + Savings = w\bar{T} + \Pi$, where Π stands for aggregate profit at any instant of time. In the Grossman & Helpman set up, real savings (i.e., savings in wage units in the present exercise) are equal to real investment in the research sector. The latter equals $T_A = \dot{A}/a$. Hence, $E/w = \bar{T} + \Pi/w - \dot{A}/a$. Consequently, given that $\dot{A}$ is unchanged at all $s > t$,

$$\frac{d(E/w)}{dA} = \frac{d(\Pi/w)}{dA}, \ \forall \ s > t$$

$$= -(1-\alpha)\frac{E/w}{A} + (1-\alpha)\frac{d(E/w)}{dA},$$

i.e.,

$$\frac{d(E/w)}{dA} = -\frac{1-\alpha}{\alpha}\frac{E/w}{A}. \tag{5.52}$$

With this expression in hand, we may proceed to calculate the effect of the proposed change on (5.51). It is not hard to show that

$$\frac{dU_t}{dA} = \int_t^\infty e^{-\rho(s-t)}\frac{1}{E/w}\frac{d(E/w)}{dA}ds + \int_t^\infty e^{-\rho(s-t)}\frac{1-\alpha}{\alpha}\frac{1}{A}ds.$$

Equation (5.52) implies that the last expression is zero. Thus, the consumers' surplus effect is exactly destroyed by the profit destruction effect. In other words, there is no dynamic distortion in the model. Thus, the Command economy will not be able to improve upon the Private economy path.[18]

PROPOSITION **5.4** *When all knowledge is privately owned, the brand proliferation model displays a zero growth, perfect foresight equilibrium in the long run. The Private economy equilibrium is socially optimal. The equilibrium may be realised instantaneously or asymptotically, depending on initial conditions.*

5.3.4 Research with Public Knowledge

In this case, (5.41) is replaced by (5.11). Consequently, (5.42) and (5.43) change to

$$p_A a A - w \leq 0, \text{ if } \dot{A} \geq 0$$

$$= 0, \text{ if } \dot{A} > 0. \tag{5.53}$$

and

$$\bar{T} = \frac{1}{a} \frac{\dot{A}}{A} + \frac{E}{p}. \tag{5.54}$$

Equation (5.54) demonstrates immediately that the model will now permit balanced growth equilibrium, i.e., a positive constant value of $\dot{A}/A$. The remainder of the section will derive the equilibrium balanced growth rate. Proceeding as in Section 5.3.2, but taking account of (5.11), we see that (5.47) changes to

$$\frac{1}{a} \frac{\dot{A}(t)}{A(t)} = \bar{T} - T_x(t)$$

$$= \bar{T} - \frac{\alpha}{1 - \alpha} \frac{1}{\int_t^\infty e^{-\rho(s-t)}(1/A(s)) \, ds} \frac{1}{aA(t)}. \tag{5.55}$$

---

[18]The reader should verify the truth of the above intuitive argument by working out the algebra for the Command economy via the Hamiltonian approach.

Under balanced growth, $\dot{A}/A = g$ (say). Thus, $A(s) = A(t)$ $e^{g(s-t)}$. Consequently, the integral in the extreme right hand denominator of (5.55) is written

$$\left(\int_t^\infty e^{-\rho(s-t)}(1/A(s)) \, ds \right)$$

$$\times aA(t) \;=\; a \int_t^\infty e^{-\rho(s-t)}(1/A(s))$$

$$\times (A(t) \, e^{g(s-t)}) \, e^{-g(s-t)} \, ds$$

$$=\; a \int_t^\infty e^{-\rho(s-t)}(1/A(s))$$

$$\times A(s) \, e^{-g(s-t)} \, ds$$

$$=\; a \int_t^\infty e^{-(\rho+g)(s-t)} \, ds$$

$$=\; a/(\rho + g).$$

Substituting the above in (5.55),

$$\frac{1}{a} \frac{\dot{A}(t)}{A(t)} \;=\; \frac{1}{a} g$$

$$=\; \bar{T} - \frac{\alpha}{1-\alpha} \frac{\rho+g}{a}. \tag{5.56}$$

We argued in Section 5.3.2 that (5.47) captured the motion of A in a dynamic equilibrium. The arguments apply *mutatis mutandis* to (5.56) also. Consequently, the solution $g = g^*$ to (5.56) represents the equilibrium balanced growth rate for the economy.[19] Solving, we get

$$g^* = a \, (1-\alpha) \, \bar{T} - \alpha \, \rho. \tag{5.57}$$

---

[19]We may view (5.56) to be a generalisation of the requirement that the demand and the supply rates of growth be equal.

It is clear that no positive balanced growth equilibrium is possible if

$$\frac{\rho}{1-\alpha} > \frac{a\bar{T}}{\alpha}.$$

The above inequality admits the following interpretations. (i) A high ρ $\Rightarrow$ present consumption is preferred to future consumption, hence low rate of growth; (ii) a high α $\Rightarrow$ high substitutability between $x(j)$'s, low preferences for variety, hence low growth rate; (iii) a low value of "a" implies low productivity in research, hence low growth rate.

Balanced growth is not characterised by constant growth in the output of the final goods sector. Indeed, as opposed to previous exercises, the final goods sector does not produce a single commodity. With the total stock of human capital fixed, the output x of each monopoly firm falls as the number A of firms rises. The latter increase, however, more than compensates for the former fall, so that $ln\ D$ rises with $\dot{D}/D > 0$. To prove this, observe that p/E is constant under balanced growth. This follows from (5.54), since $g = constant$. Next, by definition, $E = Apx$. Thus, $E/p = Ax$, or, $\dot{A}/A = -\dot{x}/x$, since $E/p = constant$. Now, $D = \int_0^A (x^\alpha dj)^{1/\alpha} = A^{1/\alpha}x$. Therefore, $\dot{D}/D = ((1 - \alpha)/\alpha)\ \dot{A}/A > 0$, as claimed. Welfare increases through variety expansion, even though consumption of each type of "x" declines.[20]

5.3.5   The Command Economy

From our discussion of the private knowledge case, it is straightforward that there will be no inefficiency caused by monopoly. However, the research sector will now generate a non-internalisable externality as in the Romer model. This will be reflected in the growth rate chosen by the Command economy.

The Command Economy's problem (like most of our earlier exercises) consists of a static and a dynamic exercise. The

---

[20]Grossman & Helpman argue further that the balanced growth path is the only possible perfect foresight path for the economy.

static exercise consists of allocating a given total of human capital, say χ, across the existing brands $[0, A]$. Formally, the planner maximises

$$D = \left(\int_0^A (x(j))^\alpha dj \right)^{1/\alpha}$$

subject to $$\int_0^A x(j)dj \leq \chi.$$

Since $0 < \alpha < 1$, optimality requires equal distribution, χ/A across all brands. This implies in turn that $D = \chi\, A^{1-\alpha/\alpha}$.

Given this information, the dynamic problem is stated as

Maximise

$$\int_0^\infty e^{-\rho t}\, ln\, D\, dj = \int_0^\infty e^{-\rho t} \left(ln\, \chi + \frac{1-\alpha}{\alpha}\, lnA \right) dj$$

subject to

$$\frac{1}{a}\frac{\dot{A}}{A} + \chi = \bar{T}. \tag{5.58}$$

In what follows, we shall restrict our attention to balanced growth paths only. Thus, by assumption, T_A and χ are constants. The problem is solved by setting up the Hamiltonian

$$\mathcal{H} = \left(\frac{1-\alpha}{\alpha}\, ln\, A + ln\, \chi \right) + \xi(\bar{T} - \chi)\, a\, A. \tag{5.59}$$

The *FOC*'s are

$$\frac{1}{\chi} = \xi\, a\, A, \tag{5.60}$$

$$\dot{\xi} = -\frac{1-\alpha}{\alpha}\frac{1}{A} - \xi\, a\, (\bar{T} - \chi) + \rho\, \xi, \tag{5.61}$$

$$e^{-\rho t}\, \xi \rightarrow 0 \text{ as } t \rightarrow \infty. \tag{5.62}$$

Notice that under the assumption of balanced growth, (5.60)

implies that ξA is a constant. Hence, (5.62) may be rewritten as

$$e^{-\rho t} \xi A \to 0 \text{ as } t \to \infty. \tag{5.63}$$

Equations (5.60), (5.61) and (5.63) are now used to derive the balanced growth rate for the Command economy. Define a new variable $M = \xi A$, so that $\dot{M}/M = \dot{\xi}/\xi + \dot{A}/A$. Then, using the constraint in (5.58), equation (5.61) reduces to

$$\dot{M} = \rho M - \frac{1-\alpha}{\alpha}, \tag{5.64}$$

while (5.63) is rewritten as

$$e^{-\rho t} M \to 0 \text{ as } t \to \infty. \tag{5.65}$$

The solution to (5.64) (under the constraint (5.65)) is[21]

$$M(t) = \frac{1-\alpha}{\alpha \rho} = \text{ constant.} \tag{5.66}$$

Thus, by definition of M and (5.60), $\chi = \alpha \rho / a (1-\alpha)$. Hence, using the constraint for (5.58), the growth rate G^* for the Command economy is

$$\begin{aligned}
G^* &= \frac{\dot{A}}{A} \\
&= a\,\bar{T} - a\,\chi \\
&= a\,\bar{T} - \frac{\alpha \rho}{1-\alpha} \\
&= \frac{1}{1-\alpha}(a\,(1-\alpha)\,\bar{T} - \alpha\,\rho).
\end{aligned} \tag{5.67}$$

Comparing with (5.57), we see that $G^* > g^*$, as expected.[22]

---

[21]The equation is solved as follows. Multiplying both sides by the integrating factor $e^{-\rho t}$, we get $\dot{M} e^{-\rho t} - \rho M e^{-\rho t} = -(1-\alpha/\alpha) e^{-\rho t}$. Integrating out, $M e^{-\rho t} = (1 - \alpha/\alpha) e^{-\rho t}/\rho + \text{ constant}$. Using (5.65), the result follows.

[22]While this completes our discussion of the brand proliferation model of Grossman & Helpman, it would be in the interest of the reader to follow up the original reference for details of the model's policy implications.

PROPOSITION **5.5** *When knowledge is a free good in research, the brand proliferation model displays a positive balanced growth equilibrium. The Private economy equilibrium is socially sub-optimal and grows at a smaller balanced rate than the Command economy.*

We have now introduced ourselves to two classic works on knowledge capital accumulation and growth. While they bring out some special points of interest regarding knowledge capital, there are other important features of knowledge that they ignore. One of the vital aspects of knowledge capital they do not pay attention to is the fact that research on knowledge accumulation is normally characterised by uncertainty of arrival of new ideas. The other side of the coin is that the arrival of new knowledge often renders existing knowledge obsolete. We consider these issues in the final chapter of this book.

Chapter 6

Research and Uncertainty

6.1 Uncertainty and Obsolescence

The preceding chapter attempted to capture an important aspect of reality, the role of knowledge capital accumulation in economic growth. Both models viewed new pieces of knowledge to be determinate outputs of a research technology. However, the assumption of a deterministic output flow from a research activity, though admissible as a first approximation, must ultimately be dispensed with in the interest of realism. A second defect of the earlier models lies in the fact that each new invention brings about a novel product that keeps contributing to either productivity or utility forever. Once again, the nature of competition in the actual world appears to be far more drastic. More often than not, the appearance of a new technique (Romer's intermediate input) renders many of the existing technologies obsolete.[1]

---

[1] The idea that new products and/ideas render older ones extinct goes back to Domar (1946) and Schumpeter (1934), who pointed out the inevitability of any exercise in economic growth to be associated with a simultaneous process of destruction of existing facilities prior to maturity. The fact that market competition does not internalise the capital losses

This chapter will present two models, due to Aghion & Howitt (1992, 1998) and Grossman & Helpman (1991-a, 1991-b) respectively, which attempt to fill out the lacuna. Although the two models address similar issues, they differ in their analytical structures. The Aghion & Howitt exercise is closer to the Romer (1990) model, while the Grossman & Helpman model has several features resembling their own deterministic exercise considered in the last chapter.

6.2 Aghion and Howitt: Description of the Economy

Structurally, the Aghion & Howitt work shares features of the Romer (1990) as well as the Grossman & Helpman (1991-b) worlds. As far as similarity with the latter goes, Aghion & Howitt rely entirely on knowledge capital as the engine of growth, thus abstracting from physical capital. However, the concrete form in which new knowledge manifests itself assumes the form of a Romer type of intermediate input that improves the productivity of the competitive final goods sector and is itself produced by a monopolist. Unlike the Romer exercise though, the arrival of each new variety renders any existing variety obsolete.[2] Consequently, the form of the production function (5.1) loses relevance. The productivity increase brought about by each new generation of intermediate input is therefore assumed to be exogenously given. Unlike the Solow model, this does not determine the rate of growth of the economy in balanced growth, since the arrival of new inputs follows a stochastic path. As a result, the concept of rate of growth of the economy is replaced by its expected rate of growth. The latter is endogenously determined.

---

implies that an increase in the growth rate is not unambiguously welfare improving. Recall that a similar phenomenon was noted in a different context in the Dasgupta & Marjit Quality of life model of Chapter 3, Section 3.3.

[2]The reason underlying obsolescence is that new inputs involve higher productivity. Aghion & Howitt also consider the possibility of simultaneous use of different varieties, i.e., of non-drastic innovations. See Young (1993) for a non-stochastic version of the problem.

The endogenous determination of the expected rate of growth is explained as follows. The blueprint for each new variety of input is a product of research in Romer-Grossman-Helpman fashion. The novel feature introduced is that the arrival rate of blueprints is a stochastic variable, with the probability of success in research rising with a rise in labour input. The desire to advance the flow of profits in the intermediate input sector induces a *potential* monopolist to raise the demand for research labour (say, indirectly, by offering a higher price for the blueprint or, directly, by running a research firm where it offers higher wages). As against this, there is a disincentive for the *potential* monopolist to encourage research. He realises that once current research is successful and he actually sets up a monopoly firm, he will be threatened with extinction by potential rivals engaged in or supporting research on the next generation of the input. So, the lure of profits affects labour input into research positively, while the risk of survival implied by future competition exerts a negative pressure on research. The equilibrium employment of research labour is determined in standard neoclassical manner by balancing the pain against the pleasure. Once this is known, the probability of success is solved for using the distribution governing the arrival rate of ideas and this in turn determines the expected growth rate of the economy.

6.2.1   The Private Economy: Drastic Innovation

In this section, we shall restrict attention to the case of drastic innovations, i.e., to the case where the arrival of new technology makes old technology infeasible. The possibility of non-drastic innovations will be considered subsequently. Time is denoted by the continuous variable t and the chronological order of new inventions by the discrete variable τ. The time distance separating the τ-th from the $\tau + 1$-th invention will be referred to as the τ-th *time interval*. The time point t at which the τ-th invention occurs is not known with certainty. Hence, the length of the τ-th time interval is a stochastic variable. The variable x_τ denotes the specialised input used during the τ-th time interval, while the research to develop a blueprint for x_τ is undertaken during the interval $\tau - 1$. Similarly, $x_{\tau+1}$ is researched during the time τ-th time interval and used during interval $\tau + 1$ and so on.

As in Romer, there are three sectors of production, a competitive final good sector, a monopolistic intermediate good sector and a competitive research sector. The final good is produced according to[3]

$$Y = Ax^\alpha, \ 0 < \alpha < 1, \tag{6.1}$$

where A is a productivity parameter whose level is determined by the generation of x in use. Thus, x_τ is associated with A_τ, $x_{\tau+1}$ with $A_{\tau+1}$, etc. Further, $A_{\tau+1} = \gamma A_\tau$, $\gamma > 1$, where γ is a nonstochastic variable. If successive generations of the inputs were to be available in a *deterministic* chronological sequence, the economy's growth rate would be fairly transparent. However, as noted already, the arrival time of a new input is a stochastic variable.

The entire quantum of Y is consumed (as in Rebelo II), so that there is no direct savings out of Y. Nevertheless, savings occurs since the level of Y depends on that of x and the latter is determined by the allocation of human capital to the production of x. The larger (smaller) the allocation in favour of x, the larger (smaller) is current consumption. Thus, a decision to produce less of x amounts a decision to save more.

The input x_τ is produced by means of human capital, but the latter has a competitive use in research also. A fixed quantity $\bar{T}$ of skilled labour is allocated between these alternative uses. (In Romer, it is allocated between research and the final good.) The two activities involving labour use will be described in turn and it is simpler to begin with x_τ. Any x is produced by the linear technology:

$$x_\tau = T_x^\tau, \tag{6.2}$$

where T_x^τ stands for labour used in producing x_τ. As with Romer, the producer of x_τ is a monopolist, with the price p_τ

---

[3]The presentation of this section depends on Aghion & Howitt (1998). A somewhat more general treatment may be found in Aghion & Howitt (1992).

of x_τ satisfying the inverse demand relationship

$$p_\tau = \alpha \, A_\tau \, x_\tau^{\alpha-1}. \tag{6.3}$$

The equilibrium condition for this sector is found by maximising profit

$$\pi(x_\tau) = \alpha \, A_\tau \, x_\tau^{\alpha-1} \, x_\tau - w_\tau \, x_\tau,$$

for which the *FOC* is

$$w_\tau = A_\tau \, \alpha^2 \, x_\tau^{\alpha-1}. \tag{6.4}$$

The corresponding optimal choice of x_τ is

$$\text{argmax} \,_{x_\tau} \pi(x_\tau) = \left(\frac{\alpha^2}{w_\tau/A_\tau} \right)^{1/1-\alpha}. \tag{6.5}$$

The above may be expressed as a functional relationship

$$x_\tau = \tilde{x} \left(\frac{w_\tau}{A_\tau} \right)$$

$$= \tilde{x}(\omega_\tau), \tag{6.6}$$

where $\omega_\tau = w_\tau/A_\tau$. An increase in ω_τ lowers x_τ, hence the demand for T^τ_x. On the other hand, the inelastic supply of human capital is assumed to be $\bar{T}$ at each t. The availability of labour for the research sector rises therefore as ω_τ goes up. Thus, $\bar{T} - \tilde{x}(\omega_\tau)$ may be interpreted as the residual supply of labour for the research sector after ensuring equilibrium for the x-sector. We denote $\bar{T} - \tilde{x}(\omega_\tau)$ by $T^s_A(\omega_\tau)$ and show it as the upward rising curve in Figure 6.1. The intercept of the curve on the vertical axis is given by $\alpha^2/\bar{T}^{1-\alpha}$. At any ω_τ rate below this, $\bar{T}$ is entirely devoted to producing x_τ.

Using (6.4), the expression for profit is rewritten

$$\pi(x_\tau) = ((1-\alpha)/\alpha) \, w_\tau \, x_\tau. \tag{6.7}$$

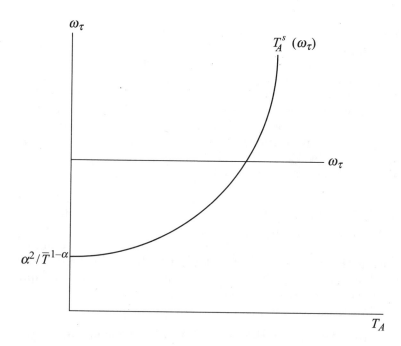

Figure 6.1

Further, productivity adjusted profit is $\tilde{\pi}(\omega_\tau) = \pi(x_\tau)/A_\tau$, which falls as ω_τ rises (using (6.5)). This function will appear once again in the discussion of equilibrium for the research sector. The equilibrium in question will be determined once we have specified the demand function for research labour. This will be done in two steps. The first step consists of assigning a value to the research product, while the second involves writing down the condition of profit maximisation in that sector.

Towards the first step, we begin by noting a crucial difference between (5.11) and the specification of the research technology in the Aghion & Howitt model. The models of Chapter 5 visualised a non-stochastic link between human capital input and the rate of flow of ideas. Consequently, the equilibrium allocation of human capital to the research sector determined the supply rate of growth of the economy. The present set up specifies the common rate of growth of productivity associated with any new idea exogenously. Equilibrium labour allocation in the research sector merely helps to fix the probability of arrival of a new idea and hence the expected rate of growth of the economy. Keeping this in mind, let us denote the price of the $\tau + 1$-th innovation, i.e., the *idea* behind the specialised input $x_{\tau+1}$, by $V_{\tau+1}$. (Recall that the research labour force of interval τ is engaged developing the said idea.)

No arbitrage will require $V_{\tau+1}$ to be equal to the discounted present value of the stream of expected profit for the monopoly firm using $x_{\tau+1}$ in the $\tau+1$-th interval. In order to calculate the expected profit, let T_A^τ be the level of human capital employed during the τ-th interval for developing the blueprint for the product $x_{\tau+1}$. Similarly, $T_A^{\tau+1}$ is the level of human capital employed in research during the $\tau+1$-th interval for developing the blueprint for the product $x_{\tau+2}$.

We shall assume the probability of success at any point of time t (in the τ-th interval) to be λT_A^τ, $\lambda > 0$. The assumption is governed by the following considerations. First, the specification is based on the assumption that the flow of ideas follows a Poisson process. Thus, let us consider the following Poisson distribution

$$f(n) = \frac{e^{-\lambda t} (\lambda t)^n}{n!}, \ m > 0$$

governing the number of arrivals (n) of a random variable (more concretely, the number of ideas or blueprints) during a time interval $[0, t]$, where λ stands for the parameter of the Poisson distribution. According to this distribution, the probability of zero arrival during $[0, t]$ is $e^{-\lambda t}$. Consequently, the probability of at least one arrival during $[0, t]$ is $1 - e^{-\lambda t}$. The latter yields the density function $\lambda e^{-\lambda t}$, which stands for the probability that the waiting time for an arrival is *exactly t*. As $t \to 0$, we obtain the probability of instantaneous arrival as λ.

Suppose now that researches carried out by distinct researchers are statistically independent processes. In particular, let X_1 and X_2 be random variables governed by two independent Poisson processes with instantaneous arrival rates λ_1 and λ_2. The probability that at least one success will occur is $\lambda_1 + \lambda_2$. The Aghion & Howitt model assumes that $\lambda_1 = \lambda_2 = \lambda$. Thus, when the size of research labour is T_A^τ, the Poisson arrival rate of innovations for the *economy as a whole* is the "sum" of the individual arrival rates, viz. $\lambda\, T_A^\tau$.

A second characteristic of the distribution is that it views research to be a memoryless process. Thus, firms do not derive any benefit from the experience gained from unsuccessful research efforts, so that newcomers may embark upon a research activity without having gone through any of the earlier stages of research on previous generation ideas. Essentially, one is assuming that it is sufficient for present researchers to study existing specimens of previous generation products to churn out new ideas. In other words, research satisfies the public knowledge assumption of the previous chapter. The same observations will characterise the research sector of the Grossman & Helpman model on Quality Ladders to be discussed subsequently.

The expected profit at any t in the $\tau + 1$-th interval is given by $e^{-(\lambda\, T_A^{\tau+1})\, t} \pi(x_{\tau+1})$, since $e^{(\lambda\, T_A^{\tau+1})t}$ is the probability of no success till t with respect to research on $x_{\tau+2}$. Let r stand for the prevailing rate of interest, assumed to be an exogenously given constant across time. Then, the discounted present value of expected profit is

$$\int_0^\infty e^{-rt}\, e^{-\lambda\, T_A^{\tau+1}\, t}\, \pi(x_{\tau+1})\, dt = \int_0^\infty e^{-(r + \lambda\, T_A^{\tau+1})\, t}$$

$$\times \pi(x_{\tau+1})\, dt$$

$$= \frac{\pi(x_{\tau+1})}{r + \lambda\, T_A^{\tau+1}}.$$

On account of no arbitrage therefore,

$$V_{\tau+1} = \frac{\pi(x_{\tau+1})}{r + \lambda\, T_A^{\tau+1}}, \tag{6.8}$$

or,

$$r\, V_{\tau+1} = \pi(x_{\tau+1}) - \lambda\, T_A^{\tau+1}\, V_{\tau+1}.$$

The last equation has the following interpretation. The opportunity cost of investing in the research product is $r\, V_{\tau+1}$. On the other hand, the monopolist purchasing the blueprint for $x_{\tau+1}$ earns $\pi(x_{\tau+1})$ at each instant and suffers the uncertainty of capital loss due to the possible arrival of $x_{\tau+2}$, the next generation input. The probability of this event is $\lambda\, T_A^{\tau+1}$, so that the expected loss is $\lambda\, T_A^{\tau+1}\, V_{\tau+1}$. The *RHS* of the above equation captures the monopolist's expected net return at each t. Opportunity cost then is equated to the expected marginal gain.[4] Equation (6.8) completes the first step towards specifying the demand function for L_A^{τ} in the research sector in the interval τ.

The second step in deriving the demand for research labour during τ involves noting that it is the product of research labour T_A^{τ} that is priced $V_{\tau+1}$. The probability of success at any t in τ being $\lambda\, T_A^{\tau}$, the associated expected revenue of research firms is $\lambda\, T_A^{\tau}\, V_{\tau+1}$ and expected profit is therefore given by $\lambda\, T_A^{\tau}\, V_{\tau+1} - w_{\tau}\, T_A^{\tau}$. The corresponding *FOC* for expected profit maximisation by research firms is

$$w_{\tau} = \lambda\, V_{\tau+1}. \tag{6.9}$$

We may combine (6.8) and (6.9) to get

$$\omega_{\tau} = \frac{\lambda}{A_{\tau}}\, V_{\tau+1}$$

$$= \lambda\, \frac{\pi(x_{\tau+1})/A_{\tau}}{r + \lambda\, T_A^{\tau+1}}$$

$$= \frac{\lambda\,(A_{\tau+1}/A_{\tau})\, \tilde{\pi}(\omega_{\tau+1})}{r + \lambda\, T_A^{\tau+1}}.$$

---

[4]Compare with the interpretation of (2.11).

In other words,

$$\omega_\tau = \lambda \, \frac{\gamma \, \tilde{\pi}(\omega_{\tau+1})}{r + \lambda \, T_A^{\tau+1}}. \tag{6.10}$$

This fixes ω_τ, given $\omega_{\tau+1}$ and $T_A^{\tau+1}$ and defines, finally, an infinitely elastic demand curve for T_A^τ at the fixed ω_τ.[5] The equilibrium value of L_A^τ in interval τ occurs where $T_A^{\tau \, s}(\omega_\tau)$ intersects the horizontal demand curve. See Figure 6.1, which shows how the equilibrium pair (ω_τ, T_A^τ) is solved for, given $(r, \omega_{\tau+1}, T_A^{\tau+1})$.

The equilibrium allocation of human capital helps to fix an expected growth rate of the Y-sector. To explain the nature of this expected rate, note that the flow of Y during two successive innovations is

$$
\begin{aligned}
Y_\tau &= A_\tau \, x_\tau^\alpha \\
Y_{\tau+1} &= A_{\tau+1} \, x_{\tau+1}^\alpha \\
&= \gamma \, A_\tau \, x_{\tau+1}^\alpha.
\end{aligned}
$$

Since τ is a discrete variable, the rate of growth of Y is $\ln Y_{\tau+1} - \ln Y_\tau$. To get a handle on this expression, we may divide up the analysis into two parts. The first relates to the special case where the equilibrium human capital allocation derived above repeats across time. In this case, x_τ as well as T_A^τ would be constants for all τ and a state parallel to the balanced growth equilibrium of earlier chapters will emerge, with important variables like Y_τ, π_τ, w_τ growing at the same rate as the rate of growth of A_τ. In the second case, the equilibrium is non-repetitive.

Repetitive Equilibrium

In this case, $\omega_\tau = \omega$ and $T_A^\tau = T_A$ (say) $\forall \, \tau$. As a result, (6.10) is replaced by

$$
\begin{aligned}
\omega &= \lambda \, \frac{\gamma \, \tilde{\pi}(\omega)}{r + \lambda \, T_A} \\
&= \omega_d(T_A; r). \tag{6.11}
\end{aligned}
$$

---

[5]See Aghion & Howitt (1992) for a more general demand curve.

The function $\omega_d(T_A; r)$ may be interpreted to yield the demand price of research labour as a function of the quantity T_A. Similarly, the monotonic property of $\tilde{x}(\omega)$ and

$$T_A^s(\omega) = \bar{T} - \tilde{x}(\omega)$$

may be used to write the supply price as a function of the quantity T_A. Thus,

$$\omega = \omega_s(T_A), \tag{6.12}$$

The function $\omega_d(T_A; r)$ is decreasing and $\omega_s(T_A)$ increasing in T_A. The repetitive equilibrium $(\hat{T}_A, \hat{\omega})$ occurs at the intersection of these two curves. Plugging the equilibrium values back in (6.11) and recalling (6.7),

$$\omega = \frac{\lambda \, \gamma \, . \, ((1 - \alpha)/\alpha) \, . \, \omega \, . \, (\bar{T} - \hat{T}_A)}{r + \lambda \, \hat{T}_A},$$

or,

$$\frac{\lambda \, \gamma \, ((1 - \alpha)/\alpha) \, (\bar{T} - \hat{T}_A)}{r + \lambda \, \hat{T}_A} = 1. \tag{6.13}$$

For the repetitive equilibrium, we have $x_\tau = constant$, so that $Y_{\tau+1} = \gamma \, Y_\tau$. Thus, $\ln Y$ increases by $\ln \gamma$ each time an innovation occurs. Suppose that during a unit interval of time, there has occurred $\epsilon(t)$ innovations. Then, during this interval, $\ln Y$ rises by $\epsilon(t) \ln \gamma$ and

$$\ln Y(t + 1) - \ln Y(t) = \epsilon(t) \ln \gamma.$$

The probability of $\epsilon(t)$ innovations occurring in the unit interval is $((\lambda \, T_A)^{\epsilon(t)} e^{\lambda \, T_A}/\epsilon(t)!)$. The mean of this distribution is $\lambda \, T_A$. Hence,

$$E[\ln Y(t + 1) - \ln Y(t)] = \lambda \, T_A \ln \gamma$$

and the expected rate of growth of the Y-sector is

$$g(r) = \lambda \, T_A \ln \gamma, \tag{6.14}$$

where the dependence on r arises from (6.11). With a rise in r, the discounted stream of profits falls (as per (6.8)), $w_\tau =$

λ $V_{\tau+1}$ falls, x rises and T_A falls according to (6.11). Thus, $g(r)$ falls with r. With reference to earlier exercises, we may identify this relationship as the supply rate curve, since its derivations involve only profit maximisation by the firms.

The natural question to ask is whether one can superimpose a demand curve on the supply curve following our adopted procedure. As far as preferences go, the representative household is assumed to maximise

$$U = \int_0^\infty Y(t) \, e^{-rt} dt. \qquad (6.15)$$

This function is significantly different from (2.1). In particular, instantaneous utility is now a linear function of consumption. An important role played by this deviation from (2.1) will be discussed below in connection with the nature of capital markets that may sustain the equilibrium over time. As we have already seen, the level of Y is determined at best as a random variable. Hence, the only sensible maximand for the household is the expected value of U in (6.15). On the other hand, this requires knowledge of the distribution governing the arrival of ideas. This knowledge, however, is restricted to the firm sector alone, since it depends on the equilibrium level of human capital employment in research. Normally, the household is not expected to be able to internalise this knowledge. Thus, the model as posed leaves the demand curve unsolved for.[6] As a result, the equilibrium rate of interest cannot be endogenously determined and continues to be an exogenously specified variable.

PROPOSITION **6.1** *In the presence of obsolescence with new ideas arriving according to a stochastic law, supply forces determine an expected rate of growth for the economy even*

---

[6] An alternative procedure, one followed by Grossman & Helpman and to be discussed in Section 6.3 below, is to pose the household's demand problem in nominal terms by solving for the growth rate of optimal expenditure on consumption. In this case, random changes in the level of Y cause proportionate changes in its price, leaving the non-stochastically determined expenditure term unaffected.

when the allocation of human capital to the different sectors of production is invariant over time. This rate of growth is a monotone decreasing function of the exogenously specified interest rate prevailing in the market.

Non-repetitive Equilibrium

In case of a non-repetitive equilibrium, we shall have an infinite sequence $\{(\cdots, (\omega_{\tau-1}, T_A^{\tau-1}), (\omega_\tau, T_A^\tau), (\omega_{\tau+1}, T_A^{\tau+1}), \cdots\}$ satisfying (6.10). This sequence constitutes a perfect foresight equilibrium in the sense that its expectation leads to its fulfilment. To understand the nature of the path followed by the sequence, note that a rise in equilibrium $T_A^{\tau+1}$ causes equilibrium $x_{\tau+1}$ and therefore equilibrium $\hat{\pi}(\omega_{\tau+1})$ to fall. Equation

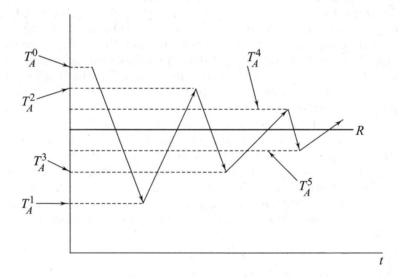

Figure 6.2

(6.10) implies then a corresponding fall in equilibrium w_τ, a rise in x_τ and finally a fall in T_A^τ also. Hence, there is a monotone decreasing function $T_A^\tau = \psi(T_A^{\tau+1})$ connecting consecutive pairs $(T_A^\tau, T_A^{\tau+1})$. Depending on the slope of the function ψ, alternative scenarios emerge. One such, a converging sequence to the repetitive equilibrium, is depicted by Figure 6.2. (See Figure 2.3 in Aghion & Howitt (1998) for more insight into the nature of a repetitive equilibrium.) The perfect foresight equilibrium portrayed by the diagram may be understood as follows. The expectation of T_A^2 gives rise to the employment of $T_A^1 = \Psi(T_A^2)$. Similarly, the expectation of T_A^1 causes $T_A^0 = \Psi(T_A^1)$. The sequence of T_A^τ so generated, when read forwards (following the direction of the arrowheads) converges to a repetitive equilibrium at the level R. Another interesting special case arises when $T_A^0 = \psi(T_A^1)$ and $T_A^1 = \psi(T_A^0)$. If both $T_A^0 > 0$ and $T_A^1 > 0$, then research employment fluctuates without any tendency for convergence. The reader is encouraged to prove that if either T_A^0 or T_A^1 is zero, then the economy is caught in a zero growth trap.

6.2.2 The Private Economy: Non-drastic Innovation

In the drastic innovation case, the incumbent monopolist is not constrained by competition from the holders of previous patents. Non-drastic innovation, by contrast, refers to the case where the incumbent's pricing policy is constrained by the threat of undercutting by past monopolists. In the non-drastic case, the need to keep competitors out leads a monopolist to charge less than in the case of drastic innovation. This means that in both cases, two vintages of intermediate products do not coexist.

We shall derive first a necessary and sufficient condition under which innovation will be drastic. The previous patent holder will stay out of the market if he is allowed a maximum profit of zero. This will be possible if the price of the product is driven down to the average cost of production. Given (6.2), it follows that the price should equal w_τ. The corresponding cost of producing Y by means of the previous generation $x_{\tau-1}$ will be denoted by $C_{\tau-1}(w_\tau, Y)$. Since, $Y = A_{\tau-1} \, x^\alpha_{\tau-1}$ when the previous patent holder supplies x, it follows that

$$C_{\tau-1}(w_\tau, Y) = w_\tau \, x_{\tau-1}$$

$$= w_\tau \left(\frac{Y}{A_{\tau-1}} \right)^{1/\alpha}. \qquad (6.16)$$

The innovation will be drastic if unconstrained monopoly pricing by the latest generation x producer leads to a cost of production of Y that is lower than $C_{\tau-1}(w_\tau, Y)$. Let us calculate this cost. The solutions for x and π in the drastic case are given by (6.5) and (6.7). Further, using (6.3), the price charged by the monopolist causing drastic innovation is

$$p_\tau = \frac{w_\tau}{\alpha}. \qquad (6.17)$$

Hence, the cost function for Y when x_τ replaces $x_{\tau-1}$ is

$$C_\tau(p_\tau, Y) = p_\tau \, x_\tau$$

$$= \frac{1}{\alpha} \, w_\tau \left(\frac{Y}{A_\tau} \right)^{1/\alpha}. \qquad (6.18)$$

According to the argument developed above, the innovation is drastic *iff*

$$C_\tau(p_\tau, Y) \leq C_{\tau-1}(w_\tau, Y)$$

or, after manipulation,

$$\gamma \geq \alpha^{-\alpha}. \qquad (6.19)$$

Alternatively, the innovation is non-drastic *iff*

$$\gamma < \alpha^{-\alpha}. \qquad (6.20)$$

In this case,

$$C_\tau(p_\tau, Y) > C_{\tau-1}(w_\tau, Y),$$

which suggests that the latest product must be charged a price $\tilde{p}$ lower than p_τ so that $C_\tau(p_\tau, Y)$ falls to

$$C_\tau(\tilde{p}, Y) = C_{\tau-1}(w_\tau, Y).$$

The above equation reduces to

$$\tilde{p} \left(\frac{Y}{A_\tau}\right)^{1/\alpha} = w_\tau \left(\frac{Y}{A_{\tau-1}}\right)^{1/\alpha},$$

or,

$$\tilde{p} = \gamma^{1/\alpha} \, w_\tau$$

$$< \frac{1}{\alpha} \, w_\tau, \text{ given (6.20)} .$$

The corresponding level of profit earned is

$$\tilde{\pi}_\tau = \tilde{p} \, \tilde{x}_\tau - w_\tau \, \tilde{x}_\tau$$

$$= (\gamma^{1/\alpha} - 1) \, w_\tau \, \tilde{x}_\tau$$

$$> 0,$$

where $\tilde{x}_\tau$ maximises $A_\tau \, x^\alpha - \tilde{p} \, x$. For the repetitive equilibrium case, (6.13) is replaced by

$$\frac{\lambda \, \gamma \, (\gamma^{1/\alpha} - 1) \, \tilde{x}}{r + \lambda \, \tilde{T}_A} = 1. \tag{6.21}$$

6.2.3 The Private Economy: Capital Markets

A problem associated with the uncertain nature of research output is that wages to be paid to human capital may not be coterminous with the arrival of revenue even in the repetitive equilibrium case discussed above. Under the circumstance, the financing of wage payment to research workers would appear to pose a problem. The form of the welfare function (6.15), however, simplifies the problem.

To appreciate this, note that according to (6.9), $w_\tau = \lambda \, V_{\tau+1}$ stands for the expected wage rate of a researcher at each t in the τ-th interval. Thus, aggregate expected wages equal $V_{\tau+1}$ itself when $1/\lambda$ workers are employed. On the

other hand, $V_{\tau+1}$ is also the discounted present value of the
expected flow of profits to the monopoly firm in possession of
$x_{\tau+1}$. According to (6.15), researchers would be indifferent between an expected payment of $V_{\tau+1}$ *now* and the expected flow
of returns from an investment of $V_{\tau+1}$ calculated at the rate
of interest r.[7] Thus, one may view the Aghion-Howitt world
to be organised according to the following plan. At each instant of time, the owners of an existing monopoly firm consume
the profit and non-research workers consume the wages. Research workers are treated as potential owners of the monopoly
firm that will be set up once they innovate successfully. Consequently, they are indifferent between the expected value of
current wages and the expected value of the profit stream.

The above arrangement is equivalent to a perfect credit
market where the return to capital loaned out will be equalised
with the market rate of interest r.[8]

6.2.4   The Command Economy: Repetitive Equilibrium

In his optimisation exercise, the social planner is in a position
to internalise the probability of arrival. Consequently, in a
repetitive equilibrium, he will maximise the expected value of
U, i.e.,

$$E\,U \;=\; \int_0^\infty e^{-rt}\,(E\,Y(t))\,dt$$

$$\;=\; A_0\,x^\alpha \int_0^\infty e^{-rt}\left(\sum_0^\infty \frac{e^{-\lambda\,T_A\,t}\,(\lambda\,T_A\,t)^\tau}{\tau!}\right)\gamma^\tau\,dt$$

---

[7] As per (6.15), the household is indifferent between a unit of consumption at t_0 and $e^{r\,(t_1-t_0)}$ units of consumption at t_1.

[8] Note, however, treating r as the market rate of interest leaves open
the question of its determination. In our earlier models, the equilibrium
rate of interest was determined endogenously with the equilibrium rate of
balanced growth. See remarks at the end of our discussion of the Repetitive Equilibrium. Problems related to capital market imperfections are
discussed by Aghion & Howitt (1998), King & Levine (1993).

$$= A_0\, x^\alpha \int_0^\infty e^{-(r - \lambda\, T_A\, (\gamma - 1))t}\, dt$$

$$= \frac{A_0\, (\bar{T} - T_A)^\alpha}{r - \lambda\, T_A\, (\gamma - 1)}. \tag{6.22}$$

The derivation of (6.22) uses the fact that

$$\sum_{\tau=0}^{\infty} \frac{(\lambda\, T_A\, \gamma\, t)^\tau\, e^{-\lambda\, T_A\, t}}{\tau!} = e^{-\lambda\, T_A\, t} \sum_{\tau=0}^{\infty} \frac{(\lambda\, T_A\, \gamma\, t)^\tau}{\tau!}$$

$$= e^{\lambda\, T_A\, (\gamma - 1)\, t}.$$

The planner maximises (6.22) *wrt* T_A, the *FOC* for which reduces to

$$1 = \frac{\lambda\, (\gamma - 1)\, (1/\alpha)\, (\bar{T} - T_A^*)}{r - \lambda\, T_A^*\, (\gamma - 1)}, \tag{6.23}$$

where T_A^* stands for the optimal choice by the planner. Comparison with (6.13) as well as (6.21) reveals that the planners choice of T_A^* may be lower than $\hat{T}_A$ or $\tilde{T}_A$. Consequently, the expected rate of growth in the Command economy could fall short of that achieved by the Private economy. (See (6.14).) The result is reminiscent of our findings in Chapter 3 in connection with the Quality of life model. Aghion & Howitt explain it by noting that the planner is likely to internalise the profits/ losses of an incumbent monopolist on account of early arrival of the next generation input in calculating the social gain from innovation. This could cause him to reduce the equilibrium input into the research sector. The Private economy on the other hand, will not internalise the losses arising from obsolescence and might end up growing faster. The penultimate line of (6.22), however, suggests an alternative interpretation of the result, one that is comparable to the intuition underlying the Quality of life model, or indeed, any model of optimum growth. As we can see, the expression involves a trade-off between consumption (the term $A_0\, x^\alpha$) and rate of growth (the term $e^{\lambda\, T_A\, (\gamma - 1)}$). The planner's choice of T_A^* balances off one against the other. The Private economy, as we have seen, engages in no optimisation exercise at all as far as the household's welfare goes. Profit maximisation by the firms, without reference to the growth consumption trade-off incorporated in the welfare function, can therefore give rise to excessive growth and sub-optimal consumption.

PROPOSITION **6.2** *The Command economy for the Aghion & Howitt model internalises losses on account of excessive growth, arising either due to losses from obsolescence or consumption, and may end up growing at a rate lower than the Private economy.*

6.3 Quality Ladders—Grossman & Helpman: Description of the Economy

The second model we proceed to discuss in this chapter goes back to Grossman & Helpman. They called it the Quality ladder model and meant it to complement their Brand proliferation model of the previous chapter. This model bears to the Aghion & Howitt exercise roughly the same relationship that the Brand proliferation model bore to the Romer (1990) model. Thus, the intermediate input sector is avoided, new ideas being incorporated directly in final products. Moreover, as against the Aghion & Howitt model, the final goods sector manufactures a fixed set of commodities, represented by a continuum of size unity. Each commodity j in the set $(0, 1]$, however, faces a random prospect of quality upgradation at each point of time.[9] Thus, a commodity can be improved in a discrete sequence of endlessly many vertically differentiated varieties.

---

[9]Quality upgradation is to be understood as new innovative goods replacing old ones and offering more services per unit of expenditure on them. "... a compact disc player would be regarded as a superior version of the phonograph. [The] treatment abstracts from the obvious reality that these, like most, sophisticated products are distinguished by more than a single characteristic ..." Grossman & Helpman (1991-b), Chapter 4, p. 85.

The τ-th quality of product j is indicated by a quantitative index A_j^τ, $\tau = 1, 2, \cdots$, with $A_j^{\tau+1} = \gamma \, A_j^\tau$, independent of j and τ. We shall further normalise $A_j^0 = 1$, $\forall j$ and denote by x_j^τ the level of consumption of the A_j^τ-th variety of commodity j.

In case of Aghion & Howitt, we argued that there was no point in solving the household's dynamic optimisation exercise, since the household is not in a position to internalise the uncertainty associated with the emergence of new intermediate inputs. In the Quality ladder model, however, this problem is avoided by posing the household's choice problem with reference to its "expenditure" on the fixed set of final goods. Each commodity in the set is viewed as an imperfect substitute of each other. However, given any commodity in the set, a unit of quality incorporated in any specific variety of it is a perfect substitute of a unit of quality in any other. Define the composite commodity index[10] as

$$\ln \, D(t) = \int_0^1 \ln \, \sum_\tau A_j^\tau \, x_j^\tau \, dj. \qquad (6.24)$$

[10]Writing $\sum_\tau A_j^\tau \, x_j^\tau = X(j)$ for simplicity, this may be seen as a special case of (5.28) obtained by letting $\alpha \to 0$. Rewrite (5.28) as

$$D^\alpha = \int_0^1 X(j)^\alpha \, dj,$$

$$\text{or, } D^\alpha - 1 = \int_0^1 X(j)^\alpha \, dj - 1,$$

$$\text{or, } \frac{D^\alpha - 1}{\alpha} = \int_0^1 \frac{X(j)^\alpha - 1}{\alpha} \, dj,$$

$$\text{or, } \lim_{\alpha \to 0} \frac{D^\alpha - 1}{\alpha} = \int_0^1 \lim_{\alpha \to 0} \frac{X(j)^\alpha - 1}{\alpha} \, dj,$$

$$\text{or, } \ln \, D = \int_0^1 \ln \, X(j) \, dj.$$

The form $(X(j)^\alpha - 1)/\alpha$ is reminiscent of (2.24). With $\alpha \to 0$, we can see that the elasticity of substitution between commodity pairs is unity. Thus, as noted above, any two commodities in the set $(0, 1]$ are imperfect substitutes.

The linear term $\sum_\tau A_j^\tau x_j^\tau$ confirms our observation above that a unit of A_j^τ is a perfect substitute for a unit of $A_j^{\tau'}$, $\tau \neq \tau'$. The corresponding welfare function is assumed to be

$$U = \int_0^\infty e^{-\rho\,t} \ln D(t)\, dt, \qquad (6.25)$$

As in the case of Chapter 5, we choose to represent prices in some abstract unit. Denoting total expenditure on manufactured products by the household at any instant by E, it is easy to see (by maximising (6.24) subject to an appropriate budget constraint) that expenditure is distributed uniformly across all commodities. Moreover, the cardinality of the set of commodities being unity, the expenditure on each variety is E.

We may note trivially that the household will spend only on that variety of a commodity which yields the maximum quality per unit of expenditure. Let $\hat\tau$ be that variety and p_j^τ be the price of variety τ. Then the household's demand function for commodity j at any instant is given by

$$x_j^\tau = \begin{cases} E/p_j^\tau, & \text{if } \tau = \hat\tau \\ 0 & \text{otherwise}. \end{cases}$$

The above function assumes the absence of a tie between two different varieties of j.[11]

The above constitutes a solution to the household's static optimisation problem. To solve the dynamic optimisation exercise, we begin by constructing a price index for the composite product $[x_j^{\hat\tau}]_0^1$. We proceed as in Chapter 5 by viewing D as a production function and maximising profits for a competitive producer of the product. Using (6.24), the production function is written in explicit form as

$$D = e^{\int_0^1 \ln A_j^{\hat\tau}\, x_j^{\hat\tau}\, dj}.$$

---

[11]The reason underlying this fact will be evident once we explain the nature of oligopolistic competition underlying the manufacturing sector.

The competitive producer maximises $p_D \, D - \int_0^1 p_j^{\hat{\tau}} \, x_j^{\hat{\tau}} \, dj$, where p_D is the price of the composite good D. The FOC for this problem is

$$p_D \left(e^{\int_0^1 \ln \, A_j^{\hat{\tau}} \, x_j^{\hat{\tau}} \, dj} \right) \frac{1}{x_j^{\hat{\tau}}} = p_j^{\hat{\tau}} \; \forall \; j.$$

Applying logarithm to both sides and simplifying

$$p_D = e^{\int_0^1 \ln \, (p_j^{\hat{\tau}})/(A_j^{\hat{\tau}}) \, dj}.$$

Given this expression, the household's dynamic optimisation problem is solved precisely the same way as in Section 5.3 and the solution is identical with (5.37).

We may proceed now to a discussion of the producers' behaviour.

6.3.1 Manufacturing and Research Sector.

Let us begin with producers of the final goods. Parallel to Chapter 5, each variety of a product j requires a unit of human capital to be produced. Thus, the marginal cost of production equals the wage rate w irrespective of variety as well as product type. Each industry j is characterised by oligopolistic competition. The outcome of the competition, however, is that there is effectively a single producer in industry j producing the latest variety of the product.[12] Imagine first that there are multiple producers producing a particular variety of the product. There are two possibilities here. First, one is a successful innovator and the other is an imitator. Price competition will drive the price down to marginal cost (i.e., the wage rate). The innovator's profit will be zero and the imitator, who will have an imitation cost in addition to the cost of production, will earn negative profit. The latter, therefore, cannot survive. The second case involves two simultaneous innovators. This possibility has very low probability. To see this, assume that the probability of success[13] in research during an interval

---

[12]Refer to the immediately preceding footnote.

[13]The probability distribution is assumed to have the same features as in the Aghion & Howitt model.

dt is $\lambda\, T^\tau_{A_j}\, dt$ if T_{A_j} units of labour are employed to carry out research. When simultaneously running research projects are characterised by two statistically independent probability distributions, the probability of joint occurrence of two successes is $(\lambda\, T^\tau_{A_j}\, dt)^2$, which is negligibly small (even if the two processes employ different quantities of labour, say $T^\tau_{A_{j1}}$ and $T^\tau_{A_{j2}}$).

For reasons similar to the ones characterising the case of nondrastic innovation in the Aghion & Howitt model, the market will follow a pricing mechanism that ensures that two producers, one using the latest technology and the other lagging a step behind, cannot coexist. In order to drive the older technology out, the state of the art producer will charge a price marginally below $\gamma\, w$, if w is the ruling wage rate.[14] Consequently, he will earn a profit approximately equal to

$$\pi = \gamma\, w\, x - w\, x \qquad (6.26)$$

$$= \left(1 - \frac{1}{\gamma}\right) \gamma\, w\, x$$

$$= \left(1 - \frac{1}{\gamma}\right) p\, x$$

$$= \left(1 - \frac{1}{\gamma}\right) E. \qquad (6.27)$$

It is revealing to note that the successful monopolist will never wish to stay more than one step ahead of the one he ousts. Assume to the contrary that he is two steps ahead. Then, he will charge a price slightly below $\gamma^2\, w$ and his profit from the new venture will be approximately

$$p\, x - w\, x = \gamma^2\, w\, \frac{E}{\gamma^2\, w} - w\, \frac{E}{\gamma^2\, w}$$

$$= \left(1 - \frac{1}{\gamma^2}\right) E.$$

---

[14]The reader should work this out.

Against this, however, he will have to set off the loss he causes to himself by scrapping the previous generation product. Thus, his net return will be

$$\left(1 - \frac{1}{\gamma^2}\right) E - \left(1 - \frac{1}{\gamma}\right) E = \frac{1}{\gamma} \left(1 - \frac{1}{\gamma}\right) E,$$

which falls short of $(1 - 1/\gamma) E$ in (6.27).

The industries being symmetric, the employment of human capital in each line of production may be taken to be identical, independent of the generation of the product being researched (i.e., the value of τ). We may therefore denote the value of this variable by $T_A(t)$ at time t. The size of the set of products being unity, $T_A(t)$ stands for the aggregate quantity of human capital employed in research also. In the same vein, $p_j^\tau(t) = p(t) = \gamma \, w(t)$, $\forall \, j$. Thus, total human capital employed in manufacturing is $E(t)/\gamma \, w(t)$. The market for human capital will be in equilibrium at each t if

$$T_A(t) + \frac{E(t)}{\gamma \, w(t)} = \bar{T}, \qquad (6.28)$$

where $\bar{T}$ stands for the fixed quantum of human capital at all t, as in the previous model.

6.3.2 Repetitive Equilibrium

To describe the equilibrium, let us first solve for the value $V(t)$ of a research firm. This is easily done, given our derivation of (4.30). Thus,

$$
\begin{aligned}
V(t) &= \int_t^\infty e^{-\int_t^s r(i)di} e^{\int_t^s -\lambda \, T_A(i)di} \, \pi(s) \, ds \\
&= \int_t^\infty e^{-\int_t^s (r(i)+\lambda \, T_A(i))di} \left(1 - \frac{1}{\gamma}\right) E(s) \, ds.
\end{aligned}
$$

$$(6.29)$$

In a repetitive equilibrium, $T_A(t) = T_A \, \forall \, t$. Hence, from (6.28), $E(t)/\gamma \, w(t) = constant$. Following the procedure of Section

5.3.2, we substitute from (5.37) and write $u(t) = V(t)/E(t)$ to conclude

$$u(t) = \left(1 - \frac{1}{\gamma}\right) \int_t^\infty e^{-(\rho + \lambda\, T_A)(s-t)}\, ds.$$

Thus, in a repetitive equilibrium, u is a constant for all t. Upon differentiation, we obtain

$$\frac{\dot{u}}{u} = (\rho + \lambda\, T_A) - \left(1 - \frac{1}{\gamma}\right)\frac{1}{u} \qquad (6.30)$$

Let $\bar{V} = 1/u$, which is a *constant* in repetitive equilibrium. Then, (6.30) reduces to

$$\dot{\bar{V}}/\bar{V} = \left(1 - \frac{1}{\gamma}\right)\bar{V} - (\rho + \lambda\, T_A)$$

$$= 0. \qquad (6.31)$$

Equation (6.28) is rewritten

$$T_A = \bar{T} - \frac{1}{\lambda\,\gamma}\,\bar{V}, \qquad (6.32)$$

using (6.9) and the definition of $\bar{V}$. The solution to (6.31) and (6.32) yields the repetitive equilibrium values of T_A and $\bar{V}$.[15]

It is of interest to appreciate the nature of the balanced growth equilibrium. Similar to the Aghion & Howitt model, an industry does not grow in a deterministic fashion. Each industry progresses in random jumps, following a Poisson distribution. By virtue of the law of large numbers though, the ratio of successful industries in the set of all industries at each t is $\lambda\, T_A$. As a result, the growth rate g_D of the consumption

---

[15]The reader should be able to argue (following Grossman & Helpman (1991-a, 1991-b)) that the economy jumps to the balanced growth equilibrium solution as in the models of Chapter 3. Grossman & Helpman demonstrate further that any trajectory other than the balanced growth path cannot define a perfect foresight equilibrium.

index D turns out to be a constant. To calculate g_D, denote $A_j^\tau(t) = \hat{A}_j(t)$ and $x_j^\tau(t) = \hat{x}_j(t)$ and rewrite (6.24) as

$$\ln\ D(t) = \int_0^1 \ln\ \hat{A}_j(t)\ \hat{x}_j(t)\ dj.$$

Note that $\hat{x}_j(t) = E(t)/p_j(t) = E(t)/\gamma\ w(t)$. Hence,

$$\ln\ D(t) = \int_0^1 \ln\ \hat{A}_j(t)\ dj + \ln\ E(t) - \ln\ w(t) - \ln\ \gamma.$$

Since $\bar{V} = E/V$, $w = \lambda\ V$ and $\dot{V}/\bar{V} = 0$, it follows that $\dot{w}/w = \dot{E}/E$. Consequently,

$$g_D = \frac{d\ \ln\ D(t)}{dt} = \frac{d}{dt}\int_0^1 \ln\ \hat{A}_j(t)\ dj.$$

The expression $\int_0^1 \ln\ \hat{A}_j(t)$ may be viewed as the mean of the logarithms of qualities across all products. Consider now the Poisson probability that a given product will take exactly m steps up the quality ladder in an interval $[0, t]$. The set of industries being a continuum, the Law of Large Numbers implies that the probability equals the fraction of industries experiencing m quality improvements in $[0, t]$. Normalising $\hat{A}_j(0) = 1$, it follows that

$$\int_0^1 \ln\ \hat{A}_j(t)\ dj\ =\ \sum_{m=0}^{\infty} \frac{(\lambda\ T_A\ t)^m\ e^{-\lambda\ T_A\ t}}{m!}\ \ln\ \gamma^m$$

$$=\ \ln\ \gamma \sum_0^{\infty} \frac{(\lambda\ T_A\ t)^m\ e^{-\lambda\ T_A\ t}}{m!}\ m.$$

But $[\ \sum_0^{\infty}((\lambda\ T_A\ t)^m\ e^{-\lambda\ T_A\ t}/m!)\ m\ ]$ is the expected number of improvements in $[0, t]$, which in turn equals $\lambda\ T_A\ t$. Thus,

$$\int_0^1 \ln\ \hat{A}_j(t)\ dj = \lambda\ T_A\ t\ \ln\ \gamma$$

and

$$g_D = \lambda\ T_A\ \ln\ \gamma, \tag{6.33}$$

the *RHS* of which is identically the same as (6.14). As far as the *LHS* goes, however, the Grossman-Helpman model solves for an equilibrium growth rate that is independent of r, while, as already observed, Aghion & Howitt end up only with a supply side picture. Grossman & Helpman succeed in eliminating the effect of r by incorporating demand factors in the equilibrium solution. Their method depends crucially on two factors. First, they pose the problem of demand in terms of expenditure E, which helps them convert a stochastic exercise to a deterministic one. A second and no less important reason lies in the choice of the logarithmic utility function. This second fact played an important role in the brand proliferation model of Chapter 5 too and was pointed out in the footnote following equation (5.46).[16]

PROPOSITION **6.3** *In the Quality ladder model characterised by a fixed set of final products, with new qualities arriving according to a stochastic law in each line of production, supply as well as demand forces determine an expected rate of growth of the system even when human capital allocation repeats over time. The rate of growth is independent of the rate of interest, but the model does not determine an equilibrium rate of interest for the system.*

This chapter has presented two examples of growth models based on the insight provided by Schumpeter's work. The essence of his idea was that growth inevitably proceeds through a process of "creative destruction" or "business stealing", as the discovery of higher grade products drive out existing ones. There is a significantly large literature on creative destruction led growth. Some of these are summarised in Dinopoulos (1994) and Romer (1994). Apart from the works covered by this book, one of the earliest foundations of Schumpeterian growth theory may be found in Segerstrom, Anant and Dinopoulos (1990). There has been substantial progress in

---

[16]We refrain from proceeding to discuss the direction of divergence between the Private economy growth rate and the Command economy growth rate. Grossman & Helpman arrive at conclusions similar to the ones of Aghion & Howitt and no additional insight can be gained by working through the algebra.

this area of research since then and some of the findings are adequately summarised in Dinopoulos & Sener (2003). Readers interested in finding out more on the subject may refer to this last mentioned work for more recent thoughts.

References

Aghion P. & P. Howitt (1992) 'A Model of Growth through Creative Destruction', *Econometrica*, 60, 323–51.

—— (1998) *Endogenous Growth Theory*, Cambridge, Mass.: The MIT Press.

Alesina A, & D. Rodrik (1994) 'Distributive Politics and Economic Growth', *Quarterly Journal of Economics*, 109, 465–90.

Arnold, L. G., (1997) 'Stability of the Steady–State Equilibrium in the Uzawa–Lucas Model: A Simple Proof'. *Zeitschrift fr Wirtschafts und Sozialwissenschaften*, 117, 197–207.

—— (2000) 'Stability of the Market Equilibrium in Romer's Model of Endogenous Technical Change', *Journal of Macroeconomics*, 22, 69–84.

Atsumi, H. (1965) 'Neoclassical Growth and the Efficient Programme of Capital Accumulation', *Review of Economic Studies*, 32, 127–36.

Banerjee, S. & M.R. Gupta (1997) 'The Efficiency Wage Given Long–run Employment and Concave labour Constraint', *Journal of Development Economics*, 53, 185–95.

Barro, R. (1990) 'Government Spending in a Simple Model of Endogenous Growth', *Journal of Political Economy*, 98, S 103–S125.

Barro, R. & X. Sala-i-Martin (1999)(1992) 'Public Finance in Models of Economic Growth', *Review of Economic Studies*, 59, 645–61.

—— (2003) *Economic Growth*, Second Edition, Cambridge, Mass.:, The MIT Press.

Bellman, R. (1957) *Dynamic Programming*, Princeton, NJ: Princeton University Press.

Bond, E., Ping Wang & Chong K. Yip (1996) 'A General Two Sector Model of Endogenous Growth with Human and Physical Capital: Balanced Growth and Transitional Dynamics', *Journal of Economic Theory*, 68, 149–73.

Bond, E., K. Trask & Ping Wang (2003) 'Factor Accumulation and Trade: Dynamic Comparative Adavantage with Endogenous Physical and Human Capital', *International Economic Review*, 44, 1041–60.

Burmeister, E. & R.A. Dobell (1970) *Mathematical Theories of Economic Growth*, London: Macmillan.

Cass, D. (1965) 'Optimum Growth in an Aggregative Model of Capital Accumulation', *Review of Economic Studies*, 32 233–40.

—— (1966) 'Optimum Growth in an Aggregative Model of Capital Accumulation: A Turnpike Theorem', *Econometrica*, 34, 33–50.

Chiang, A.C. (1984) *Fundamental Methods of Mathematical Economics*, Singapore: McGraw-Hill.

—— (1992) *Elements of Dynamic Optimisation*, New York: McGraw-Hill.

Dasgupta, D. (2001) 'New Growth Theory: A Supply–Demand View' in *Contemporary Macroeconomics*, ed. by Amitava Bose *et al*, New Delhi: Oxford University Press.

—— (1999) 'Growth vs Wefare in a Model of Nonrival Infrastructure', *Journal of Development Economics*, 58, 359–85.

—— (2001) 'Lindahl Pricing, Nonrival Infrastructure, and Endogenous Growth', *Journal of Public Economic Theory*, 3, 413–30.

—— (Forthcoming) 'Notes on Optimal Control Theory for the Neoclassical Model of Growth', in *Economic Theory in a Changing World: Policy Modelling for Growth*, ed. by Sajal Lahiri and Pradip Maiti, New Delhi: Oxford University Press.

Dasgupta, D. & S. Marjit (2004) 'Consumption, Quality of Life and Growth', Discussion Paper No. ERU 2002–12 (Revised).

Dasgupta, P. & D. Ray (1986) Inequality as a Determinant of Malnutrition and Underemployment: Theory, Economic Journal, 96, 1011–34.

De la Croix, David, Philippe Michel (2002) *Theory of Economic Growth*, Cambridge: Cambridge University Press.

Diamond, P. (1965) 'Disembodied Technical Change in a Two-Sector Model', *Review of Economic Studies*, XXXII, 161–8.

Dinopoulos, E. (1994) 'Schumpeterian Growth Theory: An Overview', *Osaka City University Economic Reveiew*, 21, 1–21.

Dinopoulos, E. & F. Sener (2003) 'New Directions in Schumpeterian Growth Theory', in H. Hanusch and A. Pyka (eds), *Elgar Companion to Neo-Schumpeterian Economics*, Cheltenham: Edward Elgar.

Dinopoulos, E. & P. Segerstrom (2004) 'A Theory of North-South Trade and Globalization', Mimeographed.

Dixit, A. & J. E. Stiglitz (1977) 'Monopolistic Competition and Optimum Product Diversity', *American Economic Review*, 67, 297–308.

d'Autume, A. & P. Michel (1993) 'Endogenous Growth in Arrow's Learning by Doing Model', *European Economic Review*, 37, 1175–84.

Dixit, A.K. (1990) *Optimisation in Economic Theory*, Second Edition, Oxford: Oxford University Press.

Domar, E. (1946) 'Capital Expansion, Rate of Growth and Employment', *Econometrica*, 14, 137–47.

Drandakis, E.M. & E.S. Phelps (1966) 'A Model of Induced Investment, Growth and Distributiuon', *Quarterly Journal of Economics*, 76, 304, 823–39.

EPW Research Foundation (2002): 'National Accounts Statistics of India, 1950–51 to 2000–2001', Mumbai, India.

Ethier, W.J. (1982) 'National and International Returns to Scale in the Modern Theory of International Trade', *American Economic Review* 72, 389–405.

Feenstra, R. C. (1996) 'Trade and Uneven Growth', *Journal of Development Economics*, 49, 229–56.

Frankel, M. (1962) 'The Production Function in Allocation and Growth: A Synthesis', *American Economic Review*, 52, 995–1022.

Futagami, K., Y. Morita & A. Shibata (1993) 'Dynamic Analysis of an Endogenous Growth Model with Public Capital', *Scandinavian Journal of Economics*, 95, 607–25.

Galor, O. & J. Zeira (1993) 'Income Distribution and Macroeconomics', *Review of Economic Studies*, 60, 35–52.

Galor, O. (1996) 'Convergence? Inferences from Theoretical Models', *Economic Journal*, 106, 1056–69.

Grossman, G. M. & E. Helpman (1991-a) 'Quality Ladders in the Theory of Growth', *Review of Economic Studies*, 58, 43–61.

—— (1991-b) *Innovation and Growth in the World Economy*, Cambridge MA: MIT Press.

Halkin, H. (1974) 'Necessary Conditions for Optimal Control Problems with Infinite Horizons', *Econometrica*, 42, 267–72.

Harrod, R.H. (1939) 'An Essay on Dynamic Theory',

Economic Journal, 49, 14–33.

—— (1948) *Towards a Dynamic Economics*, London: Macmillan.

Hicks, J.R. (1963) *The Theory of Wages*, London: Macmillan.

Human Development Report (2003), UNDP, Oxford University Press.

Kaldor, N. (1957) 'A Model of Economic Growth', *Economic Journal*, 67, 591–623.

King, R.G. & R. Levine (1993) 'Finance, Entrepreneurship and Growth: Theory and Evidence', *Journal of Monetary Economics*, 32, 513–42.

Koopmans, T.C. (1965) 'On the Concept of Optimal Economic Growth', Published in Pontificiae Academiae Scientiarum Scripta Varia 28, 1, Semaine D'Etude sur Le Role de L'analyse Econometrique dans la Formulation de Plans de Developpement (Also in 'The Econometric Approach to Development Planning', Amsterdam: North-Holland.)

Long, J. B. & C. I. Plosser (1983) 'Real Business Cycles', *Journal of Political Economy*, 91, 39–69.

Lucas R.E. Jr. (1988) 'On the Mechanism of Economic Development', *Journal of Monetary Economics*, 1, 3–42.

—— (2002) 'Supply Side Economics: An Analytical Review', *Oxford Economic Papers*, 42, 293–316.

—— (1990) 'The Industrial Revolution: Past and Future', in Robert E. Lucas, Jr. (ed.), *Lectures on Economic Growth*, New Delhi, Oxford University Press.

Malthus, Thomas R. (1798) *First Essay on Population*, Reprints of Economic Classics, New York, Augustus Kelly, 1965.

Mangasarian, O.L. (1966) 'Sufficient Conditions for the Optimal Control of Non-linear Systems', *SIAM Journal on Control*, 4, 139–52.

Mino, K. (1996) 'Analysis of a Two-Sector Model of Endogenous Growth with Capital Income Taxation', *International Economic Review*, 37, 227–51.

Peretto, P. (1998) 'Technological Change and Population Growth', *Journal of Economic Growth*, 3, 4, 283–311.

Perotti, R. (1993) 'Political Equilibrium, Income Distribution and Growth', *Review of Economic Studies*, 60, 775–76.

—— (1996) 'Growth, Income Distribution and Democracy: What the data Say?', *Journal of Economic Growth*, 1, 149–87.

Persson, T. & G. Tabellini (1994) 'Is Inequality Harmful for Growth?', *American Economic Review*, 84, 600–21.

Phelps, E.S. (1961) 'The Golden Rule of Accumulation: A Fable for Growthmen', *American Economic Review*, (638–643).

—— (1962) 'The New View of Investment: A Neoclassical Analysis', *Quarterly Journal of Economics*, 76, 4, 548–67.

—— (1965) 'Second Essay on the Golden Rule of Accumulation', American Economic Review, LV, 739–814.

Pontryagin, L.S., V. G. Boltyanskii, R. V. Gamkrelidze, & E. F. Mishchenko (1962) 'The Mathematical Theory of Optimal Processes.' Trans. K.N. Trirogoff, ed. by L.W. Neustadt, New York: Wiley-Interscience.

Quah, D. (1996) 'Twin Peaks: Growth and Convergence', *Models of Distribution Dynamics*, 106, 1045–55.

Ramsey, F. (1928) 'A Mathematical Theory of Saving', *Economic Journal*, 38, 543–59.

Ray, Debraj (1998) Development Economics, New Delhi, Oxford University Press.

Rebelo, S. (1991) 'Long-Run Policy Analysis and Long-Run Growth', *Journal of Political Economy*, 99, 501–21.

Ricardo, David (1951) (1817) 'On the Principles of Political Economy and Taxation', in Pierro Sraffa (ed) *The Works and Correspondences of David Ricardo*, vol. 1, Cambridge: Cambridge University Press.

Rivera-Batiz, L. A. & P.M. Romer (1991) 'Economic Integration and Endogenous Growth', *Quarterly Journal of Economics*, 106, 531–55.

Robinson, Joan (1938) 'The Classification of Inventions', *Review of Economic Studies*, 5, 139–42.

Romer, P.M. (1986) 'Increasing Returns and Long Run Growth', *Journal of Political Economy*, 94, 1002–37.

—— (1990) 'Endogenous Technical Change', *Journal of Political Economy*, 98, S71–S102.

—— (1994) 'The Origins of Endogenous Growth', *Journal of Economic Perspectives*, 8, 3–22.

Schumpeter, J. A. (1934) *The Theory of Economic Development*, Cambridge: Harvard University Press.

—— (1942) *Capitalism, Socialism and Democracy*, Harper and Row.

Segerstrom, P., T.C.A. Anant & E. Dinopoulos (1990) 'A Schumpeterian Model of Product Life Cycle', *American Economic Review*, 80, 1077–92.

Segerstrom, P. (1998) 'Endogenous Growth without Scale Effects', *American Economic Review*, 88, 1290–1310.

Shell, K. (1967) *Essays on the Theory of Optimal Economic Growth*, Cambridge: MIT Press.

Sheshinski, E. (1967) 'Optimal Accumulation with Learning by Doing', in *Shell*, 67–85.

Solow, R.M. (1956) 'A Contribution to the Theory of Economic Growth', *Quarterly Journal of Economics*, 32 (65–94).

—— (2000) *Growth Theory: An Exposition*, Oxford: Oxford University Press.

Stokey, N. (1996) 'Free Trade, Factor Returns and Factor Accumulation', *Journal of Economic Growth*, 1, 421–47.

Swan, T. W. (1956) 'Economic Growth and Capital Accumulation', *The Economic Record*, 332, 334–61.

The India Infrastructure Report (1996) National Council of Applied Economic Rresearch, New Delhi.

Uzawa, H. (1961-a) 'Neutral Inventions and the Stability of Growth Equilibrium', *Review of Economic Studies*, 28, 117–24.

—— (1961-b) 'On a Two-Sector Model of Economic Growth: I', *Review of Economic Studies*, 29, 40–47.

—— (1963) 'On a Two-Sector Model of Economic Growth: II', *Review of Economic Studies*, 30, 105–118.

—— (1965) 'Optimum Technical Change in an Aggregative Model of Economic Growth', *International Economic Review*, 6, 19–31.

von Neumann, J. (1945–6) 'A Model of General Economic Equilibrium', *Review of Economic Studies*, 13, 1–9 (Translated from original German article (1938) by G. Morgenstern).

von Weizäcker, C. C. (1965) 'Existence of Optimal Programmes of Accumulation for an Infinite Time Horizon', *Review of Economic Studies*, 32, 85–104.

World Bank, Development Report, 1994.

Young, A. (1993) 'Substitution and Complementarity in Endogenous Innovation', *Quarterly Journal of Economics*, 108, 775–807.

Xie, D. (1994) 'Divergence in Economic Performance: Transitional Dynamics with Multiple Equilibria', *Journal of Economic Theory*, 63, 97–112.

Index